Coaching Psychology for Learning

The contribution of coaching psychology to educational fields is increasingly recognised. This timely book introduces coaching psychology as a facilitative method to support learning in different educational contexts.

Coaching Psychology for Learning: Facilitating Growth in Education is conveniently organised into three parts:

- Part 1 begins with a detailed account of educational paradigms, learning theories and coaching psychology theories; it then reviews important studies of coaching applied to the educational field and identifies a number of gaps to which coaching psychology for learning can contribute;
- Part 2 presents two empirical participatory studies of coaching psychology for learning, which draw from both doctoral research conducted in the UK and educational work in Mainland China; two original and evidence-based coaching models are also illustrated;
- Part 3 consolidates the empirical evidence and original coaching models by exploring the nature of educational coaching, including the context, purpose, processes, and people and their interrelations.

The review of learning theories and coaching psychology theories in Part 1 enables the reader to gain a quick understanding of coaching psychology and its role in education, while the empirical studies in Part 2 are particularly useful for undergraduate and postgraduate students, providing practical examples of how to conduct coaching psychology research in the field of education, in both the West and the East. The book also offers advice on design and implementation issues, which will benefit educational psychologists and coaching psychologists who wish to focus their professional practice in education.

Coaching Psychology for Learning is essential reading for any teacher, student or practitioner who wishes to become an educational coach to facilitate learning. It will appeal to coaches and coaching psychologists, including those in training and at postgraduate level, as well as professionals in educational settings, such as school leaders, student counsellors, coaches and educational psychologists.

Qing Wang is an educational psychologist, a chartered psychologist, an ISCP accredited coaching psychologist and a passionate lecturer. She is currently Associate Professor in Educational Psychology at the School of Psychology and Cognitive Science in East China Normal University. She has 10 years' experience in coaching psychology in the field of education. With a genuine interest in coaching psychology for learning, she explores, designs, delivers, and evaluates coaching models and approaches with teachers and students in secondary schools, medical schools, vocational schools, universities and in parents' education. She uses ideas from CBT, mindfulness, narratives, motivational interviewing, solution-focused and positive psychology approaches to provide a comprehensive service that encompasses professional and personal issues.

Coaching Psychology
Series Editor: Stephen Palmer

Coaching psychology is a distinct branch of academic and applied psychology that focuses on enhancement of performance, development and wellbeing in the broader population. Written by leading experts, the **Coaching Psychology** series will highlight innovations in the field, linking theory, research and practice. These books will interest professionals from psychology, coaching, mentoring, business, health, human resources and management as well as those interested in the psychology underpinning their coaching and mentoring practice.

https://www.routledge.com/Coaching-Psychology/book-series/COACHPSYCH

Titles in the series:

Coaching Psychology in Schools: Enhancing Performance, Development and Wellbeing
Mark Adams

Very Brief Cognitive Behavioural Coaching (VBCBC)
Windy Dryden

Coaching Psychology for Learning: Facilitating Growth in Education
Qing Wang

Coaching Psychology for Learning

Facilitating Growth in Education

Qing Wang

LONDON AND NEW YORK

First published 2018
by Routledge
2 Park Square, Milton Park, Abingdon, Oxon OX14 4RN

and by Routledge
711 Third Avenue, New York, NY 10017

Routledge is an imprint of the Taylor & Francis Group, an informa business

© 2018 Qing Wang

The right of Qing Wang to be identified as author of this work has been asserted by her in accordance with sections 77 and 78 of the Copyright, Designs and Patents Act 1988.

All rights reserved. No part of this book may be reprinted or reproduced or utilised in any form or by any electronic, mechanical, or other means, now known or hereafter invented, including photocopying and recording, or in any information storage or retrieval system, without permission in writing from the publishers.

Trademark notice: Product or corporate names may be trademarks or registered trademarks, and are used only for identification and explanation without intent to infringe.

British Library Cataloguing in Publication Data
A catalogue record for this book is available from the British Library

Library of Congress Cataloging in Publication Data
Names: Wang, Qing, 1985- author.
Title: Coaching psychology for learning : facilitating growth in education / Qing Wang.
Description: Abingdon, Oxon ; New York, NY : Routledge, 2018. | Includes bibliographical references.
Identifiers: LCCN 2017054789 (print) | LCCN 2017058500 (ebook) | ISBN 9781315170510 (Master e-book) | ISBN 9781138047938 (hardback) | ISBN 9781138047945 (pbk.)
Subjects: LCSH: Educational psychology. | Counseling psychology. | Personal coaching. | Learning.
Classification: LCC LB1051 (ebook) | LCC LB1051 .W244 2018 (print) | DDC 370.15—dc23
LC record available at https://lccn.loc.gov/2017054789

ISBN: 978-1-138-04793-8 (hbk)
ISBN: 978-1-138-04794-5 (pbk)
ISBN: 978-1-315-17051-0 (ebk)

Typeset in Times New Roman
by Keystroke, Neville Lodge, Tettenhall, Wolverhampton

To my parents, Prof. Huiping Li and Dr Yixin Wang, for showing me the value and beauty of learning, and to my daughter Xiuxi, for inspiring me to become an authentic educational coach.

Contents

List of figures	xiii
List of tables	xv
Foreword by Stephen Palmer	xvii

1 Introduction 1

Why am I writing this book? 1
A personal narrative of learning and coaching 2
Aim of this book 3
An overview of this book 4
Introduction to each chapter 5
Who is the book for? 6
A word on language 6

PART I
An enquiry of educational paradigms, learning and coaching 9

2 Philosophy and educational paradigms examined 11

Introduction 11
Traditional education worldviews and paradigmatic shift 11
The participatory worldview and education 14
Systems thinking and education 20
Complexity theory and education 23
Summary 26
Recommended reading 26
Key points for reflection 26

3 What is learning? 31

Introduction 31
A psychological movement in the view of learning 31

x Contents

Motivational theories of learning 34
Social perspectives on learning and discursive psychology 36
Humanistic perspective and person-centred psychological
  principles 41
Learning (how) to learn and lifelong learning 43
Learning as a journey 45
A learning-centred model 51
Summary 53
Recommended reading 54
Key points for reflection 54

4 The place of coaching psychology in learning   60
Introduction 60
What is coaching psychology? 60
The meta-theory of coaching psychology 62
Comparisons of coaching with other supporting approaches 64
Psychological approaches of coaching relevant to learning 67
Coaching and coaching psychology in educational contexts 71
A call for further research on coaching and learning 78
Summary 80
Recommended reading 80
Key points for reflection 80

PART 2
**Empirical case studies of coaching psychology for
learning**   89

**5 Coaching psychology for enquiry-based learning (EBL) in
secondary education**   91
Introduction 91
Research design and methodology 91
The qualitative evidence: the thematic findings 95
The narrative evidence: students' learning stories 102
The observational evidence: interactions and communication
  between learning coaches and students 107
The quantitative evidence: development of learning power and
  engagement 110
Summary 111
Recommended reading 111
Key points for reflection 111

Contents xi

6 Towards a systems model of Coaching for Learning   113
Introduction 113
The definition of 'Coaching for Learning' 113
The systems model of Coaching for Learning 114
The context of Coaching for Learning 115
Why: the purpose of Coaching for Learning 116
How: the processes of Coaching for Learning 117
Who: people in the system 122
Evaluating the effectiveness of Coaching for Learning 125
Features of the systems model of Coaching for Learning 126
Summary 128
Recommended reading 129
Key points for reflection 129

**7 Coaching psychology for problem-based learning (PBL) in
medical education**   131
Introduction 131
What is problem-based learning in medical education? 131
PBL tutoring and facilitation 132
How coaching psychology is related to PBL 133
The commonalities between coaching psychology and PBL 134
*The (possible) differences between PBL tutoring and PBL
    coaching 135*
Research methodology: participatory and phenomenological 136
Context of the study 137
First phase of the study 137
Second phase of the study 139
Reflexive statement 141
Summary 142
Recommended reading 142
Key points for reflection 142

8 PBL coaching: towards an integrative model of CPBL   145
Introduction 145
The CPBL model 145
The structure of the CPBL model 147
The features of the CPBL model 148
The phenomenological findings 152
Synthesised discussion 158
Summary 163

xii Contents

Recommended reading 164
Key points for reflection 164

PART 3
Towards a systems approach of educational coaching 169

9 The relational and discursive aspects of educational coaching 171
Introduction 171
The definition of educational coaching 171
The psychological prerequisites to educational coaching 171
The relational aspect of educational coaching 173
Discursive aspects of educational coaching 177
Summary 182
Recommended reading 183
Key points for reflection 183

10 Reflections and concluding remarks 185
Introduction 185
A reprise of the book 185
How do we understand educational coaching? 186
How do we study educational coaching? 188
How do we apply educational coaching? 190
Future research directions of educational coaching 196
Concluding statement: an invitation 199
Recommended reading 200
Key points for reflection 200

Index 202

Figures

2.1	Extended epistemology in the participatory worldview	17
3.1	The holistic metaphor of learning	45
3.2	Three different types of centredness in education	51
4.1	The literature gap between coaching and learning	79
5.1	Interventions for teachers and students in prototyping	93
5.2	Nicole's learning journey at first narrative interview	104
5.3	Nicole's learning journey at second narrative interview	106
6.1	The systems model of Coaching for Learning	114
6.2	The context of Coaching for Learning	115
6.3	Creating environments and providing sources for learning	120
6.4	Sharing a language of learning	120
6.5	Enabling and scaffolding the knowledge construction process	121
6.6	Coaching relationship through communication	122
8.1	The CPBL model for PBL coaching	146
9.1	The psychological model of educational coaching	174

Tables

2.1	Conventional classroom	12
2.2	'Another Way' classroom	13
2.3	How systems thinking informs educational transformation	22
3.1	Views of learning	32
5.1	List of the themes from coaching psychology for EBL research	95
6.1	Coaching for Learning at four stations	118
6.2	Roles and tasks of teachers in Coaching for Learning	123
8.1	The themes in students' and tutors' experiences of PBL coaching	152
9.1	Psychological prerequisites of educational coaching	172

Foreword

Stephen Palmer

Coaching psychology as a profession and sub-discipline of psychology is going through an exciting period of development as it is being applied to a range of different fields. The evidence base for coaching psychology practice has been steadily increasing over the past two decades. Coaching psychology practice has moved beyond one-to-one coaching into teams, groups, organisations and communities. This innovative book, *Coaching Psychology for Learning: Facilitating Growth in Education*, written by Dr Qing Wang, an educational psychologist and ISCP accredited coaching psychologist, introduces coaching psychology as a facilitative method to support learning in different educational contexts. Dr Wang links theory and research, including her own research, to coaching practice in education. Importantly, she provides practical examples of how to undertake coaching psychology research in the education field, covering the West and the East. This excellent book will be of great interest to any professional wishing to apply coaching theory and practice to an educational setting, in particular, teachers, coaching and educational psychologists, researchers, consultants and school counsellors. It will be an essential resource for school-based practitioners.

Professor Stephen Palmer PhD
Work and Learning Research Centre, Middlesex University
President of the International Society for Coaching Psychology

Chapter 1

Introduction

Dear Readers,

I welcome you to this book and hope you find it interesting. This is an invitation to think about coaching psychology and learning in the current educational context. As an educational psychologist and a coaching psychologist, I have a great deal of faith in what coaching psychology has to offer in the field of education, and the benefits are being recognised by more and more people who are actively engaged in supporting student learning, development and growth. I wish to share some of my thoughts on this topic with you in this book.

Why am I writing this book?

Coaching psychology, as an emerging sub-discipline in psychology, is a rapidly developing and exciting area for academic research and professional practice. It has been widely used in commercial consultancy, leadership development, health management, sports, and personal life domains across the world. Recent changes in the field of coaching psychology have emphasised the 'scientific' side of it. For example, the Interest Group for Coaching Psychology of the Australian Psychological Society, created in 2002, was the first group for facilitating the theoretical, applied and professional development of coaching psychology. This was followed by the Special Group in Coaching Psychology (SGCP) of the British Psychological Society (BPS), which was formed in 2004; the BPS SGCP holds a Register of Coaching Psychologists in recognition of those who have a speciality in coaching psychology. The International Society for Coaching Psychology (ISCP), an international professional membership body, has developed its own definition of coaching psychology and an accreditation system of Accredited Coaching Psychologists and Accredited Coaching Psychologist Supervisors. The American Psychological Association (APA) Division 13 (consulting psychology) is also keen on coaching psychology. The division has a particular interest in executive and leadership coaching because coaching is in line with the consultative process including education, training and evaluation.

The contribution of coaching psychology to educational fields is increasingly recognised. For example, many schools across the world have adopted a coaching psychology approach to develop school principals' leadership skills (although they may not necessarily use the term 'coaching psychology'); experienced/senior teachers have used various coaching or mentoring skills to train young teachers in their professional development; and school counsellors attempt to coach students to become more resilient and successful learners. In this book, I focus on coaching psychology as a facilitative method to support learning, particularly in the context of educational paradigmatic shift. A 21st century educational paradigm calls for a stronger commitment to co-construction of knowledge, students' self-determined learning and ownership, and the role of teachers as learning facilitators. The traditional role of educator/teacher as knowledge transmitter is moving towards a coach to individual learners, or a catalyst of learning. However, the psychology of coaching and learning is often overlooked. It seems that little research/practice has been conducted regarding exactly how coaching psychology facilitates students' learning. This facilitation should not only look at students' academic performance or the general learning habits that we usually prefer them to acquire, but also their lifelong learning dispositions, attitudes, beliefs, sense of agency and overall development of learner's identity. I believe coaching psychology, as a facilitative system, can provide valuable insights into enhancing students' learning on the following levels: 1) cognitive level; 2) motivational level; 3) emotional level; 4) relational/social level; and 5) identity level. There are psychological theories and learning theories that underpin each level, and there are established coaching psychology approaches on each level. For example, on the cognitive level, cognitive coaching can enhance students' learning based on the theories of cognitive load, scaffolding and zone and proximal development. Another example: on the identity level, narrative coaching, based on theories of narrative psychology and self-theories, is an appropriate approach to encourage a learner to de-construct and re-construct his or her own identity through guided storying and re-storying processes. There is a need for this book as a systematic exploration of how learning theories and coaching psychology approaches inform each other in the age of rethinking education as an authentic learning adventure.

A personal narrative of learning and coaching

The above academic context informs the need of this book. Moreover, my personal context 'aroused' my intention to write this book. I started my scholarly journey as an overseas student from Mainland China to the UK in 2007. With the support, warmth and coaching of my supervisors, colleagues and friends, I completed my Masters and PhD with Distinction. Most importantly, I found coaching psychology a powerful tool to develop my own learning muscles. I have a different perspective of education, learning, teaching and helping from the one I used to hold. I have been working in the field of educational consultancy and student counselling, and my original interest in research was psychological counselling and psychotherapy in terms of enhancing students' positive learning dispositions and self-efficacy beliefs in learning. However, I found that counselling or therapy, with the primary goal of healing, seemed to be different from what I really believe in, which is helping learners in their active knowledge construction and meaning making. Essentially, most students in secondary schools and universities are not clinically diagnosed and some of them are highly functioning people who seek better performance, exploration of potential, development and growth as learners. Coaching psychology came into the picture of my thinking and I delved into the relevant literature and theories. During my stay in the UK, I was coached by several professional coaches who worked in large retail companies; I was also coached by my supervisors and other distinguished scholars in the field. In addition to being coached, I performed as a coaching practitioner in some areas. I coached secondary students and helped them to be more effective learners; I coached undergraduate students, particularly overseas students, to become more culturally and socially adaptive since they faced similar transformative experiences to those I had experienced. Since coming back to China, I have seen self-help or business management books with translated titles including the word 'coaching', but there is no book on explicit psychological approaches of coaching in relation to education, teaching or learning. I realise that there is much space for further reflection on and exploration of coaching psychology, learning and growth, which are intimately connected.

This book will be a welcome addition to academic research and evidence-based practice by attempting to unify psychological theories of coaching and learning based on a strong empirical foundation of nine years of study (2007–2016). The core element (and the most creative part) of this book is the development of the Coaching for Learning (CfL) model and the Coaching and Problem-Based Learning (CPBL) model that should be applicable across a range of educational settings, for example, secondary education, higher education and medical education. It is my sincere hope that you will feel inspired to work on your own understanding of coaching psychology and learning to become a reflective educator/ teacher/coach, and of course, a lifelong learner.

Aim of this book

The aim of this book is multifaceted. The main objectives are to:

✓ Examine the paradigmatic shift in education and its influence on the understanding of learning.
✓ Articulate how coaching psychology contributes to learning facilitation based on the psychological theories that underline coaching and learning.
✓ Propose two coaching psychology frameworks that specifically target enhancing the individual learner's growth in enquiry- and problem-based learning based on empirical studies and encourage new applications in various educational contexts.
✓ Introduce people who are less familiar with the role of coaching psychology to facilitating learning with scientific evidence and potential applications.

4 Introduction

✓ Stimulate further research and theory development by identifying key reflective thoughts and asking open questions.
✓ Inspire the sharing of experiences and insights between educational practitioners and researchers who are interested in coaching psychology.

An overview of this book

This book consists of three parts. Part 1 includes an enquiry of educational paradigms, learning and coaching. This part covers a comprehensive review of educational worldviews, learning theories and coaching psychology theories that are relevant to the book. Both the traditional paradigms and 21st century paradigms of education are examined, with the focus on participatory theory, systems thinking and complexity theory. This part of the book also contains major learning theories from a psychological perspective, including motivational theories, socio-cultural theories, discursive psychology, humanistic theories and learning how to learn, and I put forward a learning-centred model that clarifies a few assumptions relevant to coaching psychology. Enquiry-based learning and problem-based learning approaches are both discussed in detail because relevant empirical studies will be presented in Part 2. This part then provides definitions of coaching and coaching psychology, links between coaching psychology approaches and learning theories, and a review of coaching psychology in the domain of education, and ends with an evocation of coaching psychology for learning in research and practice.

In Part 2, there are two pieces of empirical research as cases of coaching psychology for learning. The first case is drawn from my PhD research in the UK. It describes how coaching psychology could facilitate secondary students' learning disposition development and growth as learners in enquiry-based learning, using a mixed methodology of quantitative surveys, semi-structured interviews, narrative interviews and classroom observations. The main findings in a thematic form and participants' narratives are presented and discussed. I introduce the systems model of coaching psychology and enquiry-based learning, capturing the essential elements of this case.

The second case is drawn from my work in Mainland China. It shows how coaching psychology could be combined with problem-based learning in order to optimise medical students' learning experience, higher-order learning abilities, clinical capacities and empathetic communication skills. The main findings in this case are also presented and discussed, and I establish an integrated framework of coaching psychology and problem-based learning.

These two empirical cases are dependent on their local contexts, one in a UK secondary school, another in a Chinese medical school. However, they demonstrate similar learning points and highlight the essence of coaching psychology for learning that transcends learners' age, gender, grade, major and ethnicity. Together they form an interesting background for more reflections and investigations that I shall elaborate on in Part 3.

Part 3 opens with an exploration into the nature of coaching psychology for learning, including the context, purpose, processes, people and their interactive relations. Finally, I pull my reflections and thoughts together. This part comprises the need for educational coaching, a commitment to a participatory educational paradigm, several practical issues in conducting research in coaching psychology for learning, implementation issues with different purposes, and the possibility of peer coaching and parent coaching using a similar framework. This is an open-ended journey, so that you may feel inspired and able to develop your own understanding of coaching psychology for learning in the future.

Introduction to each chapter

Chapter 1 explains my rationales and motivation regarding my focus on the field of coaching psychology and learning. It clarifies the aim and the readership of this book, and offers an overview of it. It concludes with an explanation of the language and style of this book.

The philosophy of education and worldview questions are described in Chapter 2. This chapter provides a philosophical framework of paradigm shift in education influenced by the participatory paradigm, systems thinking and complexity theory. I describe my philosophical position of ontology, epistemology, methodology and axiology and discuss how they influence my understanding of learning.

Chapter 3 provides a critical review of theories and principles in learning from a psychological perspective. It highlights motivational, socio-cultural and humanistic theories of learning that have potential relevance to coaching. I explore the journey metaphor of learning in detail. The concepts of learning power, enquiry- and problem-based learning are included in this chapter. I discuss different models of education and situate coaching psychology in a learning-centred model.

Chapter 4 addresses key definitions and theories of coaching psychology, which are grounded in the psychology of learning in the previous chapter. In addition, this chapter reviews important studies of coaching applied to the educational field, and identifies a number of gaps to which coaching psychology for learning can contribute.

In Chapter 5, I illustrate how I set out on a journey of empirical enquiry of coaching psychology and enquiry-based learning in the context of secondary education. I briefly explain the methodological approach and procedures, and elucidate main thematic findings. I present students' and teachers' narratives and their learning stories, and communications between students and teachers as learning coaches.

Chapter 6 is connected with the previous chapter. It illustrates the emerging systems model of coaching psychology for enquiry-based learning based on the empirical evidence, including its interrelated elements and features.

Chapter 7 is another empirical enquiry of coaching psychology for learning that involves problem-based learning in medical education. I briefly explain the methodological approach and procedures, students' and PBL tutors' narratives and learning stories.

In Chapter 8, I illustrate the integrated model of coaching psychology and problem-based learning based on the empirical evidence. The elements and features of the model are elaborated.

Chapter 9 consolidates the empirical evidence and the originated models in order to deepen the arguments about the relationship between coaching psychology and learning in a time of educational paradigmatic shift. These models are situated in a broader context with elements of purpose, people, processes and language as living systems. I delve into the relational and discursive aspects of the systems that connect the language of learning, knowledge construction and learning facilitation.

In Chapter 10, I conclude this book by stating a number of important reflections on educational coaching. I recapitulate my key ideas and then discuss the implications of theory development, methodological innovation and educational practice of coaching psychology for learning with various participants. This chapter sets a platform for the commencement of new exploration conducted by readers.

Who is the book for?

This book is intended to speak to you particularly if you are one of the following audiences:

- ✓ Students who are pursuing a higher degree in educational psychology, teacher training or coaching psychology applied in the field of education.
- ✓ Educational professionals (school leaders, teachers, student counsellors, coaches, administrative staff, etc.) who wish to know more about coaching psychology and its role in education and develop their understanding of coaching psychology to enhance students' performance, positive learning dispositions and identity in learning.
- ✓ Educational psychologists and coaching psychologists who wish to focus their professional practice in the field of education, especially those who are interested in culture and its role in the multi-cultural context of education.

The empirical cases presented in this book have taken place in a UK context and in China, therefore you can get a sense of how coaching psychology in learning works in both Western and Eastern cultures. The methods and principles are transferable and may be relevant to readers across the world.

A word on language

For the most part of the book, I have chosen to write in the first person, and I balance this personal style of writing with an academic style of writing, particularly in articulating the theories of coaching psychology and learning as well as in presenting the empirical cases. This is because they are about the philosophical and psychological foundations, the methodological issues and the principles used. I have used extensive references in the text to indicate my sources and demonstrate that the arguments are firmly grounded in existing literature. However, this book is not just for academic professionals, although its style may feel familiar to students who are in higher education or researchers in the field of educational psychology.

Finally, I hope you can get the most out of this book.

With best wishes from Qing Wang.

Part 1

An enquiry of educational paradigms, learning and coaching

This part covers a comprehensive review of educational worldviews, learning theories and coaching psychology theories. You will read about:

- The traditional paradigms and 21st century paradigms of education with a focus on participatory theory, systems thinking and complexity theory.
- Major learning theories from a psychological perspective: motivational theories, socio-cultural theories, discursive psychology, humanistic theories, learning how to learn, lifelong learning, and learning power.
- Learning as an enquiry journey, enquiry-based learning and problem-based learning approaches, and the learning-centred model.
- Definitions and theories of coaching and coaching psychology.
- Links between coaching psychology approaches and learning theories.
- A review of coaching psychology in the domain of education.

Chapter 2

Philosophy and educational paradigms examined

Introduction

This chapter explores the philosophical framework that influences my understanding of learning, and in doing so reveals the essential paradigmatic position that permeates this book. By exploring different worldviews and related educational paradigms, I consider that there is a gap between conventional educational paradigms and the education we may need to advocate for the 21st century. My view of learning situates itself in a participatory worldview with systems thinking and complexity theory. The chapter opens up different approaches to learning and ways to support learning that will be discussed in the next chapter. It also links to the empirical cases of coaching psychology for enquiry-based and problem-based learning that will be presented in Part 2.

Traditional education worldviews and paradigmatic shift

As a notion of an overarching framework, a paradigm or worldview organises our whole approach to being in the world and to governing subsequent research, such as defining problems and selecting methods of research (Kuhn, 1962). Admittedly, educational research involves a commitment to philosophical worldviews that needs to be recognised, admitted and articulated.

The predominant educational paradigm of today inherits the educational systems created for the industrial age in the 20th century that aimed to sort students into different working positions, disseminate knowledge and build basic skills (Reigeluth, 1994). It has been greatly influenced by Cartesian thinking on mind-body dualism, analytical thinking, and the Enlightenment with its emphasis on rationality. These have constituted a conventional educational paradigm that has been dominated by positivism, reductionism, behaviourism and instrumentalism since the 20th century. This paradigm has influenced modern educational discourse, policy making and practices of teaching and learning.

However, these early philosophical positions have major problems in explaining human learning. For example, behaviourism does explain some of the outcomes of the learning process that cannot be directly measured, but it can only explain behaviours that are driven by forces, not meanings and thoughts themselves. Being dominated by Cartesian dualism and mechanical modes of production, the 20th century model of education is built on a view that privileges the objectivity of knowledge and distances the learner from what is known. It values the primacy of knowledge and reason characterised by a pre-described curriculum typified by the themes of acquisition, independence and competition (Marshall, 1999). Thus, the teacher–student relationship is typically hierarchical. Teachers are experts in transmitting knowledge and chief orchestrators of the curriculum in order to maximise the students' ability to process and absorb it (Haste, 2009), but teachers often have little control over what content is to be covered and are usually required to use mandated learning materials such as textbooks (King & Frick, 1999). The way in which knowledge is encountered by the student is 'top-down'. Students often find the subject matter to be disconnected from their real lives, thus they have a passive interaction with the subject and teachers. In this paradigm, the primary goal of teaching and learning is students' academic performance; meaning-making is reduced to repeating pre-packed abstract, inert knowledge that has little relevance to students' lives outside a classroom wall. The classroom of this type of teaching and learning is portrayed in Palmer's (1993) 'conventional classroom':

Table 2.1 Conventional classroom

Focus of study/subject	Outward – on nature, on history, on someone else's vision of reality
Reality	Out there, apart from us, viewing it from 'outside'
Knowing	Spectator
Epistemology	Objectivism
Knower-Learner/Teacher	Blank slate, passive, inner self unexplored
Learning	Imitation of authority
Pedagogy	Isolated knowing self, competition
Ethic	Manipulators of each other and the world
Goal	Grades

However, rapid societal change has dramatically influenced our needs in education, which in turn challenges us to transform the structure and the process of our schools (King & Frick, 1999). The predominant education we have had since the beginning of the industrial age was appropriate in the 20th century; but disseminating inert knowledge and building basic skills may no longer serve educational purposes in the informational or communication age (Thornburg, 1995). We should ask: what kind of learners do we need in the 21st century? Can the conventional classroom nurture young people to become effective lifelong learners in the 21st century? If not, what kind of education can perhaps do better?

Bentley (1998) argues that the goal of 21st century education should be 'the development of understanding which can be applied and extended by taking it into the spheres of thought and action which, in the real world, demand intelligent behaviour' (p. 19). Educators talk about enhancing attainment or achievement, which is not simply about getting children to perform better. It is about getting them to be more motivated, more confident and happier, and about the idea that feeling good in these ways leads to success at school and in life generally (Cigman, 2009).

Learners in the 21st century are facing a rapidly changing world and they need to acquire a series of learning capacities in order not only to adapt to the environment but also to build a better society. Besides, students' experiences of reality unfold in terms of interrogations of overlapping systems of knowledge (Jaros & Deakin-Crick, 2007). Our schools should help young people to obtain the qualities mentioned above and become skilful synthesisers and creators of knowledge when entering an era of global communication and collaboration (King & Frick, 1999). The educational purposes of the 21st century require new ways of managing, teaching and learning to cultivate generic and active knowledge workers. Education should be designed with that goal in mind.

We have been aware that traditional approaches in education over-emphasise extrinsic success and performance of tasks; they give little support for the development of genuine understanding and risk damaging effective mind habits of learning, let alone an authentic happiness of learning and living. Since the conventional classroom is insufficient to equip young students with lifelong learning capacities, values, attitudes, dispositions and identities that are integral components of learning in the new context, the traditional didactic teaching–studying setting needs to evolve into an ecologic, dialogic and collaborative learning environment. 'Another Way' classroom (Palmer, 1993) demonstrates this sort of teaching and learning practice:

Table 2.2 'Another Way' classroom

Focus of study/subject	Partnership with nature, history, society and ourselves
Reality	We are in the world and the world is within us, a living relationship between ourselves and the world
Knowing	Active participation
Epistemology	Relationship – community of mutual knowing
Knower-Learner/Teacher	Understand self in the world, selves in conversation
Learning	Interacting, original enquiry, dialogue of knower and known
Pedagogy	Community, selves in conversation
Ethic	Mutually responsible participants and co-creators
Goal	Transformation

This evolution involves a paradigmatic shift of what we want ourselves to be and what we want our next generation to become, a transformation of values and beliefs about what counts as a good education, and a change of attitudes and dispositions towards what learners need.

The nature of the paradigmatic shift in education seems to underpin major educational thinkers' theories and writings, for instance, Dewey's (1938/1997) thinking of education and experiential learning; Roger's *Freedom to learn* (1969) and *On becoming a person* (1961); Hargreaves' (2004–2006) personalised learning; Perkins' (2008) theories of human value, education, knowledge and learning; Gardner's (2007) *Five minds for the future*; and Leadbeater's (2010) proposal of '21 ideas for the 21st century education'. Although they may have different emphases, the worldviews underpinning these contemporary educational innovations share similarities in 1) advocating an educational paradigm marked by participation, relatedness, systems and contexuality; 2) encouraging local and institutional decision-making on education; 3) indicating a reassertion of learner-centredness and experiential, exploratory learning; 4) implying a rejection of tight prescription curriculum and linear programming of teaching, and a break from heavily standardised rates of progression in learning; and 5) leading a movement towards a 'bottom-up' development and educational innovations that are internally sustainable.

However, I want to emphasise that *an educational innovation is not a revolution*. There is no standardised formula for education, and there is no predetermined path to innovation. There is no ultimate single solution to the educational problems we are having. Coaching psychology for learning may be a small trial among different kinds of innovative approaches, and it is a new idea that is developed on the shoulders of a variety of ideas and theories within a situated and participatory paradigm. It should be blended into a frame that combines closure with openness, 'a modest rigidity with a structured flexibility' (Doll, 2008, p. 193). What I would like to make clear is that *my view of learning positions itself in the new paradigm of education*. In the traditional educational paradigm, coaching may be essentially corrective: set me straight, help us out and fix our learning problems. In a more participatory and systemic educational paradigm, coaching is a process that certainly has direction, but does not have to be based on righting errors. It is more about coaches and learners co-experiencing new thinking and multiple options; its approach of problem-solving is more generative and involves drawing resources from learners themselves. Whilst young learners in the old paradigm are busy finding what is wrong or supplementing a deficiency or just catching up, students in the new paradigm gain a new perspective and fresh approaches, and become more productive in their own learning with the indirect guidance of coaching.

The participatory worldview and systems thinking greatly influence the advance of a new educational paradigm. In the next section, I will elaborate on the participatory worldview underpinning my thinking of education.

The participatory worldview and education

There are four recurring and interrelated philosophical considerations underpinning my view of education and learning: 1) an ontology of subjective–objective interaction; 2) extended epistemology and critical inter-subjectivity; 3) non-linear dynamics and participation in research methodology; and 4) authenticity, wholeness, transformation and emancipation of human beings as ultimate values. These four considerations fundamentally resonate with the participatory worldview (Reason & Rowan, 1981; Heron, 1998; Heron & Reason, 1997).

The ontology: subjective–objective interaction

Ontology refers to a branch of philosophy concerned with articulating the nature and structure of the world (Wand & Weber, 1993). The ontological question is about what the form and nature of reality is, and then, what there can be known (Guba & Lincoln, 1994). It is argued that there is an underlying dualism between the knowing subject and the objects to be known: behind this rests the whole idea of ontology as a synonym for metaphysics (Kivinen & Piiroinen, 2004). Rather than taking a firm orthodox stance, I regard reality as subjective–objective, in that the mind and the given cosmos are engaged with each other (Heron & Reason, 1997; Berman, 1981; Tarnas, 1991; Varela *et al.*, 1993; Skolimowski, 1994). The reality is the result (in Reason and Heron's word, the 'fruit') of an interaction of the mind and the world. What we meet are the world and people in the world (*Others*), but the encountering is shaped by our own terms of reference (*Self*). Heron (1996) summed up that 'it is subjective because it is only known through the form the mind gives it; and it is objective because the mind interpenetrates the given cosmos which it shapes' (p. 11).

The participatory ontology explicitly holds objections to positivism which accepts the empiricist account of the natural sciences (Reason & Rowan, 1981). Whilst positivism views the world as comprised of distinct objects independent of enquiring observers and focuses on causal relationships, formal logic and precise definitions, participatory ontology argues that positivism reduces people to models, a set of variables which are somehow equivalent across persons and situations by being manipulated, controlled and tested in an experimental environment and summarised in statistical significance. Therefore, in positivism people are alienated, isolated from their social contexts, and they can never understand human phenomena as a whole in depth (ibid.). This critique on positivism is closer to the rationalist in interpretive approaches that the social sciences are qualitatively different from the natural sciences, and human life is essentially a life of meaning, of language and reflective thoughts and communication (Giddens, 1984).

The ontology of subjective–objective interaction is in line with Marx's version of good society, in which the alienation among and between humans themselves and nature would be overcome. A similar claim is made by Blumber (1969) that people act on the basis of the meaning that objects have for them; these meanings are developed through interaction and modified through interpretive processes employed by further interaction. Abram (1996) stated that there is a deeply participatory relation and a felt reciprocity to things and to the earth. This is also reflected in phenomenological philosophers Husserl (1965) and Merleau-Ponty's

16 An enquiry of educational paradigms

(1962) work that perception itself is participatory as a certain way of linking up with phenomena and communicating with it. Skolimowski (1994) embraced this point by saying that 'things become what our consciousness makes of them through the active participation of our mind' (pp. 27–28). Furthermore, this subjective–objective notion shares an ontological assumption with pragmatism, which adopts a combination of evolutionary theory and Hegelian idealism. Pragmatism views that there is some pre-existent association of human beings in the world, but to understand these associations requires the interaction of persons with each other (Dewey, 1939). Finally the ontology is in accordance with Zen Buddhism's claim that what is to be known as reality comes from a two-way mutual relationship between subject and object rather than a one-way one, and humans should be an integrated part of the world. There is a mutual, reciprocal relation between subject and object: the subject creates the object in the sense that humans experience the object in their own individual way, and the object creates the subject in the sense that the subject is open to experiencing the object (Berger & Luckmann, 1966/1991).

The subjective–objective interplay raises an epistemological question about what the relationship is between the knower and the known. The division between knower and known has been bridged in the course of humans' action and interaction, through the negotiation and co-construction of the meanings of objects in the world (Benton & Craib, 2001). The tension of self–other distinction is dissolved through interfusion of self and other (Gaskins, 1999). We should open ourselves to meet the given, so that we can truly engage with it, interact with it and resonate with it.

Perspectives on knowledge: extended epistemology and critical inter-subjectivity

My epistemological perspectives involve an extended epistemology of four ways of knowing (experiential, presentational, propositional and practical) and the relationships between these (Heron & Reason, 1997) illlustrated in Figure 2.1. Experiential knowing is the knowledge obtained through encounter, sustained acquaintance and interaction (Heron, 1981). Presentational knowing involves seeing the apparently presented reality as a whole, and seeing a sequence of presentations as a total cycle process. Presentational construing, in which there is an active and aware use of imagination and metaphor, can be argued as a necessary condition of language acquisition and propositional knowing (Reason, 1994) that involves concepts, categories and identification of propositions (Heron, 1981). Practical knowledge, which rests in an awareness of oneself and behaviours (Reason, 1994), is demonstrated in a skill or competence that 'presupposes a conceptual grasp of principles and standards of practice, presentational elegance, and experiential grounding in the situation within which the action occurs' (Heron & Reason, 1997, p. 6). Hence, practical knowledge fulfils the three prior forms of knowing in that it can be seen as 'consciousness in the midst of action' (Torbert, 1991, p. 221).

Philosophy and educational paradigms 17

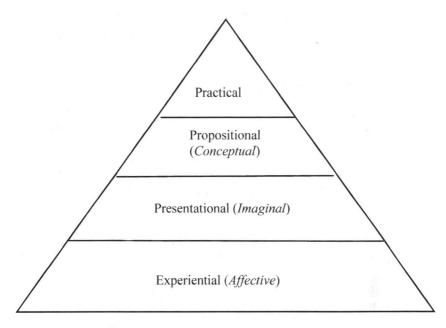

Figure 2.1 Extended epistemology in the participatory worldview

The 'systemic wisdom' (Reason, 1994, p. 12) is a smooth flow between experiential, presentational, propositional and practical knowing. However, Western epistemology is closely connected to an emphasis on intellect as the primary means of knowing and the power of conceptual language (ibid.). Experiential knowing is often overshadowed by propositional knowing, which is 'articulatable' concepts and ideas. The dominance of propositional knowing results in the separation of intellect from experience, thus knowledge coming in propositional form is valued more highly than affective, intuitive knowledge and knowing coming from practice. It also means that immediate conscious purpose is valued more highly than systemic wisdom.

Holding a sense of the extended epistemology, I think that critical inter-subjectivity is of paramount importance in learning. Critical inter-subjectivity is a critical consciousness about our knowing, including shared experiences, dialogue, feedback and exchange with others in a context of both linguistic-cultural and experiential shared meaning (Heron & Reason, 1997). It emphasises a cyclical dialectic of action and reflection, and a consciousness in which they interpenetrate (Torbert, 1991). The process of critical inter-subjectivity sets the investigator between deep engagement, participation and commitment to the moment, and self-awareness in a wider context, standing back and simultaneous reflection (Reason, 1994). These perspectives on knowing lead to the following discussion of knowledge acquisition behaviour, which should be original creative activity

18 An enquiry of educational paradigms

based on the subjective–objective ontology, extended epistemology and critical inter-subjectivity.

How do we know what we know? Rethinking methodology in educational enquiry

Since this book includes empirical studies of coaching psychology for learning, I would like to discuss participatory-informed methodology in research. The methodological question concerns how an enquirer can find out what is to be known. The acquisition of knowledge and meaning is rarely a linear process. Kuhn (1962) stated that scientific knowledge progresses by a process of perpetual paradigm shifts. A shift in paradigm produces a 'quantum leap' in understanding rather than assimilation of new knowledge into an existing paradigm. Popper (1963) suggests that individual enquirers can experience 'mini quantum leaps' at critical stages following successive cycles of experimentation. It is at these moments that an enquirer can gain greater insight and understanding of the complexities of the phenomenon under investigation.

A particular research methodology incorporates a particular educational philosophy (Carr, 1995). Empirical research, as the most common research form, is described as involving the collection, analysis and presentation of primary data in a rigorous, systematic and methodical way (Scott & Usher, 1996). The epistemological considerations relate to a problem experienced by social scientists conducting empirical research, namely 'objectivity in the research process' or the level of confidence that research findings are independent of the enquirer's involvement. We need to examine this issue in depth together with its effects on research methodology. In any educational research involving learning, some of the important data to be examined are subjective inner experiences. To systematically collect and analyse this data requires a disciplined examination of first person subjective experience. Even for the 'objective data' that is collected by proven and established linear models to examine cause and effect relationships or dependent variable/independent variable relationships, we cannot ignore the subjective elements because it very often involves personal responses on self-reported questionnaires. However, it does not mean that we have to sacrifice scientific rigour (Capra, 2003). What is needed is a methodology that is more suited to investigating complex researcher/participant interactions, a methodology that combines nonlinear dynamics and the analysis of first-person experience.

Hence I conclude that a participatory or collaborative research methodology, in which all members engage together in democratic dialogue as co-researchers and as co-subjects (Heron & Reason, 1997; Heron, 1996), is critically important for educational enquiries. First, the participatory methodology allows us to know that we are part of the world, rather than separated as minds against matter, and it allows us to join with fellow humans in collaborative forms of enquiry (Heron & Reason, 1997). Participatory enquirers assert that we can only truly do research *with* people rather than *on* people if we engage with them as persons and thus as research partners (Reason, 1994). This kind of enquiry places people in relation with the living world, with the rest of creation as relatives, with all the rights and obligations that this implies (Storm, 1972, 1994).

Second, I emphasise the importance of context. As Maturana (1991) states, 'science takes place within the context of human co-existence' (p. 30), and research becomes a critical activity when it significantly locates itself within that context. Therefore, when enquirers investigate a particular social context, the validity of knowledge comes from being located within that context. The specific contexts of coaching psychology for enquiry-based learning and problem-based learning are included in this book, and I shall elaborate them in the following chapters.

The third key point of my methodological understanding relates to Existentialism, especially in the authenticity of the enquirer, who is involved as a whole person during the process of enquiry. Self-reflexivity can be seen as one of the fundamental qualities of participatory research (Heron & Reason, 1997). Reason (1994) stated that whilst holding on to the scientific ideals of critical self-reflective enquiry and openness to public scrutiny, the practice of human enquiry engages deeply and sensitively with experience and aims to integrate action and reflection. The consequence for me in researching coaching psychology for learning is to adopt a participatory research mindset that involves:

- being open-minded;
- rigorous testing and critical examination of data and findings (using successful and appropriate criteria to check validity and reliability);
- collecting different perspectives and voices of participants as well as my own voice;
- taking risks and learning from mistakes;
- acknowledging complexity and interactive effects in the field;
- anticipating emergent discoveries;
- following the dynamic cycles of co-researching and co-learning with my participants

Axiological orientation: authenticity, wholeness, transformation and emancipation

The axiological question is asking what is intrinsically valued in being and in the human condition. Including an axiological aspect is necessary to fully define an enquiry paradigm and to make whole the concern with truth exhibited by ontological, epistemological and methodological questions (Heron & Reason, 1997).

I consider my answers to the axiological question are related to human flourishing 'as an enabling balance within and between people of hierarchy, co-operation and autonomy' (ibid., p. 10). This kind of flourishing is 'practical knowing and consummated in the process of choosing and acting' (ibid., p. 11). Autonomy relates to my axiological orientation that human *authenticity* should be addressed in living and enquiring, which expresses the creative, congruent, deep authorisation and a developmental emergence of personal and social fulfilment.

My axiological stance also involves *wholeness*. Wholeness means restoring human experience with meaning and mystery in the world as 'a sacred place' (Reason, 1994, p. 10). Participatory enquiry is to make whole and holy: 'to heal the spirit that characterises modern existence' (ibid., p. 10). This healing means to restore an individual to the community and to the context of the wider natural world, and such restoration further indicates that human experiences have a sacred dimension. It is concluded that wholeness is a political process (Bookchin, 1991; Bachrach & Botwinick, 1992) and that individuals have a basic right to be involved in the knowledge creation process that affects their lives.

I argue that this political value relates to 'emancipatory interest' (Habermas, 1971) in critical theory, which frames propositional research in terms of its impact on transformative actions seeking to free people from the domination of others. Heron (1998) suggested that lived enquiry in participatory paradigm means simply the active, innovative and examined life, which seeks both 'to transform and understand more deeply the human condition' (p. 17). However, the *emancipation* and *transformation* in my axiological perspective is not only a relief of oppression, but also an appreciation of person as an embodied experiencing subject with integration of feelings, knowing and actions, whose practical enquiry is 'a celebration of the flowering of humanity and of the co-existing cosmos' (Heron & Reason, 1997, p. 12).

Systems thinking and education

Key ideas of systems thinking

Systems thinking emerged in the 20th century as a response to and a critique of the prevailing reductionism (Flood, 2010) and Descartes' analytical thinking that focus on separating the individual pieces of what is studied (Aronson, 1996; Capra, 1994). A systems thinking approach focuses on studying the totality and the interactions of constituents of the system and becomes a philosophy for solving many practical, complex issues (Blockley, 2010). It is defined as 'getting the right information (what) to the right people (who) at the right time (when) for the right purpose (why) in the right form (where) and in the right way (how)' (Blockley, 2010). Recently systems thinking has been divided into a number of emphases, methodologies and applications. It has moved to explore the application of complexity theory and holistic science, particularly in relation to a participatory worldview (Capra, 1996, 2003).

At the heart of delivering systems thinking exists *thinking in layers, thinking about connections and loops,* and *thinking about new processes* (Blockley, 2010). I found Capra's (1994) summary of the key characteristics of systems thinking particularly helpful:

- *Shift from the parts to the whole*: the new way of thinking is thinking in terms of connectedness, contexts and relationships.
- *Shift from analysis to context*: in a living system, the properties of the parts are not intrinsic properties, but can be understood only within the context of the larger whole.
- *Shift from objects to relationships*: the objects themselves – the organisms in an ecosystem or the people in a community – are networks of relationships, embedded in larger networks.
- *Shift from hierarchies to networks*: a living system tends to form multilevelled structures of systems within systems, but there are no pyramids and no hierarchies. There are only networks nesting within other networks. There is a free flow within a network of relationships that is nurtured.
- *Shift from structure to process*: every structure is seen as the manifestation of underlying processes. Structure and process always go together.
- *Open systems*: there is a continual cyclical flow through the system and each component maintains itself in a state of dynamic balance. Therefore, feedback loops are needed from all parts of the system.

These key ideas of systems thinking prepare us to move on to the discussion of how systems thinking relates to education.

School as a living system

Before we discuss how systems thinking enlightens education, we need to consider the type of system that a school constitutes. School, or any learning community or organisation, can be regarded as a living system (Capra, 1994), a human-activities system (Newhofer, 2003), or a soft system with multiple layers of interacting human intentionality (Blockley, 2010). A soft system is organically based, mostly constructionist, and is concerned with understanding and influencing change (Sterling, 2003). In contrast, a hard system is more mechanistically based, more objectivity oriented, and is concerned with problem-solving, control and feedback. It is suggested that all hard systems are embedded in soft systems because it is through soft systems that we understand the world around us (Checkland, 1981; Blockley & Godfrey, 2000).

I would extend the notion that even in a soft system there are hard processes and soft processes. Hard processes deal with a physical, objective, material set of things, whilst soft processes involve subjective content and probably vague and imprecise information. In schools, hard processes involve relatively more 'objective' elements, such as assessment of students' academic performance, whilst soft processes are concerned with relatively more 'subjective' elements, such as learning dispositions or learning relationships. Systems thinkers are required to integrate and manage a set of hard and soft processes (Blockley, 2010). We can construct such integration through shared inter-subjective perceptions, noted in the participatory worldview.

22 An enquiry of educational paradigms

Systems thinking and education transformation

A systems approach is essential in thinking about education because schools are more like living systems that prioritise the process of improvement (Newhofer, 2003). Given that education and learning practices reflect and promote a view of the world and a certain kind of relationship between the learners and the world, an educational transformation requires a new way of valuing and thinking about human learning and being. The key benefit of systems thinking is its ability to deal with or raise creative thinking in situations marked by complexity, large numbers of interactions and the absence or ineffectiveness of immediate apparent solutions (Aronson, 1996). Thus, systems thinking can contribute to the process of educational transformation.

It is assumed that transformational change is possible by changing thinking. By explicitly drawing on systems thinking in establishing principles of change, Goldspink (2007) suggested a complex systems approach to discuss, evaluate and design aspects of educational transformation as opposites to managerialism. This approach advocates working with and harnessing self-organisation whilst revealing the basis for strategic intervention and change (ibid.). The emphasis is on human values and qualities, providing an environment in which all parties (administrators, teachers, parents and children) could learn their way forward (Foster, 2001). Clarke (2001) confirmed that a systems approach necessarily involves levels of scale that need consideration. He asserted that 'teaching results in change, not only in individuals, but also in organisations and, ultimately, in society' (p. 21). Thus it makes sense to pay attention to the components of a system that are directly and indirectly affected by change (Linnen, 2007).

Again, Capra's (1994) summary of characteristics of systems thinking helps to derive concepts and principles from the perceptual shifts, and to think how they can inform educational transformation (see Table 2.3). In this transformation an educator should be a reflective practitioner (Schon, 1983; Blockley, 1999; Dias & Blockley, 1995).

Table 2.3 How systems thinking informs educational transformation

Perceptual shift in systems thinking	Informed educational transformation
From the parts to the whole	Deeply integrate current fragment curriculum and understand their patterns of connectedness.
From analysis to context	Define diverse elements of knowledge and make connections to students' experiences within the context of their lives.
From objects to relationships	Establish collaborative learning communities, balance cooperation and competition, and nurture extended learning relationships.
From hierarchies to networks	Create an environment of networked wholeness through varying organisational levels.

Perceptual shift in systems thinking	Informed educational transformation
From structure to process	Acknowledge learning as a process, adapt academic structures to the underlying processes of change and development, and increase the sustainability of the learning community.
Open systems	Maintain energy, information and materials flowing in a flexible state, facilitate error management, and build communication channels.

What is particularly relevant to systems thinking and educational transformation is complexity theory. In order not to confuse it with systems thinking, I would like to discuss complexity theory in a separate section and examine how it impacts the paradigmatic shift in education.

Complexity theory and education

Key ideas of complexity theory

Complexity theory is systems thinking applied to the behaviour of natural systems (McElroy, 2000). Complexity studies indicate that the most creative phase of a system lies between order and chaos. Patterns which enhance a system's ability to adapt successfully to its environment are stabilised and repeated; those that do not are rejected in favour of radically new ones (ibid.). As complexity theory seeks to understand how order and stability arise from the interactions of components, emergence, self-organisation (Ball, 2004, p. 5), autoanalysis (Keith, 2006, p. 2), open systems, learning feedback, adaptability and communication (Prigogine & Stengers, 1985; Cohen & Stewart, 1995) are the main themes in complexity theory.

Complexity theory recognises that human organisations are groups of independent, autonomous agents sharing certain goals and operating in accordance with individually and collectively held rules. These rules are not necessarily in harmony with one another; the tension between them gives rise to the emergence of new ideas to replace the old ones over time (Holland, 1995; McElroy, 2000). This aspect of complexity theory, similar to field theory in Gestalt psychology (Lewin, 1952), requires holistic and interactionist approaches to understanding change in unpredictable and nonlinear circumstances. Instead of reducing complex interactive phenomena to separate elements, the overall picture or total situation is appreciated as a whole; its organised, interconnected and interdependent nature is investigated with its co-existing aspects (Parlett, 1991). Behaviours and phenomenal experiences which are seen as part of the total field are contextualised and organised (Lewin, 1952).

24   An enquiry of educational paradigms

Complexity theory and educational transformation

Complexity theory offers useful insights into the nature of continuity and change, so it is of considerable importance in the philosophical understanding of educational and institutional change in terms of 'its critique of positivism, its affinity to Dewey and Habermas, its arguments for openness, diversity, and its emphasis on relationships, agency and creativity' (Mason, 2008, p. 6). Davis and Sumara (2006) also considered how complexity theory might be appropriate to the concerns of educators and educational researchers as 'a properly educational discourse' (p. 1).

Complexity thinkers argue that knowledge management, which offers a theory of how cognition happens in human social systems, is closely related to complexity theory. A complex adaptive systems theory offers explanations of how knowledge naturally unfolds and how learning happens in living systems: every new idea that replaces an old one can be thought of as an innovation; innovation that leads to changes in knowledge and practice can be thought of as a learning event (Holland, 1995).

Educational systems, institutions and organisations exhibit many features of complex adaptive systems, being dynamic and emergent. The practices in these systems shape societal change through learning, adaptation, development and co-evolution between them and their environments (Stewart, 2001; Keith, 2006). The theory is of pedagogical significance by balancing novelty and confirmation in a self-organised system (Semetsky, 2008). This is associated with a rejection of structuralism as a consequence of considering educational systems, as characterised by the principles of openness, indeterminism, unpredictability and uncertainty (Olssen, 2008).

Research methodology for complexity theory

Thinking about context, holism and process is emphasised in complexity theory, which points to methodological, paradigmatic and theoretical pluralism (Mason, 2008). Cilliers (2005) noted that there is a need to observe complex human systems as comprised of interactive agents, which highlights the importance of researching from an ethical perspective. Horn (2008) suggested interactive and reflexive research practice is based on this recognition and fulfils this ethical ideal by engaging participants and researchers in the ongoing communication. It is also proposed that complexity theory allows for different ways of thinking about context and provides rationales for the investigation of individuals, difference and specificity (Haggis, 2008). This proposal was echoed by a number of scholars, that our thinking about research on education is moving away from casual models, single interventions and simplistic solutions to modelling the actual interconnections across multiple levels of organisation with its constraining or enabling contexts and resources (Lewin & Regine, 2000; Morrison, 2002; Lemke & Sabelli, 2008).

Specifically, Keith (2006) proposed that *case studies*, rather than randomised controlled trials, are an appropriate research methodology in complexity theory as

Philosophy and educational paradigms   25

'case studies catch complexity, specificity and the need to locate individual acts within multiple contexts and environment' (p. 4). Mason (2008) stated that 'complexity theory suggests the need for case study methodology, qualitative research and participatory, multi-perspective and collaborative, self-organised, partnership-based forms of research, premised on interactionist, qualitative and interpretive accounts' (p. 6). Rather than providing evidence for prescription, educational research should be understood as descriptive and explanatory within a range of interpretive possibilities (ibid.). These views influenced how I would approach the research on coaching psychology for learning.

Challenges of complexity theory to philosophy of education

Whilst complexity theory successfully challenges educational philosophy to rethink accepted paradigms of teaching and learning, it has difficulties in relation to the philosophy of education.

The first challenge is its axiology to educational philosophy. Morrison (2002) elucidated that complexity theory is in its nature a descriptive theory that is easily misunderstood as a prescriptive theory. Mason (2008) argued that the theory is silent on key issues of values and ethics that educational philosophy should embrace. However, this issue may be resolved by redefining the basis of education as inter-disciplinary and emergent. The basis obtains essential ethics and values and itself can be viewed as a reassertion of freedom in education (Doll, 1993), though these values are not neatly stated in the theory. Complexity theory provides the opportunity for a renaissance of educational issues which have been relatively silent in the climates of highly controlled education, with curriculum-centred or teacher-centred classrooms, heavily prescriptive and mandated contents and with assessment systems over-emphasising academic performance.

The second challenge is to explore how useful complexity theory actually is in offering explanations of change and evolution in particular situations (Keith, 2006). Davis and Sumara (2006) stated that 'complexity science will not tell educators or educational researchers what to do in any prescriptive sense . . . but it can provide direct advice on how to focus efforts when preparing for teaching' (p. 318). If educators cannot predict what is going to be an outcome, how far can this theory lead educational innovators to take responsibility for what happens or what turns out to be the situation (Stacey, 1996)? Galbraith (2004) asked why complexity theory should be any better at improving schools than its alternative (e.g., linear theories), and where the evidence is to support its advantages. Thus, how comfortably the theory sits within educational contexts is questionable in terms of its own unpredictability and questionable internal consistency, especially for educational policy makers and practitioners who seek efficiency, control, comprehensibility and immediate solutions to educational problems (Levin, 1991).

A similar problem is posed in systems thinking: if educators cannot figure out what elements are critical in the improvement of the whole system, what shall we focus on? Is systems thinking or complexity theory simply an excuse for ambiguity, inefficiency and lack of accountability towards an uncertain future? I argue that its own uncertainty is not necessarily a weakness, but we need to make more effort to justify it when identifying its benefits to educational improvements.

Summary

Engaging with philosophical exploration is likely to cause some debate on educational, psychological, sociological and political issues. The differentiated perspectives are encouraged to co-exist and challenge each other in order to inform a paradigmatic change in education. This chapter reflects and reinforces my engagement with philosophical thinking of learning in the age of paradigmatic shift in education, integrating 1) a participatory worldview, 2) systems thinking and 3) complexity theory. This integration has helped me to identify the purpose and the epistemological understanding of knowing and learning, the ethical awareness of having democratic dialogues with learners and the methodological considerations of employing a participatory approach in studying coaching psychology for learning. Following the clarification of my philosophical foundation, I will examine learning theories from a psychological perspective in the next chapter. I would like to draw the attention of researchers and practitioners to the current issue of coaching psychology and learning for dispositional development, to engage them in the discussion and debate how we can strengthen what we have done well so far and how we can do better in the future to build positive learning characters in new generations.

Recommended reading

Carr, W. (1995). *For education: Towards critical educational inquiry*. Maidenhead: Open University Press.
Gardner, H. (2007). *Five minds for the future*. Cambridge, MA: Harvard Business School Press.
Heron, J. (1996). *Co-operative inquiry: Research into the human condition*. London: Sage.
Perkins, D. (2008). *Making learning whole: How seven principles of teaching can transform education*. San Francisco: Jossey-Bass.

Key points for reflection

- How do you understand education reflecting your philosophical positioning?
- What problems does a traditional educational worldview face in the 21st century?
- How do participatory paradigm and systems thinking contribute to your understanding of learning?
- What kind of learning and what kind of learner do you want to cultivate as a teacher?

References

Abram, D. (1996). *The spell of the sensuous*. New York: Pantheon.

Aronson, D. (1996). *Overview of systems thinking*. Retrieved from www.thinking.net/SystemsThinking/OverviewSTarticle.pdf

Bachrach, P., & Botwinick, A. (1992). *Power and empowerment: A radical theory of participatory democracy*. Philadelphia: Temple University Press.

Ball, P. (2004). *Critical mass: How one thing leads to another*. London: Arrow Books.

Bentley, T. (1998). *Learning beyond the classroom: Education for a changing world*. London: Routledge.

Benton, T., & Craib, I. (2001). *Philosophy of social science: Philosophical issues in social thought*. Basingstoke: Palgrave Macmillan.

Berger, P., & Luckmann, T. (1966/1991). *The social construction of reality: A treatise in the sociology of knowledge*. Harmondsworth: Penguin.

Berman, M. (1981). *The reenchantment of the world*. Ithaca, NY: Cornell University Press.

Blockley, D. (1999). Process modelling from reflective practice for engineering quality. *Civil Engineering and Environmental Systems, 16*(4), 287–313.

Blockley, D. (2010). The importance of being process. *Civil Engineering and Environmental Systems, 27*(3), 189–199.

Blockley, D., & Godfrey, P. (2000). *Doing it differently: Systems for rethinking construction*. London: Thomas Telford Ltd.

Blumber, H. (1969). *Symbolic interactionism: perspectives and method*. Englewood Cliffs, NJ: Prentice-Hall.

Bookchin, M. (1991). *The ecology of freedom: The emergence and dissolution of hierarchy*. New York: Black Rose.

Capra, F. (1994). *From the parts to the whole: Systems thinking in ecology and education*. Seminar Mill Valley School District.

Capra, F. (1996). *The web of life: A new synthesis of mind and matter*. London: Harper Collins.

Capra, F. (2003). *The hidden connections: A science for sustainable living*. London: Harper Collins.

Carr, W. (1995). *For education: Towards critical educational inquiry*. Maidenhead: Open University Press.

Checkland, P. (1981). *Systems thinking, systems practice*. Chichester: John Wiley & Sons.

Cigman, R. (2009). Enhancing children. In R. Cigman & D. Andrew (Eds). *New philosophies of learning*. West Sussex: John Wiley & Sons.

Cilliers, P. (2005). Knowledge, limits and boundaries. *Futures, 37*, 605–613.

Clarke, M. A. (2001). *Introduction spring 2001*. Denver, CO: University of Colorado at Denver.

Cohen, J., & Stewart, I. (1995). *The collapse of chaos*. Harmondsworth: Penguin.

Davis, B., & Sumara, D. (2006). *Complexity and education: Inquiries into learning, teaching, and research*. Mahwah, NJ: Lawrence Erlbaum Associates.

Dewey, J. (1938). *Experience and education*. New York: Simon & Schuster.

Dewey, J. (1939). *Logic: The theory of inquiry*. London: Allen & Unwin.

Dias, W., & Blockley, D. (1995). Reflective practice in engineering design. *Proceedings – Institution of Civil Engineers, 108*, 160–168.

Doll, W. (1993). *A postmodern perspective on curriculum*. New York: Teachers College Press.

28 An enquiry of educational paradigms

Doll, W. (2008). Complexity and the culture of curriculum. *Educational Philosophy and Theory, 40*(1), 190–212.

Flood, R. L. (2010). The relationship of 'systems thinking' to action research. *Systemic Practice and Action Research, 23*(4), 269–284.

Foster, M. (2001). *Learning our way forward*. Department of education, training and employment, Government of South Australia.

Galbraith, P. (2004). Organizational leadership and chaos theory: let's be careful. *Journal of Educational Administration, 42*(1), 9–28.

Gardner, H. (2007). *Five minds for the future*. Cambridge, MA: Harvard Business School Press.

Gaskins, R. W. (1999). 'Adding legs to a snake': A reanalysis of motivation and the pursuit of happiness from a Zen Buddhist perspective. *Journal of Educational Psychology, 91*(2), 204–215.

Giddens, A. (1984). The *constitution of society, outline of the theory of structuralism*. Cambridge: Policy Press.

Goldspink, C. (2007). Transforming education: Evidential support for a complex systems approach. *Transforming Education, 9*(1–2), 77–92.

Guba, E. G., & Lincoln, Y. S. (1994). Competing paradigms in qualitative research. In N. K. Denzin & Y. S. Lincoln (Eds), *Handbook of qualitative research* (pp. 105–117). Thousand Oaks, CA: SAGE.

Habermas, J. (1971). *Knowledge and human interests*. Boston: Beacon Press.

Haggis, T. (2008). Knowledge must be contextual: Exploring some possible implications of complexity and dynamic systems theories for educational research. *Educational Philosophy and Theory, 40*(1), 159–176.

Hargreaves, D. (2004–2006). *Personalising learning pamphlet* (Series). London: Specialist Schools Trust.

Haste, H. (2009). What is 'competence' and how should education incorporate new technology's tools to generate 'competent civic agents'. *Curriculum Journal, 20*(3), 207–223.

Heron, J. (1981). Philosophical basis for a new paradigm. In P. Reason & J. Rowan (Eds), *Human inquiry: A sourcebook of new paradigm research*. Chichester: John Wiley & Sons.

Heron, J. (1996). *Co-operative inquiry: Research into the human condition*. London: Sage.

Heron, J. (1998). *Sacred science: person-centred inquiry into the spiritual and the subtle*. Ross-on-Wye: PCCS Books.

Heron, J., & Reason, P. (1997). A participatory inquiry paradigm. *Qualitative Inquiry, 3*(3), 274–294.

Holland, J. H. (1995). *Hidden order: How adaptation builds complexity*. Reading, Mass: Addison-Wesley.

Horn, J. (2008). Human research and complexity theory. *Educational Philosophy and Theory, 40*, 130–143.

Husserl, E. (1965). Philosophy as rigorous science. In *Phenomenology and the crisis of philosophy* (Q. Laurer, Trans. & Ed.) (pp. 71–147). New York: Harper. (Original work published 1911.)

Jaros, M., & Deakin-Crick, R. (2007). Personalised learning in the post mechanical age. *Journal of Curriculum Studies, 39*(4), 423–440.

Keith, M. (2006, November). *Complexity theory and education*. Paper presented at the APERA Conference, Hong Kong.

King, K., & Frick, T. (1999, April). *Transforming education: Case studies in systems thinking*. Paper presented at the annual meeting of the American Educational Research Association, Montreal, Canada.

Kivinen, O., & Piiroinen, T. (2004). The relevance of ontological commitments in social science: Realist and pragmatist viewpoints. *Journal for the Theory of Social Behaviour, 34*(3), 231–248.

Kuhn, T. (1962). *The structure of scientific revolutions*. Chicago: University of Chicago Press.

Leadbeater, C. (2010). *What's next? 21 ideas for 21st century education*. Innovation Unit. Retrieved from: http://charlesleadbeater.net/wp-content/uploads/2010/01/Next2.pdf

Lemke, J. L., & Sabelli, N. H. (2008). Complex systems and educational change: Towards a new research agenda. *Educational Philosophy and Theory, 40*(1), 118–129.

Levin, H. M. (1991). Why isn't educational research more useful? In D. S. Anderson & B. J. Biddle (Eds), *Knowledge for policy: Improving education through research* (pp. 70–78). London: Falmer.

Lewin, K. (1952). *Field theory in social science*. London: Tavistock.

Lewin, R., & Regine, B. (2000). *The soul at work: Listen, respond, let go: Embracing complexity science for business success*. New York: Simon and Schuster.

Linnen, L. (2007, September). *The effects of coaching on one teacher's classroom discourse*. Paper presented at the British Research Association Annual Conference, Institution of Education, University of London.

Marshall, S. (1999). Principles for the new story of learning. *New Horizons for Learning Online Journal, 6*(1), March.

Mason, M. (2008). Complexity theory and the philosophy of education. *Educational Philosophy and Theory, 40*(1), 4–18.

Maturana, H. (1991). Science and daily life: The ontology of scientific explanations. In F. Steier (Ed.), *Research and reflexivity* (pp. 30–52). London: Sage.

McElroy, M. (2000). Integrating complexity theory, knowledge management and organisation learning. *Journal of Knowledge Management, 4*(3), 195–208.

Merleau-Ponty, M. (1962). *Phenomenology of Perception* (S. Colin, Trans.). London: Routledge & Kegan Paul.

Morrison, K. R. B. (2002). *School leadership and complexity theory*. London: Routledge.

Newhofer, F. (2003). Systems thinking in education. *Forum, 45*(2), 75–77.

Olssen, M. (2008). Foucault as complexity theorist. *Educational Philosophy and Theory, 40*(1), 96–117.

Palmer, P. (1993). *To know as we are known: Education as a spiritual journey*. New York: Harper Collins.

Parlett, M. (1991). Reflections on field theory. *British Gestalt Journal, 1*, 69–81.

Perkins, D. (2008). *Making learning whole: How seven principles of teaching can transform education*. San Francisco: Jossey-Bass.

Popper, K. (1963). *Conjectures and refutations: The growth of scientific knowledge*. London: Routledge.

Prigogine, I., & Stengers, I. (1985). *Order out of chaos*. London: Flamingo.

Reason, P. (1994). Three approaches to participative inquiry. In N.K. Denzin & Y.S. Lincoln (Eds), *Handbook of qualitative research* (pp. 324–339). London: Sage.

Reason, P., & Rowan, J. (1981). *Human inquiry: A sourcebook of new paradigm research*. Chichester: John Wiley & Sons.

30 An enquiry of educational paradigms

Reigeluth, C. M. (1994). The imperative for systemic change. In C. M. Reigeluth & R. J. Garfinkle (Eds), *Systemic change in education* (pp. 3–11). Englewood Cliffs, NJ: Educational Technology Publications.

Rogers, C. (1961). *On becoming a person: A therapist's view of psychotherapy*. London: Constable.

Rogers, C. (1969). *Freedom to learn*. Columbus, OH: Merrill.

Schon, D. A. (1983). *The reflective practitioner: How professionals think in action*. New York: Basic Books.

Scott, D., & Usher, R. (1996). *Understanding educational research*. London: Routledge.

Semetsky, I. (2008). The transversal communication, or: reconciling science and magic. *Cybernetics & Human Knowing, 15*(2), 33–48.

Skolimowski, H. (1994). *The participatory mind*. New York: Ballantine.

Stacey, R. D. (1996). *Complexity and creativity in organizations*. San Francisco: Berrett-Koehler.

Sterling, S. (2003). *Whole systems thinking as a basis for paradigm change in education: Explorations in the context of sustainability* (Unpublished doctoral dissertation). Bath: Centre for Research in Education and the Environment, University of Bath.

Stewart, M. (2001). *The co-evolving organization*. Rutland: Decomplexity Associates Ltd.

Storm, H. (1972). *Seven arrows*. New York: Harper & Row.

Storm, H. (1994). *Lightningbolt*. New York: Ballantine.

Tarnas, R. (1991). *The passion of the western mind: Understanding the ideas that shaped our worldview*. New York: Ballantine.

Thornburg, D. (1995). Welcome to the communication age. *Internet Research, 5*(1), 64–70.

Torbert, W. R. (1991). *The power of balance*. Newbury Park, CA: Sage.

Varela, F., Thompson, E., & Rosch, E. (1993). *The embodied mind*. Cambridge, Mass: MIT Press.

Wand, Y., & Weber, R. (1993). On the ontological expressiveness of information systems analysis and design grammars. *Journal of Information Systems, 3*(4), 217–237.

Chapter 3

What is learning?

Introduction

This chapter is an investigation into and critique about a number of rigorous existing psychological and learning theories with particular relevance to my philosophical understanding of education. The feature of this comprehensive investigation is to view learning as a process and as a participative experience that is 'transformative, active, interactive, intrinsically motivating and lifelong' (Collins *et al.*, 2002, p. 11). This chapter thus paves the platform to discuss what coaching means to this learning and helps to establish the foundation of coaching psychology for learning.

A psychological movement in the view of learning

Educational psychology began at the beginning of the 20th century as a 'guiding science of the school' (Cubberley, 1920, p. 755), 'a discipline the content of which was defined by the problems of education and the methods of which were defined by the science of psychology' (Mayer, 1992, p. 406). There is a strong link between educational psychology theorising and research and the teaching–learning process (McInerney, 2005).

According to Mayer (1992), the view of learning and instruction influenced by psychology has changed over the course of the 20th century and it has gone through three main stages: learning as a *response acquisition*, learning as *knowledge acquisition*, and learning as *knowledge construction*. The changes in views of learning have straightforward implications for instruction and teaching, including the goal of instruction, the role of teacher and students, and the evaluation of learning outcomes. I summarise Mayer's arguments in Table 3.1 below. Nevertheless, Mayer's arguments of learning have not gone beyond the view of the learner as an active processor of information within subject-matter domains. The first problem is that the motivation and intentionality of a learner seems to be ignored. The second problem rests on the fact that the social-cultural element underpinning learning as knowledge co-construction is clearly missing from the table. The third problem is that the above theories seem to overly emphasise the 'cold' (Silberman *et al.*, 1976) aspect of learning.

Table 3.1 Views of learning

	Learning as response acquisition	*Learning as knowledge acquisition*	*Learning as knowledge construction*
Historical context	1930s – 1940s	1950s – 1960s	1970s – 1980s
Psychological dominance	Behaviourism	Cognitive psychology (information processing)	Cognitive psychology (socio-cultural)
Nature of learning	A mechanistic process in which: • successful responses are automatically strengthened; • unsuccessful responses are automatically weakened; • associations are strengthened or weakened according to environmental feedback.	A process of acquiring knowledge in which the learner: • subdivides each topic into studies; • subdivides each study into lessons; • subdivides each lesson into specific facts and formulae; • proceeds step by step to master each one of these separate parts; • covers the entire ground of knowledge.	A process of knowledge construction in which: • the learner studies subject-based learning in more realistic situations, and selects relevant information and interprets it through one's existing knowledge; • learning becomes active involving reaching out of one's mind and organic assimilation from within.
Instructional approach	Creating situations that elicit responses from learners and providing appropriate reinforcement for each response.	Curriculum-centred approach; teaching basic information from textbooks and lectures.	Child-centred approach; the child is the starting point, the centre, the end. His development and his growth is the ideal.
Goal of instruction	To increase the number of correct behaviours in the learner's repertoire.	To increase the amount of knowledge in the learner's repertoire	To develop learning and thinking strategies that are appropriate for working within various subject domains.

	Learning as response acquisition	*Learning as knowledge acquisition*	*Learning as knowledge construction*
Teacher's role in learning	An active dispenser of feedback, who rewards correct responses and punishes incorrect ones.	A dispenser of knowledge and information.	A participant with the learner in the process of shared cognition and the process of constructing meaning in a given situation.
Student's role in learning	A response-acquisition machine; a passive being whose repertoire of behaviours is determined by rewards and punishments encountered in the environment.	A recipient of knowledge	A constructor of knowledge; an autonomous learner with meta-cognitive skills for controlling his or her cognitive processes during learning.
Evaluation of learning outcomes	By measuring the amount of behaviour change.	By measuring the amount of knowledge acquired.	Evaluation is qualitative rather than quantitative, determining how the student structures and processes knowledge rather than how much is learned.

34   An enquiry of educational paradigms

McInerney (2005) presented an overview of developments in educational psychology over the past 25 years and noted an expansion of range of topics. He identified four basic emphases in educational psychology: behavioural psychology, cognitive psychology, social cognitive theory and humanism. This overview resolves the last two problems in Mayer's arguments to some extent: social cognitive psychology has been added to the list and humanism has been given more consideration. However, the motivational aspect of learning is not well elaborated in these emphases. The motivational, social and humanistic perspectives on learning are essential for understanding what kind of 'learning' I refer to in this book.

Motivational theories of learning

Affective and cognitive models of motivation

Motivation concerns the energisation and direction of behaviour and it attempts to answer questions about what gets individuals moving and toward what activities or tasks (Pintrich & Schunk, 2002). Most recent research on learners' motivation has focused on social-cognitive models that parallel the general cognitive revolution in psychology (Pintrich, 2003). In contrast, Covington (1998) proposed a motivational theory based on the need for self-worth and self-esteem. In this theory, social-cognitive constructs also play an important role in mediating between the need of self-worth and behaviours, but this model includes more affective and emotional components (Covington, 1998; Covington & Dray, 2002). Affections serve a major guiding and regulatory role in cognitive and motivational systems (Schutz & DeCuir, 2002). When implicit motives and explicit goals are congruent, individuals are more motivated and perform better (Schultheiss, 2001). This theory has an important application in learning – when learning tasks are designed with clear goals that are congruent with students' intrinsic needs and feelings, the effectiveness of learning can be maximised.

Self-determination theory (SDT) integrates both needs and social-cognitive constructs: the reward is in the process itself and in the recognition of being in control of, and responsible for, one's own learning (Deci & Ryan, 1985, 2000). Three basic needs are addressed: 1) *competence*, the desire to master and be competent in interactions with the environment; 2) *autonomy*, the desire to be in control or to feel autonomous in terms of one's own behaviour; and 3) *relatedness*, a wanting to belong or be attached to a group. The effects of these needs are mediated by social-cognitive constructs such as perceived competence, control beliefs and regulatory styles (Deci & Ryan, 2000). The theory also shares similarities in content with achievement motives that concern the need for achievement, power and affiliation (Pintrick & Schunk, 2002). What seems to be of most interest for me in SDT is that it expands the traditional distinction between intrinsic and extrinsic motivation to a more complex differentiation of motivation from mostly externally controlled to mostly self-determined (Deci & Ryan, 2000). Students who are intrinsically motivated feel autonomous and self-determined, and experience high levels of interest and inherent satisfaction from involvement in learning (Deci & Ryan, 1985).

Self-efficacy and mindset theory

Self-efficacy, probably at the centre of the mechanisms of personal agency, refers to people's beliefs about their capacities to exercise control over their own level of functioning and over events that affect their lives (Bandura, 1989, 1991). Self-efficacy can be seen as a self-concept that generates self-directness and determines motivation to learn (Lyons, 2003). Motivation and self-directedness stem from the fact that people respond evaluatively to their own behaviour, from the combined influence of goals with performance feedback (Bandura, 1991; Bandura & Cervone, 1983; Locke & Latham, 1990). Since learning involves complex tasks that make heavy attentional and cognitive demands, self-satisfaction with personal progress towards challenging standards provides a positive motivational orientation for performance accomplishments (Bandura, 1991).

People who regard ability as an acquirable skill that can be increased by gaining knowledge and perfecting competencies adopt a functional learning goal – they seek challenges that provide opportunities to expand their knowledge and competencies, and regard errors and mistakes as a natural part of the acquisition process. They judge their capabilities more in terms of personal improvement than by comparison against the achievement of others. Construing ability as an acquirable skill fosters a highly resilient sense of personal efficacy (Wood & Bandura, 1989).

The above notion is similar to the mindset theory proposed by psychologist Carol Dweck (2006). A *growth mindset* entails that mind habits can grow and change through effort rather than remain as a fixed entity. People with a growth mindset tend to invest their self-satisfaction in the attainment of challenging goals. In contrast, people who have a *fixed mindset* tend to view ability as an inherent capacity. They regard errors and deficient performances as carrying a high evaluative threat, therefore they prefer tasks that minimise errors and permit ready display of intellectual proficiency, avoid making effort, and adopt easily attainable goals as sufficing at the expense of expanding their knowledge and competencies. The motivation for learning in the growth or fixed mindset decides whether learners want to *improve* or *prove* themselves, and thus determines whether they can truly learn something or just want to look smart.

Situated and social perspective of motivation

The self-efficacy and mindset theories deal with the intra-psychological process of learners. The external dynamics also lead to action. It would seem from a social-cognitive motivational perspective that having as high as possible efficacy and competence beliefs would be useful to keep students motivated in learning contexts (Pintrich, 2003).

36 An enquiry of educational paradigms

Situated motivation (Hickey, 1997) suggests that contextual and cultural factors are paramount in the operation of cognition and motivation. Students' motivation is situated in, influenced by and changed through the nature of learning culture, interactions, tasks, activities and practices. What teachers do in terms of instruction does make a difference to students' motivation. Based on motivational literature, Pintrich (2003) listed the implication for the design principles of instruction:

- providing clear and accurate feedback regarding competence and self-efficacy;
- focusing on the development of competence, expertise and skills;
- designing tasks that offer opportunities to exercise choice and control, but also challenge students;
- providing feedback that stresses the process nature of learning, including the importance of effort, strategies and potential self-control of learning;
- providing materials and activities that are personally meaningful and interesting to the students, allowing for some personal identification with school;
- using a classroom discourse focusing on mastery, learning and understanding.

There are multiple pathways in applying design principles to create motivating learning environments for students. Exploring motivation for learning particularly from a contextually, socially grounded viewpoint leads to a broader view of social perspectives and discursive psychology that contributes to my understanding of learning.

Social perspectives on learning and discursive psychology

Piaget or Vygostsky?

Piaget's theory of *personal cognitive constructivism* deals with children growing through a discrete set of cognitive stages (sensori-motor, preoperational, concrete operational and formal operational) and developing increasingly sophisticated ways of handling knowledge (Piaget, 1937/1954). The notion that children construct their own schemas through personal interaction with the world of experiences regards *social interaction as a source of modelling* through which learned behaviours are acquired via the observation of others and reinforcement that may reflect behavioural principles. However, Marx (1859) challenged individuals as to their own subjectivity: 'it is not the consciousness of men that determines their being but, on the contrary, their social being that determines their consciousness' (p. 328). The social dimensions of learning gain considerable attention in Vygotsky's (1978) *socio-cultural constructivism*, which throws emphasis on learners constructing their own meanings within the wider social, cultural, and historical contexts of learning. The reciprocal interactions of these contexts with the individuals' learning give rise to the construction of shared knowledge

What is learning?   37

(John-Steiner & Mahn, 1996; Marshall, 1996). In this sense, I take Vygotsky's socio-cultural perspective of learning in this book.

Social interactions in learning and perezhivanie

Learning involves a dynamic, interdependent, communicative process of social and individual aspects where knowledge and understandings are shared and co-constructed in culturally formed contexts, mediated by language and other symbol systems (John-Steiner & Mahn, 1996). Lave and Wenger (1991) and other social constructionists taking a Vygotskian perspective (e.g., Bruner, Wood, Claxton) rejected the notion of learning as merely the acquisition of certain forms of knowledge. They locate learning in social relationships or situations of participation. Learning refers 'not just to local events of engagement in certain activities with certain people, but to a more encompassing process of being active participants in the practices of social communities and constructing identities in relation to these communicates' (Wenger, 1999). As a social process rather than an individual one, learning occurs in social interactions that help people bring together a range of different perspectives, explicitly share knowledge, make sense of the world and transform individuals through involvement in collective activities (Livingston & Shiach, 2010).

Vygotsky (1978) emphasised the emotional aspect of social interaction and its impact on learning. The way in which learners perceive, experience and process the emotional aspects refers to a concept of *perezhivanie* (Vygotsky, 1978). Perezhivanie indicates that the affective processes of language and human connection in social interaction are individually perceived, appropriated and represented by the learner. These interactions occur in the learner's zone of proximal development.

Zone of proximal development

The term 'zone of proximal development' (ZPD) is perhaps one of the most well-known ideas associated with the Vygotskian perspective of learning and development (Chaiklin, 2003). It is 'the distance between the actual development level (of the learner) as determined by independent problem solving and the level of potential development as determined through problem solving under adult guidance or in collaboration with more capable peers' (Vygotsky, 1978, p. 86).

ZPD has two significant impacts on my understanding of facilitating learning. First, ZPD suggests that there are upper and lower limits (the zone of the learner), within which new learning will occur (Hammond & Gibbons, 2005). The zone can be simply put as the distance between what a person can do with and without help (Verenikina, 2003). The point here is that coaching or any other kind of facilitation provided should complement and build on the learner's existing abilities and go just slightly beyond their current competence (Cole & Cole, 2001). If the coaching is pitched too high, the learner is likely to be frustrated or anxious; if the coaching is too low, the learner is presented with no challenge and simply feels bored

38 An enquiry of educational paradigms

(Mariani, 1997). So there should be an appropriate combination of challenge and support to make sure that the learners are working *within* their current ZPD in order to extend their knowledge and understanding without pushing them too much.

Secondly, ZPD is not a kind of individual attribute that is possessed or assessed by each learner; a student does not *have* a ZPD, but rather, *shares* and *co-constructs* one with a coach through the activities in which they jointly participate (Hammond & Gibbons, 2005). This means rather than having 'fixed' limits, ZPD 'constitutes a potential space for learning that is created in the interactions between participants as they engage in a particular activity together' (Wells, 1999, p. 330). Measuring the level of potential development is just as important as measuring the actual developmental level (Wertsch & Tulviste, 1992). The upper limit of ZPD may change as the activity unfolds, so the level of potential development may rise higher. Effective facilitation of learning is able to extend the upper limit of ZPD and make it possible for learners to reach beyond what they are supposed to be capable of.

Scaffolding

The concept of scaffolding, which is 'a way of operationalising Vygotsky's concept of working in the zone of proximal development' (Wells, 1999, p. 127), was firstly used by Wood *et al.* (1976) as a metaphor in the learning context to describe the nature of parental tutoring in the language development of young children. Just as builders provide essential but temporary support around the outside of a new building before the building is able to support itself, teachers need to provide temporary supporting structures to assist students to develop new understandings and new abilities that they cannot manage on their own in the classroom context (Hammond & Gibbons, 2005). Scaffolding consists essentially of the adult 'controlling' elements of the task that are initially beyond the learner's unassisted efforts, thus permitting them to concentrate on completing only those elements that are within their range of competence (Wood *et al.*, 1976). In that sense, scaffolding assumes a more competent person (a teacher or a coach) and a less competent person (a child or a student) on a jointly accomplished learning task through mediating; it is often the case that learners' efforts are assisted and fostered by others who are more skilful (Kaye, 1992). However, scaffolding in the classroom is easily narrowed as a one-way process as the interactions in the classroom are predominantly one-sided and teacher-driven. Donovan and Smolkin's (2002) study of scaffolding revealed that when scaffolding is understood as direct instruction and guidelines, it might become counterproductive: scaffolding might hinder children in demonstrating their full range of genre knowledge. I would adopt a *facilitative* approach to supporting learning, which is different from an instructional approach.

Three metaphors of learning: a linguistic turn

The discussion of learning from a socio-cultural perspective so far leads to a linguistic turn that relates to different metaphors of learning. Sfard (1998) proposed that there are two dominant metaphors of learning in our education: the *acquisition metaphor* in which learning is treated as gaining possession over some commodity, and the *participation metaphor* in which learning is conceptualised as changing roles and identities within communities of shared practice. In the acquisition metaphor of learning, basic units of knowledge can be accumulated, gradually refined, and combined to form a richer cognitive structure; a human mind that acquires meaning is analogous to a container to be filled with certain materials. There is a rich terminological assortment that denotes the action of gaining ownership over some kind of self-sustained entity: *reception, acquisition, construction, internalisation, appropriation, transmission, attainment, development, accumulation* and *grasp* (ibid.). The teachers help the students to attain these goals by telling, instructing, conveying and delivering.

In contrast, the participation metaphor of learning places its attention on activities; it does not imply a clear end point to the process of learning, and the ongoing learning activities are never considered separately from the context within which they take place. The participation metaphor that brings the message of *situatedness, contextuality, social mediation, discourse, communication, togetherness* and *collaboration* potentially leads to a more democratic practice of teaching and learning. It suggests that learners should be viewed as people who participate in certain kinds of activities rather than accumulate conceptual entities, and learning a subject is conceived as a process of becoming a member of a certain community. Nevertheless, seeing learning as pure participation might produce a distorted picture of the full unfolding process, and it might pose pedagogical issues on subject teaching and learning. Moreover, I find the dichotomy between acquisition and participation might risk placing individualistic and social perspectives of learning at opposite poles of the individual/social axis.

Therefore, I suggest that we need to live with both metaphors and embrace the metaphorical pluralism. The competition between these two metaphors reveals the arbitrary nature of the generally accepted classification of learning, thus opening up an opportunity for producing a critical theory of learning that has an emancipatory and engaging effect on educational communities. I agree with Koschmann's (1999) third metaphor for learning based on Dewey and Bentley's (1946) notion of transactionalism that *learning is an inter-subjective co-construction of reality*. This metaphor sees learning as a transaction taking place between the learner and the environment, including both changes to the individual and to the learner's social environment. This transactional process entails a dialogic and discursive perspective of learning.

Discursive psychology and learning

Learning intimately relates to and depends upon internal and external speech; it develops and is maintained through interpersonal experience. The higher voluntary forms of human behaviour have their roots in social interaction and in an individual's participation in social behaviours that are mediated by speech

(Vygotsky, 1981). Individual speech is not a personal activity, but is 'a part of dialogue, of cooperation and social interaction' (Vygotsky, 1984/1998, p. 356). Language, together with other forms of semiotic mediation, is the key to all aspects of knowledge co-construction that mediates social and individual functioning (Wertsch & Stone, 1985).

Dialogue plays an indispensable role in social interactions of the learning process. Bohm (1996) contrasted dialogue with discussion, stating that dialogue is a process where meaning is socially constructed through collaboration and is constantly changing. In discussion, individual ideas are asserted but a collaborative outcome is not necessarily intended (Burley & Pomphrey, 2011). The most relevant dialogic process within a learning relationship takes place in collaboration (Burley & Pomphrey, 2011); learning is about 'becoming' participants in social practices (Wenger, 1999) that are discursively constituted (Lerman, 2000). People become part of practices as practices become part of them. Discourse is the vital medium for social influences throughout the developmental period and across the domains of cognitive activities (Potter, 2003). In addition, discourse plays a role as an 'identity kit' which comes complete with the appropriate ways of acting, talking and writing, so as to display membership of a particular social group or social network and take a particular social role (Gee, 1990). As Harre and Gillett stated, 'the subject matter of psychology has to take account of discourses, significations, subjectivities and positioning, for it is in these that psychological phenomena actually exist' (1994, p. 22). Discursive psychology can be seen as a particular focusing lens in socio-cultural studies of learning to provide a language that enables the link between the actions of individuals and groups in the classroom and history and culture (Lerman, 2001).

Discursive psychology emphasises the critical mediating role of language, discourse and other communicative, linguistic tools in developing human consciousness and identities. For example, the focus for teacher-as-coach would be on developing the identities of students as agents of their own learning and actors in the classroom. In the development of identities in the practices, there is a range of *positions* for students and teachers, depending on the degree of their participation and what roles they take, and these positions are produced by practices. Nonetheless, as Lerman (2001) stated, 'classroom discourse does not offer the observer a window on the mind precisely because the mind is not static, or decontextualised, but responds to the context, the activity, and power/ knowledge, and it is oriented to communicate and to act'. The discursive understanding of learning should take into account both structure and agency, not dialogue *per se*. Moreover, the distribution of powerlessness and powerfulness through positioning subjects (Evans, 2000) inspires me to think about what kind of discourse emerging in the classroom would bestow power on the learners. I consider this discourse must put the learners at the centre, which leads to the next section, where I shall explore a learner-centred perspective in educational psychology.

Humanistic perspective and person-centred psychological principles

As I mentioned at the beginning of the chapter, the movement from the behaviourist-dominated metaphor to the cognitive-inspired view of learning reflects that 'an important aspect of the cognitive movement in education was the conscious recognition of the learner as an active participant in the learning process' (Di Vesta, 1987, p. 54). A humanistic perspective has been developed when we involve learners as agents in learning.

Humanism, originally identified by Rogers (1961, 1969, 1983) and Maslow (1968), is regarded as an antidote to cognitive approaches and it has seen a rebirth in the 1990s in schools and communities of learners (McInerney, 2005). These writers claimed that the significant nature of learning is a result of a combination of logic and intuition, intellect and feelings, concepts and experiences, idea and meaning, i.e., involving *the whole person*. Furthermore, Rogers and Freiberg (1994) stated: 'all personal growth is marked by a certain degree of disorganisation followed by reorganisation. The pain of new understandings, of acceptance of new facets of oneself; the feeling of uncertainty, vacillation and even turmoil within oneself are all an integral part of the pleasure and satisfaction of being more of oneself, more fully oneself, more fully functioning' (p. 323). The holistic view of learners based on a humanistic, learner-centred orientation and the paradox of learning and growth both advance understandings of thinking, behavioural, cognitive and motivational processes. These views contribute directly to improvements in teaching, learning, the educational process and the whole enterprise of schooling (American Psychological Association, 1997).

Person-centred psychological principles are of critical importance in education. These principles also strongly support coaching and coaching psychology, which I will discuss in the next chapter. Growing from the person-centred theories, a person-centred approach of learning has its goal centred on the facilitation of the whole and fully functioning person, hypothesising that people learn best when reciprocally facilitated with empathy, warmth and genuineness (Motschnig-Pitrik & Mallich, 2004). The focus is on the psychological, emotional and social needs of individual learners, as well as interventions that maximise healthy functioning and promote motivation, learning and achievement for all learners (Deakin-Crick *et al.*, 2007).

McCombs and Whisler (1997) proposed a learner-centred educational model that is rooted in the American Psychological Association's (1997) 14 learner-centred psychological principles. These principles are grouped into four domains: 1) cognitive and metacognitive, 2) motivational and affective, 3) developmental and social, and 4) individual differences factors. Though these principles are primarily internal to the learners, they also acknowledge external and contextual factors that interact with the internal factors. These principles provide a knowledge base for understanding learning as a natural process that occurs when the relationships, conditions and contexts of learning are supportive to individual

42 An enquiry of educational paradigms

learners' needs, capacities, experiences and interests (Deakin-Crick *et al.*, 2007). What can be synthesised from these principles is that educators, teachers and coaches can assist learners to develop internal factors and optimise external factors by relating to learners in a positive, supportive and person-centred way.

Rogers (1969) held that classic person-centred education includes certain attitudinal qualities existing in the personal relationship between the facilitator and the learner that can yield significant learning. These qualities embrace at least an initial genuine *trust* in learners with the facilitator, followed by the creation of an acceptant and empathic climate. Trust means more than affirmation and encouragement; it involves challenges of uncertainty, inequality and differences and most importantly the confidence of both the facilitators and learners to take these risks (Bond, 2007). Poplin and Weeres (1994) reported that 'students desire authentic relationships where they are trusted, given responsibility, spoken to honestly and warmly, and treated with dignity' (p. 20). The importance of relationships is advocated by McCombs (2003, 2004), who saw that 'learning is enhanced in contexts where learners have supportive relationships, have a sense of ownership and control over the learning process, and can learn with and from each other in a safe and trusting learning environment' (p. 7). A meta-analysis study of learner-centred teacher–student relationship showed that positive teacher–student relationships are associated with optimal, holistic learning (Cornelius-White, 2007). This relationship emphasises empathy, unconditional positive regard, genuineness, non-directivity and encouragement of critical thinking. It also includes teachers' flexibility in teaching methods, transparent compromise with learners, collaborative and student self-evaluation, and the provision of human and learning resources.

The person-centred approach of learning stimulates my understanding of coaching. Coaching should reconnect learners and their experiences as well as focus on the human process of personal and interpersonal relationships, beliefs and perceptions. The ability of the coach to form a connection with the coaching process can be the determinative factor of the effectiveness of coaching interventions. What particularly interests me about the research into learner-centred relationships is that students' and observers' perspectives of relationship are more predictive of student success than teachers' views of themselves (Cornelius-White, 2007). This finding mirrors that in psychotherapy clients' and observers' perspectives of therapists' empathy and alliance are better predictors of clients' success than counsellors' own views (Bergin & Garfield, 1994). This understanding of person-centred relationships inspires me to pay special attention to students' voices in their experiences of coaching as well as to the observation of affective and behavioural outcomes. Both teachers' and students' perceptions of the coach–learner relationship could be an informative area of potential research, because the coaching relationship is not only a putative factor in coaching outcomes, but also *a mixture of the teacher–student relationship and the coach–learner relationship.*

Learning (how) to learn and lifelong learning

The point of discussing learning to learn (L2L) is to raise the realisation that 'learning is learnable' (Claxton, 2002), which leads to my argument that 'learning to learn is coachable'. Because of the perceived potential of L2L to underpin lifelong learning (Fredriksson & Hoskins, 2007; Black *et al.*, 2006), I intend to include these two notions in this section.

The concept of L2L has become prominent in the discourses of education, particularly in the European context (Education Council, 2006). It is identified as a quintessential tool for lifelong learning (Fredriksson & Hoskins, 2007). L2L refers to a complex mixture of knowledge, skills and understanding, as well as values, attitudes and dispositions, and incorporates the concept of self-awareness and agency with the concept of learning relationships, context, motivation and story, which collectively support the individual in becoming a lifelong learner (Hoskins & Deakin-Crick, 2008). L2L is a robust and sophisticated concept which is often confused with the notion of 'learning how to learn' (LH2L). Though the ideas of L2L and LH2L are relevant to each other in terms of philosophy, psychology, socio-cultural theory and educational research, they may have subtle differences. Whilst the notion of L2L refers to a *capacity* or a *competence*, seeing it as a general-purpose ability, the term of LH2L is intended to draw attention to the primary focus on learning *practice* and *process*. The significance of 'how to' arises from an interest in the development of learning practices and in the implications for teaching and learning for such development (Black *et al.*, 2006).

The concept of L2L contains affective and cognitive dimensions (Fredriksson & Hoskins, 2007). A framework of measuring L2L was proposed by Bonnet and colleagues (2006) in relation to these dimensions: 1) the affective dimension that contains learning motivation, learning strategies and orientation towards change, academic self-concept and self-esteem, learning environment, perceived support from significant others and learning relationships; 2) the cognitive dimension that contains identifying a proposition, using rules, testing rules or propositions, and using mental tools. However, this measurement of L2L does not include the lifelong and 'life-wide' dimensions, which are emphasised in the definition. It needs to take into account the necessary *length*, *breadth* and *depth* of learning and reflection as well as the multiple learning opportunities and environments where this competence can be utilised (Rawson, 2000). This development needs to be viewed as a dialectical process between the developing, growing individual and a developing, evolving society (Tennant, 1996).

Lifelong learning relates to learning that takes place throughout a lifespan. However, it is more than the learning that takes place through the natural processes of living; it is a form of learning that requires active awareness and engagement of the learner in a community (Deakin-Crick & Wilson, 2005). The scopes and boundaries of lifelong learning include the main types and subjects of learning: informal and formal education and self-directed learning. Smith and

Spurling (1999) offered a holistic notion of lifelong learning: a personal element of continuity, intention and unfolding strategy, a moral element of personal commitment to learning, social commitment to learning, respect for others' learning and respect for truth. The development of lifelong learning requires an intention to learn, the development of self-awareness, the capacity to take responsibility for one's own learning, and the centrality of relationship for growth and development (Deakin-Crick & Wilson, 2005). Longworth (2003) stated that lifelong learning is 'not teaching, training, and not even education in its narrow didactic sense' (p. 12). It means a 180-degree shift of emphasis and power from provider to receiver: giving ownership of learning to the learner him or herself and not to the teacher. It moves teaching from the concept of 'the sage on the stage' to the idea of 'the guide at the side'. It denotes that people should develop a positive attitude towards intellectual, aesthetic, moral and social growth so that the understandings they will need during their lives in different functioning environments will evolve.

Learning becomes learnable particularly through *intentionality*. Initiation and participation of learning are not always voluntary processes especially in compulsory education (Lerman, 2001). Most students do not choose to be at school; the society and culture determine that children should attend school for a certain period of their life. Those children without intentionality are probably vulnerable to the regulating and institutionalising effects of schooling. Intentional learners go beyond the acquisition of learning skills and become conscious of the strategies they employ, monitoring their own understandings and directions (Resnick, 1989). Taking responsibility is a central feature of intentionality: intentional learners are required to take responsibility for their own learning and involve peers in so doing. Bruner (1996) referred to this sense of responsibility as 'agency', or 'learning autonomy', acknowledging that learning is a knowledge construction process that learners have to undertake for themselves. However, learning agency and higher-order abilities cannot be taught or trained directly through formal programmes of instruction or exhortation (Claxton, 1999; Katz, 1999). Often it is the teachers or other adults who enact these higher-order skills, but learners need to be engaged at a higher level by having opportunities to reflect strategically on their learning. Here, attention is drawn to the importance of facilitation and support of this higher-order strategic thinking and of intentional learning capabilities, and it involves my argument of 'learning to learn is coachable'. This facilitative approach is to improve students' reflective and meta-cognitive capabilities about learning, both at the intrapersonal level of the individual learner and at the interpersonal level of seeing learning as a collaborative process.

So the question is: how can we coach students to learn how to learn? I recognise that the coaching process must be embedded in a learning process that is best described as a journey. The next section focuses on the learning journey and the notion of learning power.

Learning as a journey

I elaborate the conceptual issues around learning in a holistic metaphor of learning as a journey, involving the possibility of extending ZPD through coaching, illustrated in Figure 3.1.

The journey of learning metaphor puts forward a conceptualisation grounded in a context-based, inside-outside model which leads learners from personal narratives and interests 'to the models of the world that constitute the core of the traditional instruction and assessment' (Jaros, 2009, p. 192). Deakin-Crick (2009) interpreted the metaphor as if 'there is a person with a sense of self, identity and intention, who usually has an objective or an outcome in mind, and who moves through a particular domain, engaging in particular inter- and intra-personal learning practices along the way' (p. 77). The following sections unpack the journey of learning metaphor in detail.

Four stations in the journey and learning power

There are four 'stations' that learners and their coaches visit on the journey. The first is the learning self with particular identity, stories, aspirations and relationships nested in the learners' life narratives. The second station is the personal qualities, virtues, beliefs, values, dispositions and attitudes of learning. The two stations are personal and unique to each learner; the learners have their authority to create, construct, and make decisions and judgements in these domains.

Because these two stations are about personal power to learn, the term '*learning power*' is coined here as 'a form of consciousness characterised by particular

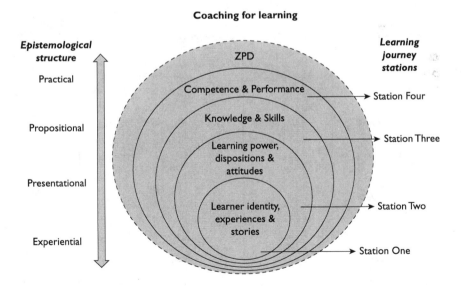

Figure 3.1 The holistic metaphor of learning

dispositions, values and attitudes, with a lateral and a temporal connectivity' (Deakin-Crick *et al.*, 2004; Deakin-Crick *et al.*, 2007). The lateral connectivity refers to the socio-cultural view that learning is mediated through the interactions of learning relationships (Rogoff & Lave, 1984; Rogoff & Wertsch, 1984; Lave & Wenger, 1991; Moseley *et al.*, 2005). The temporal connectivity means that a person is learning and changing over time, and understood in narratives shaped by different contexts (Deakin-Crick, 2009; Goodson & Deakin-Crick, 2009). Learning power includes the ingredients of learning identities, learning experiences, learning capacities, learning attitudes, learning dispositions and learning relationships, with its dimensions including affection, cognition, desire and action. The whole concept cannot be reduced to only one of these components (Deakin-Crick *et al.*, 2002, 2004; Deakin-Crick & Wilson, 2005, Deakin-Crick, 2010). I view learning power as 'energy' in the journey metaphor: the personal and autogenic features of learning power serve as fuel or energy to enable learners to move forward to their learning goals.

The first two stations are necessary but not sufficient to constitute a holistic journey. They need to be integrated into publicly accepted and valued domains where learning is not only important for learners themselves but also significant to the societies and communities where the learners live. The third station is the acquisition of publicly assessable knowledge, skills and understanding. The fourth station is the achievement of verifiable and valued competence in a particular domain. These two stations deal with knowledge and competence in the public domain. Validation and assessment of a specific body of knowledge or a particular set of competences rests with the community of practice (Deakin-Crick, 2009).

The pedagogical relationship and coaching

The hallmark of a pedagogical relationship in this journey is coaching, which enables the learner to attend iteratively to these stations and expand the learners' ZPD as indicated in Figure 3.1. The learner is coached throughout the journey by another person who supports and provides prompts, guidance and resources at key points (Deakin-Crick, 2012) in each station with various coaching techniques and formative use of learning power. Thus coaching can be regarded as a vehicle that helps learners travel more effectively towards their desired destinations. The process of the learning journey should be carefully scaffolded through coaching conversations between learners and their coach.

The major difference between coaching and traditional pedagogy is perhaps the starting point. Traditional pedagogy, which takes a more outcome-centred approach, often starts from the third station with predetermined knowledge and omits the first two stations. However, the quality enhancement of knowledge acquisition is largely determined by how well the knowledge is negotiated with and constructed through the learners' self-awareness, values and dispositions of learning. Because traditional teaching emphasises the public domains of individuals' learning without linking them to the personal domains, it may eliminate the opportunity for learners to go through successive spirals of thinking and enquiring, thus generating a gap between personally meaningful, coherent knowledge and publicly assessable knowledge presented in pre-packed sets. On the contrary, coaching, as a facilitative approach, contributes to what I believe to be the critical transition from the first two stations to the third station. Personal domains and public domains are thus integrated to create a channel for individual flexibility and intellectual rigour to travel through and enrich each other. This channel requires a robust balance between the possibilities of personal meaning and engagement and public accountability of intellectual quality and rigour (Deakin-Crick, 2009). If learning is about both acquisition and participation, then understanding this tension allows learners to increasingly take responsibility for identifying and negotiating the publicly desirable outcomes while attending to identity formation and personal purposes that are grounded in the particular place and context.

Associated with the difference between coaching and traditional pedagogy, there might be a kind of 're-professionalisation' (Williamson & Morgan, 2009) for teachers in schools. They need to go beyond their own subject specifications and develop a thorough understanding of how knowledge is constructed and of the social contexts in which it is operated, with insights into the lives of students and a willingness to engage with aspects of their cultures. They need to acquire the ability to listen to and appreciate the variety of student experiences, identify classroom activities which enable students to make sense of those experiences, permit students to make decisions about the content, processes and outcomes of their learning, and allow students to further interrogate their voiced ideas, interests and experiences with curricular knowledge. In this sense, the learners' authenticity must be acknowledged and appreciated in the journey.

Learners' authenticity

I want to address an essential aspect of the learning journey, including learners' authentic experience and participation in learning and the importance of learners' authentic relationships with others. In this holistic metaphor, the person who learns can be viewed as a traveller. Steed (2009) suggested that individuals flourish best when they 'are valued and heard, accorded respect and allowed dignity' (p. 465). So there is a fundamental recognition of personhood in learning, and the journey process is personalised through the lens of human value. My focus here is to link the notion of authenticity with this personalised journey, because committing to learning needs passion and drive that honour the learner's identity.

The conceptual roots of authenticity can be traced back to ancient Greek philosophy and the statement 'to thine own self be true' (Harter, 2002). But what is the 'true self'? Existentialism has been trying to answer that Authentic Being (*the true self*) is its own measure, in other words it does not have to justify its existence as compared with anything else (Heidegger, 1962). The concept is rooted in the existential interpretation of freedom (Grene, 1952) and reflected in humanistic psychology, in particular, the work of Carl Rogers (1961). He conceptualised the self-actualisation or fully functioning individual as: 1) open to experience with tolerance for ambiguity and accurate perception; 2) being able to live fully in the moment with adaptability and flexibility; 3) trusting of inner experiences to guide one's own behaviours; 4) experiencing freedom with choice about how to respond and feel; and 5) creative in his or her approach to living with a strong trust in one's inner experiences and a willingness to adapt to ever-changing circumstances. Authenticity has been identified as an important concept fundamental to an individual's well-being and optimal performance since Seligman and Csikszentmihalyi (2000) published their feature article on positive psychology. Authenticity is identified as a dimension of courage, one of six discrete virtues underpinning well-being and optimal functioning (Park *et al.*, 2004). According to Barrett-Lennard (1998), authenticity involves consistency between three levels: 1) people's primary experiences; 2) their symbolised awareness; and 3) their outward behaviour and communication. Thus an individual feels authentic when there is congruence between behaviour and emotional expression on one hand, and conscious awareness of physiological states, emotions or cognitions on the other, and, additionally, these are compatible from external influences.

Authenticity has important implications in learning, particularly with self-identity in the social context. Wenger (1999) suggested that 'learning as increasing participation in communities of practice concerns the whole person acting in the world' (p. 49). As we learn, we gradually internalise the diversity of viewpoints that collectively make sense of all that goes on in the community and at the same time develop values and identities (Lemke, 2002). What we do when we learn is to enter into social activities because the content of our thinking and the habits of our lives originate in our social interactions with others (Vygotsky, 1963). Who we are to ourselves and perhaps to others is partly relational and partly uniquely individual (Lemke, 2002).

Giddens (1991) argued that self-identity is continuously engaged in and negotiated through the stories we construct and reconstruct as an account of our lives, and that narratives of the self-reflexive process are indispensable for learning. Narratives and personal stories create space for learners to connect with themselves as a whole person, their selfhood and agency, and their need for meaning making and purpose in order to establish a foundation for deep engagement (Goodson & Deakin-Crick, 2009). This further explains why in authentic learning we need to start from the first station in the journey, which exclusively relates to self-knowledge and freedom of the will: the freedom of choice, decision and action in learning. If learners do not have this freedom, responsibility disappears and learning loses its significance. Once a learner has become an authentic being, the knowledge would be authentically owned. This learning is not learning for the sake of duty (as students are always required to learn in schools); instead, learning is keeping promises for the sake of duty (students are still required to learn in schools) and acting *as they choose as their own*. This commitment to the authentic self ensures learning engagement and values responsibility-taking. Moreover, there would be an integration of the social context where the learner acts, the person who learns, the knowledge that is acquired and the process of seeking that knowledge. This integration makes learning critical and meaningful and it could be achieved in an authentic enquiry-based learning, which is highlighted in the next section.

Enquiry-based learning as an authentic design

In enquiry-based learning (EBL), knowledge is not directly delivered by transmission; instead, learning is designed as an enquiry and knowledge is constructed in an authentic way to enhance interest, relevance and relatedness. The teacher's role is multiple: they can be director, designer, coach, consultant, knowledgeable other, facilitator, guide, supporter and instructor as the enquiry unfolds (Planche, 2012). It is worth noting that *not all EBL is regarded as authentic enquiry*. Publications of the Centre for Excellence in Enquiry-Based Learning in the University of Manchester have an open-ended discussion about what EBL is. The researchers at the centre agree that 'enquiry-based learning' is a term describing any process of learning through enquiry. EBL generally allows for personalisation in its design and for the integration of real-world application as learners explore an enquiry's potential (Planche, 2012). It generally refers to the process through which students acquire their knowledge by means of active learning. Students are ideally positioned to foster a deep level of engagement with problems that are multifaceted and complex (Hutchings, 2006). EBL can readily include forms of project-based, subject-based, problem-based or designed-based learning (Hutchings & O'Rourke, 2002; Planche, 2012).

Project or problem-based learning and authentic enquiry are all situated in the domain of EBL, thus they have shared common principles, such as: 1) selection and formulation of appropriate questions; 2) identification of key issues to be explored, search, interpretation; 3) assessment for valid and relevant evidence; 4) application of evidence to identified issues; 5) presentation of coherent conclusions; and 6) reflection on and assessment of the learning process. However, project or problem-based learning cannot be viewed as identical to authentic enquiry. Here I differentiate problem-based learning and authentic enquiry as an example.

First and foremost, the levels of *personal engagement* of these two kinds of enquiries are different. Problem-based learning does not necessarily involve identity, personal narratives and experiences; whereas these are the 'first station' in authentic enquiry. Authentic enquiry emphasises experiential learning, which is crucial in the epistemological development process. This builds on Dewey's (1938) original idea of learning involving experience as well as the acquisition of abstract knowledge. Experiential learning relies on the use of reflection on experience to create new knowledge or modify existing knowledge, i.e., engage in the assimilation and accommodation processes in learning. The importance of reflection is proposed in Kolb's (1984) learning cycle, which moves from actual experience to reflection on this experience, then to a process of learning and

50 An enquiry of educational paradigms

re-conceptualisation, and ends with acting on the outcomes of this process. Watkins *et al.* (2002) added to this four-stage learning cycle with another cycle of meta-learning, defined as 'the process of making sense of experience' (p. 21).

Secondly, the *learning goal* of problem-based learning is to help students develop particular problem-solving skills, especially hypothetical-deductive thinking, whereas in authentic enquiry the primary goal is to cultivate learning agency and positive dispositions. Although both enquiries involve an overlap of meta-cognitive skills and higher-order learning capabilities, problem-based enquiry may not include such a comprehensive mixture of cognitive, affective and dispositional skills that authentic enquiry attempts to develop.

Thirdly, the *transferability* and *expendability* of the content in problem-based enquiry and authentic enquiry are different. How students encounter the formal content of enquiry may influence the way that they understand learning and exert impact on their way of encountering informal and real-world learning. In problem-based learning, the problems must raise the concepts and principles relevant to the content domain, whilst in authentic enquiry students may enjoy more freedom to choose topics across different domains or disciplines. However, to advocate authentic EBL is not to propose a content-free syllabus, but to ensure that what students seek to learn rests in their own domain of interest, purpose and relevance, and they can design the pursuit of knowledge in a structured and systematic manner.

A fourth difference relates to *the role of the facilitator*. Although in both enquiries, the facilitator does not use his or her knowledge of the content to lead the learners to the 'correct' answers, problem-based learning still requires the role of a tutor or an expert to offer content-based guidance and resources. In authentic enquiry, a facilitator is more a mixture of a coach and a tutor, and much less an expert or a teacher. In addition, in an authentic enquiry the learner's affective or emotional aspects are taken into account, therefore the facilitator may simultaneously take a counsellor's role if necessary.

Today's schooling seems to pay too much attention to what children should study in school and not enough to whom they become. Teachers believe they are passing on knowledge rather than building characters. There has been a lack of real effort to integrate experiences in school and outside of school. But *if* the purpose of education is to understand the complexity of the communities we live in and to participate successfully in collaborative social activities, an education dominated by institutions and schools that isolate themselves from the rest of social life can never achieve the goal of intellectual and identity development. In authentic EBL, I would propose an increase in the awareness of the learning identities of both the teachers and the learners as a coaching dialogue deepens.

To recap, the journey metaphor articulates that learning is regarded as 'a socially embedded and embodied journey over time, from personal desire and motivation to the achievement of competence in a particular domain which is assessed and validated publicly by a particular community of practice' (Deakin-Crick, 2009, p. 187). The learner is a traveller through this journey, taking responsibility for his or her own learning and being nested in evolving relationships with people in different contexts. Coaching could be a facilitative vehicle to stimulate change, to scaffold the learning process, to move learners forward through effective support and to assist them to develop self-awareness and responsibility for their own learning. How coaching becomes this facilitative tool is underpinned by the Vygotskian socio-cultural perspective on learning and development, ZPD in particular. This holistic metaphor leads to the establishment of a learning-centred model that I want to advocate in this book.

A learning-centred model

This section draws attention to the relationships between teacher, learner and knowledge in different pedagogical models. Two kinds of models are identified from the review of education literature: a *content/curriculum centred* and a *learner-centred* model. I think there should be a third model, which is *learning-centred* (see Figure 3.2).

When education is concerned primarily with academic performance, knowledge acquisition and repetition, it features an educational model that is content or curriculum-centred. Teachers are the experts on predefined knowledge in traditional academic curricula and they are responsible for delivering the abstract knowledge to the students, who are recipients at the far end, so the focus is purely on inert knowledge. Teachers have a kind of mastery or command of certain bodies of knowledge or skills, and their professionalism is mainly defined as a capacity to

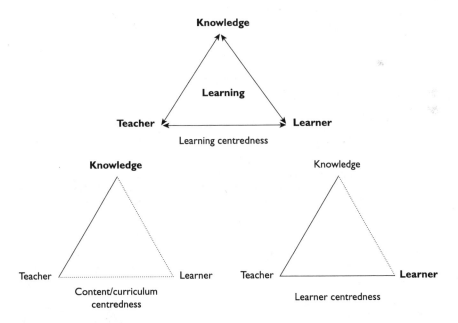

Figure 3.2 Three different types of centredness in education

52 An enquiry of educational paradigms

grasp these knowledge and skills, and effectively pass these on to their students. Hence there might be a link between teacher and knowledge. However, teachers may not authentically own what they disseminate to the students. They may use sequenced and structured materials and try to ensure an extensive coverage of content; the link, therefore, might be rather weak. Since teachers are not actively involved in and making sense of their pedagogical activities, the model is curriculum/content-centred rather than teacher-centred. The interaction between teachers and students is characterised as academic-oriented, but not necessarily authoritarian. Meanwhile, the most important connection, which is the connection between students and knowledge, is missing in this picture.

When the idea of 'person-centredness' becomes the emphasis of education, a learner-centred educational model emerges. This model puts students in the centre, taking their personal, cultural, historical and social aspects into consideration. The relationship between teachers and students is restored in the sense that teachers actively respond to students' personalised needs in learning. This potentially has 'therapeutic' effects on the overall well-being of a whole person. However, the question is: to what extent do students take responsibility for themselves rather than being taken care of in this pedagogical relationship? When personhood of the students becomes the centre, it is obvious that the connections between people (i.e. teachers and students, students and peers) are strengthened. The interaction between teachers and students is more equal than the relationship in a teacher-led classroom within content-centred education. The empathetic, nurturing way in which students are educated undoubtedly benefits their development as individuals. This learner-centred model has a number of similarities with the psycho-educational model (Brendtro & Ness, 1983) that covers six tenets: relationship is primary; assessment is ecological; behaviour is holistic; teaching is humanistic; crisis is opportunity; and practice is pragmatic. However, there is not enough evidence to claim that learners develop authentic ownership of knowledge in this model. In other words, this model arguably lacks a link between students making active meanings of what they learn inside and outside the classroom and their development. Furthermore, this model draws from a variety of humanistic theories and it may create a danger of uncritically engaging with these theories.

I think what really transforms students from recipients to participants in their own learning design is the learning-centred model. Putting learning at the centre enables the collective meaning making and knowledge construction between teachers and students as well as among students themselves in authentic contexts. The idea of learning-centred education is not an unfamiliar notion (Hubball & Poole, 2003). Learning-centred education requires a community of learners to make choices within a responsive, carefully structured learning environment. It focuses on what students are expected to know and are able to do in the context of a field, and it includes both individual and collaborative learning experiences.

The learning-centred model shares similarities with the learner-centred model in that they both emphasise *responsiveness* to the diverse needs of different learners and complex learning circumstances, acknowledge learners as active participants in the learning process, and assume that learners may be at different stages of learning and progress at different rates. However, the differences are that the learning-centred model does not necessarily imply that individual learners should have control over issues such as content coverage, learning strategies and assessment methods. Learning-centred education may reflect a pragmatic perspective on teaching and learning that 'the focus is on enduring effective learning and using whatever activities, techniques and skills best brings this about within the realities in which teachers work' (O'Sullivan, 2004, p. 597). In this sense, EBL within this model means *learning-based enquiry*, aiming to enhance learning by adopting a particular learning methodology such as authentic enquiry.

Coaching rests on the assumption of learning centredness. In line with this model, teachers are no longer viewed as the primary deliverers of information or the sole distributors of resources. They are transformed into conductors of an increasingly competent learning orchestra. They become managers of all the considerable educational and human resources in the interests of actively stimulating learning. They become catalysts of individual students' aspirations and potential for effective learning and better performance. Coaches should be able to use their knowledge and expertise from a broad repertoire of pedagogical strategies on a continuum from teacher-led to learner-centred. It is not possible to separate who is learning, what is learned, when it is learned, why it is learned, how it is learned, and in what context it is learned and used. Learning is designed to be assessable, transferable and relevant to learners' lives. Therefore, important links between teachers, students and knowledge are established.

Summary

Following the philosophical journey to explore ideological and conceptual issues of education, this chapter reviews educational and learning theories that relate to coaching from a psychological perspective. I have discussed learning with its motivational, socio-cultural and discursive aspects. Moreover, I have elaborated my understanding of learning as a journey, where a learner starts from identity, personal motivation, experiences and stories within an individual's particular social context, moves through the development of values, beliefs, attitudes and dispositions that individual learners hold when they learn, and then progresses to knowledge construction and sharing to the final presentation of learning outcomes and preparation for public assessment. One of the core notions is that learning power and higher-order learning capacities cannot be taught in a conventional teaching approach. Instead, they could be 'coached' through carefully structured, authentic EBL activities in the learning-centred model of education.

However, we should not consider the learning-centred model as a complete replacement of the current educational system in which teachers design a curriculum for learners based on what they think the learners need. There is obviously a need for some didactic component in the curriculum, and there is also a vastly increased range of competences and skills that learners will have to employ in

54 An enquiry of educational paradigms

order to function in the society. The teachers need to be initially 'de-skilled' in order to be better skilled for their new roles as effective learning facilitators. The next chapter aims to consider how coaching fits into the bigger picture of learning-centredness.

Recommended reading

Bruner, J. S. (1996). *The culture of education*. Cambridge, MA: Harvard University Press.

Claxton, G. (2002). *Building learning power: Helping young people become better learners*. Bristol: TLO.

Deakin-Crick, R. (2009). Inquiry-based learning: Reconciling the personal with the public in a democratic and archaeological pedagogy. *The Curriculum Journal, 20*(1), 73–92.

Key points for reflection

- What psychological perspectives do you think are particularly important for 21st century learning?
- What are your experiences when you guide your students travelling through the four stations in 'learning as a journey'?
- What have you done to enhance your students' 'learning power' or to cultivate their learning habits?
- What are the key differences among the content-centred model, learner-centred model and the learning-centred model in education?

References

American Psychological Association. (1997). *Learner-centred psychological principles*.

Bandura, A. (1989). Human agency in social cognitive theory. *American Psychologist, 44*, 1175–1184.

Bandura, A. (1991). Social cognitive theory of self-regulation. *Organizational Behaviour and Human Decision Processes, 50*, 248–287.

Bandura, A., & Cervone, D. (1983). Self-evaluative and self-efficacy mechanisms governing the motivational effects of goal systems. *Journal of Personality and Social Psychology, 45*, 1017–1028.

Barrett-Lennard, G. T. (1998). *Carl Rogers' helping system: Journey and substance*. London: Sage.

Bergin, A., & Garfield, S. (Eds). (1994). *Handbook of psychotherapy and behavior change* (4th Ed.). New York: Wiley.

Black, P., McCormick, R., Mary, J., & Pedder, D. (2006). Learning how to learn and assessment for learning: A theoretical inquiry. *Research Papers in Education, 21*(2), 119–132.

Bohm, D. (1996). *On dialogue*. London: Routledge.

Bond, T. (2007). Ethics and psychotherapy: An issue of trust. In R.E. Ashcroft, A. Dawson, H. Draper, & J. R. McMillan (Eds), *Principles of health care ethics* (2nd Ed.) (pp. 435–442). Hoboken, NJ: Wiley.

Bonnet, G., Svecnik, E., Hautamäki, J., Trosseille, B., Fischer, C., Meijer, J., . . . Hoskins, B. (2006). *Final report of the learning to learn expert group to the European Commission, DGEAC A6.* Paris/Brussels/Ispra.

Brendtro, L., & Ness, A. (1983). *Reeducating troubled youth: Environments for teaching and treatment.* New York: Aldine Publishing Company.

Bruner, J. S. (1996). *The culture of education.* Cambridge, MA: Harvard University Press.

Burley, S., & Pomphrey, C. (2011). *Mentoring and coaching in schools: Professional learning through collaborative inquiry.* London: Routledge.

Chaiklin, S. (2003). The zone of proximal development in Vygotsky's analysis of learning and instruction. In A. Kozulin, B. Gindix, V. S. Ageyev, & S. M. Miller (Eds), *Vygotsky's educational theory in cultural context* (pp. 39–63). Cambridge: Cambridge University Press.

Claxton, G. (1999). *Wise up: The challenge of lifelong learning.* Stoke on Trent: Network Press.

Claxton, G. (2002). *Building learning power: Helping young people become better learners.* Bristol: TLO.

Cole, M., & Cole, S. (2001). *The development of children* (4th Ed.). New York: Scientific American Books.

Collins, J., Harkins, J., & Nind, M. (2002). *Manifesto for learning: Fundamental principles.* New York: Contunuum.

Cornelius-White, J. (2007). Learner-centred teacher–student relationships are effective: A meta-analysis. *Review of Educational Research, 77,* 113–143.

Covington, M. (1998). *The will to learn: A guide for motivating young people.* New York: Cambridge University Press.

Covington, M., & Dray, E. (2002). The developmental course of achievement motivation: A need-based approach. In A. Wigfield & J. Eccles (Eds), *Development of achievement motivation* (pp. 33–56). San Diego: Academic Press.

Cubberley, E. P. (1920). *The history of education: Educational practice and progress considered as a phase of the development and spread of western civilization.* London: Constable and Company.

Deakin-Crick, R. (2009). Inquiry-based learning: Reconciling the personal with the public in a democratic and archaeological pedagogy. *The Curriculum Journal, 20*(1), 73–92.

Deakin-Crick, R. (2010). Assessment in schools – dispositions. In P. Peterson, E. Baker, & B. McGaw (Eds), *International encyclopaedia of education, Vol. 3* (pp. 181–188). Oxford: Elsevier.

Deakin-Crick, R. (2012). Personalisation: Integrating the personal with the public: A pedagogy for social sustainability. In M. Mincu (Ed.), *Personalisation of education in contexts: Policy critique and theories of personal improvement.* Rotterdam: Sense Publishers.

Deakin-Crick, R., Broadfoot, P., & Claxton, G. (2002). *Developing ELLI: The effective lifelong learning profile in practice.* Bristol: Lifelong Learning Foundation.

Deakin-Crick, R., Broadfoot, P. & Claxton, G. (2004). Developing an effective lifelong learning inventory: The ELLI project. *Assessment in Education, 11*(3), 248–272.

Deakin-Crick, R., McCombs, Haddon, A., Broadfoot, P., & Tew, M. (2007). The ecology of learning: Factors contributing to learner-centred classroom cultures. *Research Papers in Education, 22*(3), 267–307.

Deakin-Crick, R., & Wilson, K. (2005). Being a learner: A virtue for the 21st century. *British Journal of Educational Studies, 53*(3), 359–374.

56   An enquiry of educational paradigms

Deci, E. L., & Ryan, R. M. (1985). *Intrinsic motivation and self-determination in human behavior*. New York: Plenum.

Deci, E. L., & Ryan, R. M. (2000). Self-determination theory and the facilitation of intrinsic motivation, social development, and well-being. *American Psychologist, 55*, 68–78.

Dewey, J. (1938). *Experience and education*. New York: Simon & Schuster.

Dewey, J., & Bentley, A. F. (1946). Interaction and transaction. *Journal of Philosophy, 43*(19), 505–517.

Di Vesta, F. J. (1987). The cognitive movement and education. In J. A. Glover & R. R. Ronning (Eds), *Historical foundations of educational psychology* (pp. 203–233). New York: Plenum Press.

Donovan, C., & Smolkin, L. (2002) Children's genre knowledge: An examination of K–5 students performance on multiple tasks providing differing levels of scaffolding. *Reading Research Quarterly Newark, 37*(4), 428–465.

Dweck, C. S. (2006). *Mindset*. New York: Random House.

Education Council. (2006, December). *Recommendation of the European Parliament and the Council*. Paper presented at the Education Council on the Key Competencies for Lifelong Learning, Brussels: Official Journal of the European Union.

Evans, J. (2000). *Adults' mathematical thinking and emotions: A study of numerate practices*. London: RoutledgeFalmer.

Fredriksson, U., & Hoskins, B. (2007). The development of learning to learn in a European context. *Curriculum Journal, 18*(2), 127–134.

Gee, J. P. (1990). *Social linguistics and literacies: Ideology in discourses: critical perspectives on literacy and education*. London: Falmer Press.

Giddens, A. (1991). *Modernity and self-identity: Self and society in the late modern age*. Cambridge: Polity Press.

Goodson, I., & Deakin-Crick, R. (2009). Curriculum as narration: Tales from the children of the colonised. *Curriculum Journal, 20*(3), 225–236.

Grene, M. (1952). Authenticity: An existential virtue. *Ethics, 62*(4), 266–274.

Hammond, J., & Gibbons, P. (2005). Putting scaffolding to work: The contribution of scaffolding in articulating ESL education. *Prospect, Special Issue, 20*(1), 6–30.

Harre, R., & Gillett, G. (1994). The discursive mind. London: Sage.

Harter, S. (2002). Authenticity. In C. R. Synder & S. J. Lopez (Eds), Handbook of positive psychology (pp. 382–394). New York: Oxford University Press.

Heidegger, M. (1962). *Time and being* (J. Macquarrie & E. Robinson, Trans.). New York: Harper & Row.

Hickey, D. T. (1997). Motivation and contemporary socio-constructivist instructional perspectives. *Educational Psychologist, 32*, 175–193.

Hoskins, B., & Deakin-Crick, R. (2008). *Learning to learn and civic competences: Different currencies or two sides of the same coin?* Luxembourg: Office for Official Publications of the European Communities.

Hubball, H., & Poole, G. (2003). A learning-centred faculty certificate programme on university teaching. *International Journal for Academic Development, 8*(1/2), 11–24.

Hutchings, B. (2006). *Principles of enquiry-based learning*. Centre for Excellence in Enquiry-Based Learning, University of Manchester.

Hutchings, B., & O'Rourke, K. (2002). *A study of enquiry-based learning in action: An example from a literary studies third-year course*. Centre for Excellence in Enquiry-Based Learning, University of Manchester.

Jaros, M. (2009). Pedagogy for knowledge recognition and acquisition: Knowing and being at the close of the mechanical age. *Curriculum Journal, 20*(3), 191–205.

John-Steiner, V., & Mahn, H. (1996). Sociocultural approaches to learning and development: A Vygotskian framework. *Educational Psychologist, 31*(3/4), 191–206.

Katz, L. G. (1999). *Another look at what young children should be learning.* ERIC Digest. Champaign, IL: ERIC Clearinghouse on Elementary and Early Childhood Education.

Kaye, A. R. (1992). Learning together apart. In A. R. Kaye (Ed.), *Collaborative learning through computer conferencing* (pp. 1–24). London: Springer-Verlag.

Kolb, D. A. (1984). *Experiential learning: Experience as the source of knowledge and development.* Englewood Cliffs, NJ: Prentice-Hall.

Koschmann, T. (1999). Towards a dialogic theory of learning: Bakhtin's contribution to learning in settings of collaboration. In C. Hoadley & J. Roschelle (Eds), *Proceedings of the third international conference on computer supported collaborated learning* (pp. 308–313). Palo Alto, CA.

Lave, J., & Wenger, E. (1991). *Situated learning: Legitimate peripheral participation.* Cambridge: University of Cambridge Press.

Lemke, J. L. (2002). Language development and identity: Multiple timescales in the social ecology of learning. In C. Kramsch (Ed.), *Language acquisition and language socialization.* London: Continuum.

Lerman, S. (2000). The social turn in mathematics education research. In J. Boaler (Ed.), *Multiple perspectives on mathematics teaching and learning.* Westport, CT: Ablex.

Lerman, S. (2001). Cultural, discursive psychology: A sociocultural approach to studying the teaching and learning of mathematics. *Educational Studies in Mathematics, 46*(1–3), 87–113.

Livingston, K., & Shiach, L. (2010). A new model of teacher education. In A. Campell & S. Groundwater-Smith (Eds), *Connecting inquiry and professional learning.* London: Routledge.

Locke, E. A., & Latham, G. P. (1990). *A theory of goal setting and task performance.* Englewood Cliffs, NJ: Prentice-Hall.

Longworth, N. (2003). *Lifelong learning in action: transforming 21st century education.* London: Taylor and Francis.

Lyons, C. (2003). *Teaching struggling readers: How to use brain-based research to maximize learning.* Portsmouth, NH: Heinemann.

Mariani, L. (1997). Teacher support and teacher challenge in promoting learner autonomy. *Perspectives: A Journal of TESOL Italy, 23*(2), 5–19.

Marshall, W. L. (1996). Assessment, treatment and theorising about sex offenders: Developments during the past twenty years and future directions. *Criminal Justice and Behaviour, 23*(1), 162–199.

Marx, K. (1859). *A contribution to the critique of political economy.* Moscow: Progress Publishers.

Maslow, A. H. (1968). *Towards a psychology of being.* New York: D. Van Nostrand Company.

Mayer, R. E. (1992). Cognition and instruction: Their historic meeting within educational psychology. *Journal of Educational Psychology, 84,* 405–412.

McCombs, B. (2003). A framework for the redesign of K–12 education in the context of current educational reform. *Theory into Practice, 42*(2), 93–101.

McCombs, B. (2004). The learner-centered psychological principles: A framework for balancing a focus on academic achievement with a focus on social and emotional

58 An enquiry of educational paradigms

learning needs. In J. E. Zins, R. P. Weissberg, M. C. Wang, & H. J. Walberg (Eds), *Building academic success on social and emotional learning: What does the research say?* (pp. 23–39). New York: Teachers College Press.

McCombs, B., & Whisler, J. (1997). *The learner-centred classroom and school: Strategies for increasing student motivation and achievement.* San Francisco: Jossey-Bass.

McInerney, J. O. (2005). Educational psychology – theory, research, and teaching: A 25-year retrospective. *Educational Psychology, 25*(6), 585–599.

Moseley, D., Baumfield, V., Elliot, J., Gregson, M., Higgins, S., Miller, J., & Newton, D. (2005). *Frameworks for thinking: A handbook for teaching and learning.* Cambridge: Cambridge University Press.

Motschnig-Pitrik, R., & Mallich, K. (2004). Effects of person-centred attitudes on professional and social competence in a blended learning paradigm. *Journal of Educational Technology & Society, 7*(4), 176–192.

O' Sullivan, M. (2004). The reconceptualisation of learner-centred approaches: A Namibian case study. *International Journal of Educational Development, 24*(6), 585–602.

Park, N., Peterson, C., & Seligman, M. (2004). Strengths of character and wellbeing. *Journal of Social and Clinic Psychology, 23*, 603–619.

Piaget, J. (1937/1954). *The construction of reality in the child* (M. Cook, Trans.). New York: Basic Books.

Pintrich, P. R. (2003). A motivational science perspective on the role of student motivation in learning and teaching contexts. *Journal of Educational Psychology, 95*, 667–686.

Pintrich, P. R., & Schunk, D. (2002). *Motivation in education: Theory, research and applications* (2nd Ed.). Upper Saddle River, NJ: Prentice-Hall.

Planche, B. (2012). The transformative power of co-learning. *Leadership in Focus, 26*, 2–7.

Poplin, M., & Weeres, J. (1994). *Voices from the inside: A report on schooling from inside the classroom. Part one: Naming the problem.* Claremont, CA: The Institute for Education in Transformation at The Claremont Graduate School.

Potter, J. (2003). Discursive psychology: Between method and paradigm. *Discourse & Society, 14*, 783–794.

Rawson, M. (2000). Learning to learn: More than a skill set. *Studies in Higher Education, 25*(2), 226–238.

Resnick, L. B. (Ed.). (1989). *Knowing, learning, and instruction: Essays in honor of Robert Glaser.* Hilldale, NJ: Erlbaum.

Rogers, C. (1961). *On becoming a person: A therapist's view of psychotherapy.* London: Constable.

Rogers, C. (1969). *Freedom to learn.* Columbus, OH: Merrill.

Rogers, C. (1983). *Freedom to learn for the 80s.* Columbus, OH: Charles E. Merrill Publishing Company.

Rogers, C., & Freiberg, H. (1994). *Freedom to learn* (3rd Ed.). Columbus, OH: Merrill/ Macmillan.

Rogoff, B., & Lave, J. (Eds). (1984). *Everyday cognition: Its development in social context.* Cambridge, MA: Harvard University Press.

Rogoff, B., & Wertsch, J. V. (Eds). (1984). *New directions for child development: Vol. 23: Children's learning in the 'zone of proximal development'.* San Francisco: Jossey-Bass.

Schultheiss, O. C. (2001). An information processing account of implicit motive arousal. In M. L. Maehr & P. Pintrich (Eds), *Advances in motivation and achievement: Vol. 12: Methodology in Motivation Research* (pp. 1–41). Greenwich, CT: JAI Press.

Schutz, P. A., & DeCuir, J. T. (2002). Inquiry on emotions in education. *Educational Psychologist, 37*(2), 125–134.

Seligman, E. P., & Csikszentmihalyi, M. (2000). Positive psychology: An introduction. *American Psychologist,* 55(1), 5–14.

Sfard, A. (1998). On two metaphors for learning and the dangers of choosing just one. *Educational Researcher, 27*(2), 4–13.

Silberman, M. L., Allender, J. S., & Yanoff, J. M. (1976). *Real learning: A sourcebook for teachers.* Boston: Little, Brown, and Company.

Smith, J., & Spurling, A. (1999). *Understanding motivation for lifelong learning.* London: Campaign for Learning.

Steed, C. (2009). Inquiry-based learning: Personalisation or the rehabilitation of human value. *Curriculum Journal, 20*(4), 456–475.

Tennant, M. (1996). *Psychology and adult learning* (2nd Ed.). London: Routledge.

Verenikina, I. (2003). Understanding scaffolding and the ZPD in educational research. *Proceedings of the Joint AARE/NZERE Conference.*

Vygotsky, L. S. (1963). *Thought and language.* Cambridge, MA: MIT Press.

Vygotsky, L. S. (1978). *Mind in society.* London: Harvard University Press.

Vygotsky, L. S. (1981). The genesis of higher mental functions. In J. V. Wertsch (Ed.), *The concept of activity in Soviet psychology.* Armonk: Sharpe.

Vygotsky, L. S. (1984/1998). Child psychology. In R. W. Rieber (Ed.), *The collected works of L. S. Vygotsky.* New York: Plenum.

Watkins, C., Carnell, E., Lodge, C., Wagner, P., & Whalley, C. (2002). *Effective learning.* National School Improvement Network. Research Matters, number 17. London: Institute of London, University of London.

Wells, G. (1999). *Dialogic inquiries in education: Building on the legacy of Vygotsky.* Cambridge: Cambridge University Press.

Wenger, E. (1999). *Communities of practice: Learning, meaning and identity.* Cambridge: Cambridge University Press.

Wertsch, J. (1985). *Vygotsky and the social formation of mind.* Cambridge, MA: Harvard University Press.

Wertsch, J., & Stone, C. A. (1985). The concept of internalization in Vygotsky's account of the genesis of higher mental functions. In J. Wertsch (Ed.), *Culture, communication, and cognition: Vygotskian perspectives.* New York: Cambridge University Press.

Wertsch, J., & Tulviste, P. (1992). L. S. Vygotsky and contemporary developmental psychology. *Developmental Psychology, 28*(4), 548–557.

Williamson, B., & Morgan, J. (2009). Educational reform, enquiry-based learning and the re-professionalisation of teachers. *Curriculum Journal, 20*(3), 287–304.

Wood, D., Bruner, J. S., & Ross, G. (1976). The role of tutoring in problem solving. *Journal of Child Psychology & Psychiatry & Allied Disciplines, 17*(2), 89–100.

Wood, R. E., & Bandura, A. (1989). Impact of conceptions of ability on self-regulatory mechanisms and complex decision making. *Journal of Personality and Social Psychology, 56*, 407–415.

Chapter 4

The place of coaching psychology in learning

Introduction

In the last chapter, I demonstrated how the psychological investigation of learning contributes to the study of coaching psychology for learning. This chapter focuses on the theories of coaching and coaching psychology in order to see what they mean for learning. Coaching is rapidly developing as an applied discipline in a variety of contexts and it should be based on a solid psychological foundation. This chapter reviews the origins, definitions, psychological principles and theories of coaching and coaching psychology as well as the structure and characteristics of effective coaching models. I identify three perspectives of coaching psychology that are particularly useful for enhancing learning: cognitive coaching, solution-focused coaching and narrative coaching. The chapter ends with a call for further research on the relationship of coaching and learning, which leads to the next part, where I shall present my studies of coaching psychology and learning in secondary and medical schools.

It is important to note that in this chapter I often refer to the person who receives coaching as the 'coachee' or 'client' because this terminology is used interchangeably across coaching literature. I personally prefer to use 'learner', but when reviewing coaching literature, I tend to use the authors' original terminology.

What is coaching psychology?

The origin and definition of coaching

Coaching is a tool for personal and professional development, originating sometime in the late 1980s (Hudson, 1999). It is a growing field, taking many different forms and approaches (van Kessel, 2003). The pioneers of coaching drew on their own insights from a range of professional disciplines: psychotherapy, counselling, consultancy, sports, science, education and business management. The origin of coaching comes from the Middle English word 'coche', literally a vehicle which carries a person or group of people from a starting location to a desired place (Dilts, 2003). It is worth holding on to this definition when talking about coaching psychology for learning, because it is useful for my purpose of connecting it to learning as a journey.

It is not an easy task to reaching a consensual definition of coaching that integrates and appreciates different backgrounds, strategies, goals and techniques (Stojnov & Pavlovic, 2010). An early definition of coaching offered by Druckman and Bjork (1991) emphasises an instructional approach that 'coaching consists of observing students and offering hints, feedbacks, reminders, new tasks, or redirecting a student's attention to a salient feature – all with the goal of making the student's performance approximate to expert's performance as closely as possible' (p. 61). Other definitions emphasise a facilitative approach. Whitmore (1996), for example, suggested that coaching is 'unlocking a person's potential to maximise their own performance. It is helping them to learn rather than teaching them' (p. 8). Whitmore's definition of coaching brings in the theme of learning and the-coach-as-a-learning-facilitator, which is accordant with how I understand coaching, but his definition is too general and it says little about the nature of the coaching process (Grant, 2001). Hudson (1999) defined the process of coaching as occurring when a coach, 'a person who facilitates experiential learning that results in future-oriented abilities, helps a client see options for becoming a more effective human being' (p. 6). McDermott and Jago (2005) defined coaching as 'a conversational yet focused discipline that supports people in learning how to lead and manage themselves more effectively in relation to their issues, their resources, their contexts and their potential' (p. 8).

Three aspects are usually tackled as common threads running through definitions of coaching: performance, learning and development (Parsloe & Wray, 2000; Whitmore, 1996; Ives, 2008). Grant (2001) summarised that the core constructs of coaching involve:

- a collaborative rather than authoritarian relationship between coach and coachee;
- a focus on constructing solutions not analysing problems;
- the assumption that clients are capable and not dysfunctional;
- an emphasis on collaborative goal setting;
- the recognition that the coach does not necessarily need domain-specific expertise in the coachee's chosen area of learning, though the coach has expertise in facilitating learning through coaching;
- a systematic goal-directed process to foster the ongoing self-directed learning and personal growth of the coachee.

These constructs set the foundations for the definition of coaching psychology.

The definition of coaching psychology

Coaching psychology is defined by the Special Group in Coaching Psychology of the British Psychological Society as 'enhancing well-being and performance in

62 An enquiry of educational paradigms

personal life and work domains underpinned by models of coaching grounded in established learning theories or psychological approaches' (Grant & Palmer, 2002; Palmer & Whybrow, 2006). Another definition is presented by the Australian Psychological Society (2003) as 'the systematic application of behavioural science to the enhancement of life experience, work performance and well-being for individuals, groups and organisations who do not have clinically significant mental health issues or abnormal levels of distress'.

As with clinical psychology or counselling psychology, there is a big difference between coaching psychology and coaching, in that coaching psychology explicitly includes the application of appropriate psychological theories and models, and practitioners are psychologists with relevant psychology qualifications. Without any theoretical base, coaching practice may be merely based on hypothetical theories and conjecture (Biswas-Diener & Dean, 2007). It has been argued that coaching psychology research, especially evaluation on coaching effectiveness, must have a firm foundation in evidence-based principles (Short *et al.*, 2010). Moreover, there is a strong message of 'learning' in the definitions of coaching psychology, suggesting that coaching should be anchored in the psychology of learning (Law *et al.*, 2007).

The meta-theory of coaching psychology

Humanistic psychology and person-centred theory

The humanistic, person-centred theory and the positive psychology perspective together constitute a meta-theory of coaching psychology. This meta-theory of coaching psychology has a significant overlap with the learning theories discussed in the previous chapter.

The humanistic psychology can be traced back to Rogers' (1956, 1963) development of the person-centred approach in psychotherapy. The person-centred perspective views human beings as their own best experts. People have an actualising tendency, an inherent tendency toward growth and development, with optimal functioning in social environments where people feel understood, valued and accepted for who they are. This perspective draws on the self-determination theory (Deci & Ryan, 2000) that people have within themselves the potential to develop and grow given the right conditions for supporting the individual's experience of autonomy, competence and relatedness. The person-centred approach is in essence the principled stance of respecting the self-determination of others (Grant, 2004). Joseph and Worsley (2005) argued that the meta-theoretical perspective of the person-centred approach is congruent with the ethos of coaching psychology. One of the most popular coaching approaches, the facilitation approach, favoured by more than 70% of coaching sources (Palmer & Whybrow, 2007), reflects the humanistic and person-centred roots.

Theoretically, person-centred psychology is always the same, whether deployed in clinic, counselling, psychotherapy or coaching. However, these sessions would be different at the practical level. The person-centred approach is not a form of therapy or counselling per se; it is a philosophical stance that can be applied to different settings. Coaches who work on this philosophical stance view their clients as their own best experts, who have within themselves the potential to develop and grow (Joseph, 2003, 2006). The humanistic approach requires coaches to be congruent and to accept and learn to work with what actually happens rather than what should happen (McDermott & Jago, 2005). This capability links to the role of mindfulness in coaching (Passmore & Marianetti, 2007) that cultivates conscious attention and awareness of the presence in a non-judgemental way, thus providing a channel to the realisation and acceptance of 'what is'. Through congruence and mindfulness, coaches facilitate psychological growth and create an environment where clients can flourish.

Positive psychology

The person-centred approach offers a genuinely positive psychological perspective, as it unifies both the negative and the positive aspects of human functioning (Joseph & Worsley, 2005). The humanistic psychologist Maslow (1954) stated that 'the science of psychology has been far more successful on the negative than on the positive side. It has revealed to us much about man's shortcomings, his illness, his sins, but little about his potentialities, his virtues, his achievable aspirations, or his full psychological height. It is as if psychology has voluntarily restricted itself to only half its rightful jurisdiction, and that, the darker, meaner half' (p. 354). Positive psychology, which can be defined as 'the scientific study of optimal human functioning' (Seligman, 1999), tries to look at the brighter half of psychology. It revisits 'the average person with an interest in finding out what works, what is right and what is improving' (Sheldon & King, 2001, p. 216). Seligman and Csikszentmihalyi (2000) provided an understanding of positive psychology at three levels by examining: 1) valued subjective experiences: well-being, contentment and satisfaction in the past; hope and optimism for the future; and flow and happiness in the present (subjective level); 2) positive individual traits: the capacity for love, courage, interpersonal skills, aesthetic sensibility, perseverance, forgiveness, originality, future mindedness, spirituality, high talent and wisdom (individual level); and 3) the civic virtues and the institutions that move individuals towards better citizenship: responsibility, nurturance, altruism, civility, moderation, tolerance and work ethic (group level). Thus positive psychology is positioned as the study of 'the conditions and processes that contribute to the flourishing or optimal functioning of people, groups and institutions' (Gable & Haidt, 2005, p. 104). It emphasises the experience of human flourishing, subjective well-being, engagement of strengths and pursuit of meaning (Seligman, 2002).

Positive psychology provides the theoretical and empirical grounding needed by coaching psychology (Kauffman & Linley, 2007). Coaching psychology and positive psychology are natural allies: both of them resonate with people's longing for positive messages, concern the enhancement of optimal performance and well-being, attend to people's strengths and potential, and explicitly emphasise fulfilment and achievement (Linley & Harrington, 2006). Coaching psychology places a strong emphasis on self-awareness, particularly awareness of positive factors such as strengths and preferences, as one of the primary applications of positive psychology (Choong & Britton, 2007). The strong relationship between coaching psychology and positive psychology has been used to develop a number of 'positive coaching psychology' applications such as strengths coaching (Linley & Harrington, 2006; Linley *et al.*, 2010), flow coaching (Wesson & Boniwell, 2007), coaching on positive personality dispositions (Klockner & Hicks, 2008), and appreciative enquiry (Liston-Smith, 2008).

The possible application of meta-theory to coaching and learning

Incorporating person-centred orientation and the positive psychology perspective, I want to create a learning environment where students are facilitated to learn at different paces, trust and respect their self-direction, explore their strengths and resources, and enhance their self-determination in learning. Furthermore, learning activities should be designed to encourage flow in learning, have a clear set of goals, and maintain a balance between perceived challenges and perceived support, as well as provide useful, immediate feedback. The coaching approach should lead to increased engagement, energy and motivation in learning, resulting in positive emotions, greater creativity and resilience, enhanced academic performance and personal development. Positive personal virtues, learning dispositions and learning capabilities should undoubtedly be addressed. When considering the application of this meta-theory, I am also interested in looking at learners who are disengaged or resistant to learning. The purpose is to see how coaching will work with less well-functioning students.

Comparisons of coaching with other supporting approaches

Coaching is not the only approach to help people grow, learn and develop; other supporting approaches include counselling, mentoring, scaffolding, consulting and training. Williams and Irving (2001) questioned whether coaching is really any different from earlier forms of helping. Walker (2004) carefully examined the entire 'people development industry' and set up an inductive classification model, but coaching remains difficult to position in the model. It is true that the boundaries among the supporting approaches are permeable and often the same individuals participate in more than one approach. However, I consider it is useful to clarify how coaching is different from other helping styles.

Coaching, counselling and psychotherapy

Most coaching skills are based on counselling and therapeutic techniques (Richard, 1999; Neenan & Palmer, 2001; Greene & Grant, 2003; Law, 2003) such as solution-focused brief therapy, cognitive behavioural therapy, rational emotional behavioural therapy and multimodal therapy (Law *et al.*, 2007). Both coaching and therapy are based on similar theoretical constructs and similar practitioner-client issues. There is considerable overlap between counselling, psychotherapy and coaching.

Nevertheless, the differences between coaching and therapy have been identified as the focus of attention, time orientation, level of activity and type of conversations between coaches and clients (Hart *et al.*, 2001). In counselling and therapy, the focus is typically retrospective, particularly in psychodynamic and some humanistic models, dealing with unconscious issues and repairing damage from earlier experiences. In contrast, the orientation of coaching is prospective, focusing on goals, untapped potentials and critical factors in a whole person who seeks to maximise his or her fulfilment in life and work. Therapeutic dialogue typically involves expressions of feelings and emotional processing resulting in the uncovering and discovery of in-depth personal issues, whereas coaching interactions are more likely to be active, goal-directed and more action-based.

Another important distinction is the relationship. In a typical therapeutic relationship, the therapist is viewed as a 'healer', whereas coaching implies more collaboration between coach and client. The coach needs to guide but not direct the process, nor assume responsibility for the outcomes. Coaching is a joint activity shared by both parties. People have greater flexibility within the coaching relationship. They can also be in dual or multiple relationships, such as manager–employee, teacher–student or supervisor–worker relationships, whereas in counselling the relationship between a counsellor and a client is more strictly defined and professionally confined. These less restrictive boundaries for the coaching relationship may allow a coach more latitude than a therapist or counsellor.

Coaching and mentoring

Coaching and mentoring have been used interchangeably in many studies, particularly in relation to supporting learning. Without doubt they are both very valuable processes. What separates coaching and mentoring may be the direct input of subject-specific expertise (Allison & Harbour, 2009). A mentor is often used when someone is new to either a profession or a particular task. The mentor is required to have more experience than the person being mentored in that particular role, and so passes on their knowledge and skills to the mentee. Often a mentor has to make a judgement about the standard reached by the mentee. In comparison, the approach of coaching is more concerned with drawing out the resources of the coachee by effective listening, questioning, reflecting and clarifying. It is very important for a coach not to be judgemental. The feedback to the coachee is not supposed to be an assessment but a neutral message. Hence the relationships in mentoring and coaching are different: a mentoring relationship may be more hierarchical, involving more direct instruction and input of specific expertise, judgement and evaluation, whereas a coaching relationship is less hierarchical and does not depend on imparting expert knowledge.

Coaching and scaffolding

I include scaffolding in comparison with coaching because they are both important facilitative tools in students' learning and development strongly associated with ZPD.

Coaching shares a number of important features with educational scaffolding: 1) the essentially dialogic nature of discourse in which knowledge is co-constructed; 2) the significance of the authentic and cognitively challenging tasks in which knowing is embedded; 3) the role of social mediation and the establishment of inter-subjectivity as shared understandings between learners and teachers (Wells, 1999; Wertsch, 1985, 1998); and 4) the transfer of responsibility for the task to the students as the major goal (Mercer & Fisher, 1993).

Nevertheless, coaching does not assume that supporters are necessarily more knowledgeable and competent than learners in particular tasks. Vygotskian views explain that it is not the competence per se of the more knowledgeable person that is important; rather it is to understand the meaning of assistance in relation to learners' ZPD (Chaiklin, 2003). This is principally important in understanding coaching when we see learning as a highly personalised journey. Learners are supposed to generate questions that are specifically significant to themselves, and there is no reason to believe their coach would find these questions as important as the learners. In the process of collaboration of knowledge co-construction, coaching is regarded as a facilitative vehicle to support and perhaps accelerate the learner's progress, but the coach does not necessarily acquire every piece of concrete knowledge that the learners have developed. Moreover, coaching emphasises the Vygotskian theory of students as active learners in social interactions of learning and developing. The quality of interactions is seen as crucial. Coaching offers customised support and personalised facilitation that is responsive to the needs of particular learners in any situation.

To recap, coaching might be viewed as located on a continuum with other approaches of support and development. Its boundary with other types of helping approaches in the human development industry frequently becomes blurred. A coach might need to engage in counselling, training, mentoring or traditional expository teaching procedures (Munro, 1999). In other words, coaching can include the use of counselling or direct instructional procedures in the service of explicit goals. Many of the skills of good coaching, mentoring, counselling, consulting and training overlap significantly. In addition, often a blended approach of two or more helping styles is more effective (Allison & Harbour, 2009). I consider that in facilitating and supporting a learner, it is important to have an awareness of how coaching functions differently from other supporting approaches; meanwhile we should not be constrained by the labels of 'coaching', 'mentoring' or any other definitions.

Psychological approaches of coaching relevant to learning

This section aims to examine potential links between coaching with learning based on psychological approaches and emphasises valuing diversity and applying the psychology of learning to coaching (Law *et al.*, 2007). Whitmore (1996) pointed out that coaches would fail to achieve the intended results without an understanding of the psychological principles on which coaching is based. Hence there is a need for clearer differentiations between psychological approaches (Stalinski, 2003).

Based on Stober and Grant's (2006) work, Ives (2008) explored nine paradigms in coaching: 1) a humanistic perspective; 2) a behaviour-based approach; 3) an adult-development approach; 4) a cognitive approach; 5) an adult learning approach; 6) a positive psychology model; 7) an adventure-based model; 8) a systemic approach; and 9) a goal-oriented approach. He suggested that understanding more clearly the nature of the difference between approaches facilitates fitting a coaching model to specific situations. However, we do not know which approach is more effective or correct. Though the boundaries between these approaches are not firmly set, I find this categorisation helps to distinguish theoretical foundations and sheds light on the theorisation of coaching and learning across various paradigms. Due to the word limit, I cannot review all the coaching approaches. I consider three approaches are most relevant to enhancing students' learning. These approaches are based on the psychological perspectives of cognitive psychology, solution-focused and narrative psychology. I will elaborate each in turn.

Cognitive coaching

Beck (1976) argued that learning is basically a cognitive process. Cognitive coaching aims to stimulate and develop a person's thoughts, emotions and behaviours. It also offers methods and strategies that the person can use when coaching is finished (Oestrich & Johansen, 2005). Cognitive coaching deals largely with the importance of cognitions as determinates of emotional states as well as the resultant behaviours and actions (Beck, 1995; Ellis *et al.*, 1997; Neenan & Palmer, 2001). It focuses on the relationship between a person's cognitions, emotions, behaviours and physiological reactions within social contexts (Edgerton & Palmer, 2005). With its aim of increasing learners' awareness of their meta-cognition and personal thinking processes, cognitive coaching particularly emphasises coaching as a way to foster active, self-regulated learning directed to desired performance. Cognitive coaching has various theoretical sources mainly in cognitive psychology, and empirically relates to the field of cognitive therapy, including but not limited to linguistics, individualisation, mediation, constructivism, systems thinking and clinical supervision (Auerbach, 2006). Cognitive coaching does not follow the path of Freud, uncovering repressed ideas and translating unconscious

68 An enquiry of educational paradigms

thoughts into symbolic meanings, nor does it operate in a behavioural approach affecting and reinforcing actions by stimulus–response connection. Cognitive coaching assists coachees to identify critical elements in their thinking, adopt accurate and useful cognitions in order to develop better relationships, improve decision-making and achieve greater performance.

Cognitive coaching has been presented as one of the most relevant coaching approaches for educational psychologists (Munro, 1999). Cognitive coaching concerns coaching learners to improve aspects of their thinking and learning, attitudinal knowledge, learning dispositions and beliefs as well as self-esteem and self-concept as learners in different social interactive contexts (Costa & Garmston, 2002; Gottesman & Jennings, 1994). Its goal is not to teach learners new knowledge, skills or capabilities, but to mediate learners' thinking, enhance their ability in order to examine the patterns of thinking and behaviours and consider the underlying assumptions of the proceeding actions (Costa & Garmston, 2002). The mediation capability is described as: 1) knowing one's intentions and choosing congruent behaviours; 2) setting aside unproductive patterns of behaviours; 3) adjusting one's style preference; and 4) navigating through planning, reflecting and problem-solving conversations.

However, cognitive coaching is more than a set of cognitive methods (Auerbach, 2006). Cognitive coaching tools that stem from emerging cognitive theories are practical and learnable. They emphasise the whole person, who is moving towards his/her most important goals that are congruent with their vital values. Costa and Garmston (2002) pointed out that cognitive coaches should keep in mind three goals of employing this process: trust, learning and autonomy. Both parties should trust in the process, in each other and in the environment. The intention of this process is to grow intellectually, learn more about learning, mutually increase one's capacity of self-improvement and finally create and maintain a stimulating and cooperative environment deliberately designed to enhance continuous intellectual growth. This process of cognitive coaching requires a sense of deep engagement and transformation of the mind. In this sense, cognitive coaching shares common goals with lifelong learning and transformative learning.

Solution-focused coaching

Solution-focused coaching has been derived from solution-focused brief therapy (SFBT), developed by de Shazer, Dolan and Berg in the 1980s based on the work undertaken in the Milwaukee's Brief Family Therapy Centre. SFBT proposes that: 1) the development of a solution is not necessarily related to the problem; 2) the client is the expert in his or her own problems; 3) if it is not broken, do not fix it; 4) if something works, continue with it; 5) if something does not work, do something else (de Shazer, 1985). It takes a non-pathological view of people and considers searching for possibilities for action and change revealed by the client, rather than adapting therapy according to a diagnostic classification (Rossi, 1980). Whereas problem-focused therapy concentrates on decreasing problematic behaviours, SFBT concentrates on increasing behaviours desired by the clients. It is a future-focused, goal-directed approach that utilises questions designed to identify exceptions (times when the problem does not occur or occurs less often in real life), miracles (a description of what life will be like when the problem is gone or resolved), solutions (how to achieve this life without the problem) and scales (which are used to measure the client's current level of progress towards a solution) and reveal the behaviours needed to achieve or maintain further progress (Trepper *et al.*, 2006).

The theoretical basis of SFBT originates in social constructionism (Cantwell & Holmes, 1994). Opposed to the traditional medical model that assumes individuals hold the problems, SFBT contextualises solutions that arise from individuals' social contexts as a result of personal and social resources (Simon & Berg, 2002). The solution-focused questions regarding goal formulation, exceptions, scaling, miracles and competences are intended to define goals and solutions that are assumed to already exist in the clients' life questions and to extract the relevant information (Bannink, 2007). The therapist is not the expert with all the answers but the expert in asking the right solution-focused questions and structuring conversations (Bannink, 2006). It seems that SFBT offers techniques that are compatible for use within a person-centred approach (Cepeda & Davenport, 2006). SFBT is also associated with positive psychology due to its future-orientation, identification and utilisation of strengths that the client already possesses (Bannink, 2007). Hence solution-focused techniques fit into the meta-theory of coaching psychology.

Researchers have found that solution-focused techniques, based on coachees' resilience and self-efficacy, could be effectively applied to organisational coaching and personal coaching (Greene & Grant 2003; Grant, 2006; Jackson & McKergow, 2002; Szabo & Meier, 2009; Visser & Butter, 2008). The solution-focused approach to coaching emphasises the importance of asking 'how to' questions that elicit thoughts from the coachees about the best methods to attain their desired goals rather than asking 'why' questions that explore causality or the essence of the problems (Grant & O'Connor, 2010). The most useful implication of solution-focused coaching to learning is its contribution to goal attainment and self-directed learning. Coaching questions can be designed to: 1) picture the preferred future in learning situations and motivate learners; 2) find out what the small and everyday details of learners' life would be like if these hopes were realised; 3) explore what learners have already been doing that might contribute to these goals; 4) find out what might be different if learners make one step forwards realising these goals; 5) look for learners' strengths and resources that complement them; and 6) identify learners' current points of sufficient satisfaction with their learning on scales. Formulating coaching questions about learning in a solution-focused approach is based on an understanding of language and dialogue as creative and collaborative processes without a diagnostic structure that learners might feel uncomfortable about. Thus, solution-focused coaching has a significant part to play among many coaching possibilities to enhance learning.

Narrative coaching

Narrative coaching is based on the same theoretical foundation as narrative therapy (Stelter & Law, 2010), highlighting the significance of storytelling. Carr (1986) stated that 'lives are told in being lived and lived in being told' (p. 61). We use stories cognitively, discursively and socially to remember and organise our past, communicate about and negotiate our present as well as envision and act into our future (Drake, 2007). Narratives serve to establish temporal coherence and shape how events, actions, other persons and ourselves can be experienced and perceived as sensible and meaningful (Stelter, 2009). Narrative psychology is based on a systemic and dynamic view of stories as processes by which we create and navigate our world according to our unique blend of cultural and individual expectations (Chafe, 1990). It provides a structure and purpose to 'think narratively' (Drake, 2007) in coaching, seeing a story inseparable from the context in which it is performed, lived and held (Boje, 1991; Rossiter, 1999).

A key assumption in the narrative approach of coaching is the post-modern belief in the dynamic, relational and multifaceted nature of identity (Drake, 2008). According to James (1892), there is an ongoing dialogue between the self-as-subject (the sense of 'I') and the self-as-object (the sense of 'Me'). This view reflects inherent tensions in the continual process by which we construct and negotiate our narrative identities. Gergen (1991) and Keupp (1999) stated that self and identity are constructed and shaped in the specific social context, relationships and discourse. Narrative coaching works at the level of identity, which is seen as clients' primary self-concepts and orientations in narrating their lives and as both source and anchor for their behaviours (Drake, 2005). The coach should recognise that if they want their coachees to adopt new behaviours or attain new results, they must help them build an identity to which the desired behaviour is a natural response (Drake, 2007). In this sense, identity is regarded as a verb rather than a noun for a coach to engage in the narrative process (Drake, 2008).

Stelter (2009) argued for the growing importance of values as a central dimension in the reflective coaching process. Specific values are co-explored by coach and coachee so that both are equally engaged and interested in the exploration. The development of values and preferences in connection with behaviours is central for an individual's conscious and intentional orientation in situations and for the process of meaning-making in general. Narrative coaching proposes meaning-making as a central dimension in the coaching dialogue. Meaning is made through the actual experiences and implicit knowledge that the individual acquires in various contexts in life, and it is shaped through social negotiation and narratives that describe the life practice of the individual. The individual, personal meaning-making depends on how articulate, skilled and expressive people are in speaking about their experiences (Stevens, 2000). This process can be supported by coaches' sensitive questioning to get in touch with these implicit, embodied and pre-reflective dimensions of coachees' being. The socially co-constructed meaning, which is integrated with the individual meaning in coaching conversations, takes place in a given context that forms the basis for constructive, active and meaningful linguistic systems.

The coaches' contribution in narrative coaching is to provide both an interpersonal structure and a narrative structure in which coachees can engage and explore their stories (Levitt, 2002). The key role of a coach is to 'invite people to see their stories from different perspectives, to notice how they are constructed, to note their limits and to discover that there are other possible narratives' (Freedman & Combs, 1996, p. 57). As individuals realise limitations inherent in the available narratives in which they are embedded, they can see them more clearly, create a sense of distance from these narratives and allow the submerged voices of their selves to surface (Polkinghorne, 2001). The coaches and coachees then identify new meanings and alternative narratives that support a new view of who they are and how they will be in this world (Drake, 2008). Deeper changes are more likely when broader narrative patterns and narrative strategies are addressed (Mattingly, 1998). Other coaching approaches involve storytelling too. What differentiates narrative coaching from cognitive coaching and solution-focused coaching is that a narrative approach might take more time in offering a reflective space where coach and coachee have time for a thoughtful pause that allows new ways of acting in specific situations (Stelter, 2009) when stories are used to create transformative results.

A narrative perspective offers a helpful approach to strengthen a sense of coherence in the learners' identity, couple various learning events and integrate past, present and future into a whole. Based on an understanding that learners' self-awareness is fundamental for their developmental path and learning as situated in social discourse and relationships, narrative coaching can be seen as a process of co-creation of knowledge in a relational aspect (Pearce, 2007). As we shall see, a major step in the narrative coaching process is to introduce and work with the distinction between available narratives and potential stories, help learners identify narrative data from their lives, reframe available stocks of knowledge and relationships and discover and develop new options (Drake, 2003, 2004, 2007). It is assumed that the more learners consider themselves as the authors of learning stories, the stronger the sense of ownership and the sense of responsibility for their learning they would develop, and the better they might be at articulating their own learning stories in a more sophisticated language. Hence learning stories can signal where learners are relative to their development, and narratives can certainly provide rich sources for enhancing learning.

Coaching and coaching psychology in educational contexts

Fillery-Travis and Lane (2006, 2007) proposed that more research is needed to build our understanding of coaching to impact on performance for different populations and also to understand the nature of how coaching makes a difference over other learning and developing interventions. Coaching, or coaching psychology,

72 An enquiry of educational paradigms

is used in a wide range of formal educational contexts for a variety of purposes (Burley & Pomphrey, 2011). These include:

- the new teacher training process;
- the continuing professional development of teachers;
- leadership programmes which use coaching for the specific development of individuals at senior level and for broader institutional purposes;
- in the wider schools workforce to support students with learning or behavioural difficulties;
- working with school students in order to develop motivation and aspiration;
- in schools to develop abilities, skills and talents in specified areas such as music, art or sports.

My review of coaching psychology in education mainly covers the following broad themes: 1) coaching for developing leadership and executive performance in schools; 2) coaching for supporting teachers' professional development and enhancing teaching practices; 3) coaching for promoting students' motivation and aspiration in school learning and raising academic performance; and 4) coaching for enhancing students' psychological well-being.

Coaching for school leadership development

Coaching for leadership development is growing in popularity and credibility in schools. It fits well with the national agenda of personalised learning and distributed leadership (Tolhurst, 2010). For example, the Centre for the Use of Research and Evidence in Education (CUREE) has developed a suite of modules on Effective Coaching and Mentoring (2005). The leadership programmes offered by the National College for Leadership of Schools and Children's Services such as 'National Professional Qualification for Headship', 'Leading from the Middle' and 'Leadership Pathway' all use coaching as an essential tool for leadership development. These programmes identify common aims for coaching individual school leaders. They have clear guidelines for the role of the coach as an experienced professional, facilitating participants' in-school learning, challenging them to extend their practice and develop their skills, establishing trust and purposeful relationships and encouraging the use of online communities and materials (Burley & Pomphrey, 2011).

Coaching has demonstrated its effectiveness in the business world, and it has become a well-established intervention that offers opportunities for school leaders (Wise & Jacobo, 2010). Executive coaching programmes are used by schools at senior leadership level in order to develop individuals for specific goals and enable institutional development (Kampa-Kokesch & Anderson, 2001; Bloom, 2005; Creasey & Paterson, 2005; Foster & Carboni, 2008; Burley & Pomphrey, 2011; Wise & Jacobo, 2010). These programmes often use existing coaching models in business contexts to structure a goal-setting and option-generation process.

However, many executive coaching programmes do not directly address the challenges that school leaders face in their particular settings.

Bloom, Castagna and Warren (2003) designed a CLASS approach that is built around the particular needs of school leaders to support individuals with relatively limited experience to move into principal positions in schools. This approach advocates that the most effective coaches are generally 'outsiders' to the coachee's context, bringing a different perspective to the relationship, circumstances and possibilities. It blends different coaching strategies, such as cognitive coaching (Costa & Garmston, 2002) and transformative coaching (Hargrove, 1995), to convey a fluid and flexible coaching model in which the coach serves as expert consultant, collaborator and teacher. The facilitative strategies focus on building the coachee's capacity through meta-cognition and reflection. Nevertheless, this approach seems to primarily focus on individual development and it lacks a vision of how it could make a difference to the school environment and students' learning.

Foster and Carboni (2008) used a student-centred case method and an action enquiry pedagogy in leadership development as a way to demonstrate how management theories can help analytically disentangle complex phenomena. After delivering a leadership workshop on individual action enquiry projects, self-directed peer coaching and role modelling to school leaders, they evaluated the impact on leadership effectiveness by observation and interviews. Small increases in self-awareness and more significant changes in students' lives and organisations were reported. More recently, Wise and Jacobo (2010) presented a coaching framework for school transformation built on the premises of socio-cultural and organisational learning theory. In this framework, coaching provides a shared problem-solving setting where the coach seeks the principal's ZPD and utilises it to push the leader to move to a new way of thinking and acting. The framework provides a conceptual tool that coaching helps a school principal to stay on the course of constant reflection, assessment and strategic development aligned to the goal of higher achievement of all students.

These and many other studies on coaching and leadership development in schools denote that coaching can be at the heart of change. Coaching serves as a compelling tool to stimulate and inspire leaders to think and act differently thus eventually bringing desired and ongoing change to the organisations (Hargrove, 2008). It should be noted that some of these actions involve the principal becoming a coach for teachers in the school, thus building capacity through the coaching system (Wise & Jacobo, 2010). In the next section, I review the studies of coaching for enhancing teaching practices in teachers' continuing professional development (CPD).

Coaching for teachers' professional development

In recent years there has been a shift of emphasis towards continuing professional development in forward-thinking schools that it is centred around a process of ongoing, collaborative professional learning (Allison & Harbour, 2009). Kelly

74 An enquiry of educational paradigms

(2007) described CPD as 'an activity which enhances the quality of teaching and learning within the school. It should develop the school and the individual and impact directly on what goes on in the school.' (p. 12)

A growing interest in coaching, mentoring and peer-networking is documented in the national strategy for CPD (Rhodes & Beneicke, 2002). In 2004 the National Strategy materials published by the Department for Education and Skills advocated coaching as a means to embedding the developments in teaching and learning across the various strategy strands. The Department for Education (2010) suggested that coaching and feedback on teachers' practice is 'a particularly important element and can be decisive in determining whether changes in practice survive' and it 'will continue to emphasise the value that can come from teachers learning from each other – through observing lessons, feedback, coaching and mentoring'.

Coaching has been shown to be an effective teaching–learning approach for assisting individuals to improve performance, leading to increased professional knowledge and practice (Munro, 1999). Tolhurst (2010) acknowledged the essence of coaching and mentoring with staff in schools in terms of building their capacity, accelerating the personal and professional development of staff, mentoring newly qualified teachers to adapt to new roles and tasks, enhancing team morale, supporting the senior management team in decision-making and underpinning the implementation of organisational change.

There is a requirement for providers of initial teacher training to work in partnership through the use of an experienced teacher being identified to work alongside a trainee teacher (TDA, 2008). However, these experienced teachers take roles as mentors, and their relationships with trainee teachers are more like mentoring relationships. The government-initiated coaching strategy of 'Masters in Teaching and Learning' provides an explicit model of 'support and professional challenge' and further includes a need to 'motivate and inspire, encourage on-going enquiry and reflection, and identify needs relevant to the participants in school contexts, apply evidence and educational theory to real-life situations' (TDA, 2009, p. 4). The framework, including principles, core concepts and skills for coaching, is designed to help increase the impact of continuing professional development on student learning. The key principles are as follows:

- a learning conversation;
- a thoughtful relationship;
- a learning agreement;
- combining support from fellow professional learners and specialities;
- growing self-direction;
- setting challenging and personal goals;
- understanding why different approaches work;
- acknowledging the benefits to mentors and coaches;
- experimenting and observing;
- using resources effectively.

Coaching psychology in learning   75

However, the framework only specifies what roles coaches should take; it omits key concepts which can inform the coaching process. Rather, it is a combination of purposes, functions and outcomes. There is limited scope for critical and reciprocal learning. Thus the framework may reduce the complexity of coaching research in schools to a simplified categorisation of coaches' roles. It may fail to fulfil more challenging aspirations for collaborative enquiry, reflection and professional learning.

Joyce and Showers (2002) found that coaching had a dramatic impact on the transfer and application of new learning that was significantly higher than for other training methods. They studied a range of teacher developmental activities and then examined how these activities impacted on the acquisition of knowledge and skills, and whether they resulted in new strategies being applied to classroom practice. Results showed that there was little translation to a change in classroom practice when the teachers were lectured or simply had new teaching strategies demonstrated. The only way that a significant change was seen in knowledge acquisition and classroom application was when the teachers worked closely with a coach. They recommended that teachers form small peer coaching groups that would share the learning process, so that staff development might directly affect student learning. Similarly, Knight (2008) conducted a comparative educational-based study with 51 participants for implementing coaching in teacher training. The results showed that the teachers who were supported by a coach used a new instructional framework more than who were not coached.

A considerable body of literature has explored teachers' peer mentoring and coaching as CPD (Ross, 1992; Lu, 2010; Jane & Peeler, 2006; Showers & Joyce, 1996; Zanting & Verloop, 2001). However, this does not mean that coaching necessarily improves teachers' professional learning. Real improvement is mediated by a belief that teachers would make a positive effect on students' achievement when the teachers embark on coaching. This is coined by teacher efficacy (Gibson & Dembo, 1984). In Ross's (1992) study on teacher efficacy and the effects of coaching on student achievement, teachers who believe they will make a difference are more likely to see coaching as an opportunity to expand and consolidate their teaching techniques and interact more effectively with their coaches and peers. In contrast, teachers who see student learning as affected by uncontrollable forces may regard coaching as nothing but more work or another kind of training.

More recently, Burley and Pomphrey (2011) explored how coaching and mentoring can be used as a dynamic process for effective professional learning in secondary schools to bring about change in professional practice by conducting a variety of enquiries. They launched a series of professional development sessions for investigating: 1) the nature of mentoring and coaching through collaboration; 2) mentoring and coaching in a range of professional contexts outside of education; 3) one-on-one coaching and mentoring collaborations within the school context; and 4) wider mentoring and coaching collaborations within the school context for effective institutional change. They introduced each collaborative enquiry as a

76 An enquiry of educational paradigms

case study with its context, purposes, actions, processes and outcomes in terms of its effects on the coachee, the coach and the coaching process. The researchers proposed that the mentoring and coaching relationship can be seen as the learning platform that enables collaborative critical enquiry to take place. However, these enquiries have solely concentrated on teachers' and individual leaders' personal and professional development. The responses revealed that there was a need for further investigation into how coaching and mentoring affect students' learning or institutional change.

In sum, coaching meets the goals of CPD in terms of holding a strong drive for developing the quality of teaching and learning as well as establishing a learning culture amongst staff (Allison & Harbour, 2009). Coaching has gained predominance in the early and continuing professional development of teachers (Burley & Pomphrey, 2011). One central concern has been helping students benefit when their teachers learn, grow and change (Showers & Joyce, 1996). Nevertheless, it provokes more questions: how do teachers who have been coached impact on student learning in various age groups, in different subjects or in aspects outside of school learning? There remains a vague link between coaching as teachers' CPD and student learning.

Coaching for student learning and academic performance

There has been some research in the area of coaching student performance in the adult population (Grant, 2001), coaching in MBA student teams to increase team effectiveness and performance (Bolton, 1999) and coaching parents to improve student learning (Graham *et al.*, 2008). These coaching texts reflect a growing interest in coaching's potential contribution to education with a focus on studying different coaching interventions and the impacts on adult learners.

Hidi and Renninger (2006) proposed a four-phase model of interest development for deepening learning engagement with affective and cognitive factors: triggered situational interest, maintained situational interest, emerging individual interest and well-developed individual interest. The educational implications of this model were reviewed across a wide range of age groups, including secondary school students (Renninger & Hidi, 2002; Lipstein & Renninger, 2006).

Of more relevance to the non-adult population, Hamman *et al.* (2000) examined types and frequencies of coaching of learning at secondary school level and its relation to students' strategic learning. They found that students' strategic learning activities were significantly related to teachers' coaching of learning, which occurred only 9% of the instruction. It shows the potential of coaching to develop students' learning capability. However, other factors that might influence students' learning activity, such as learning relationships, were neglected in the study.

A student-focused coaching model has been developed to facilitate students' reading (Hasbrouck & Denton, 2007). The model is defined as 'a cooperative, ideally collaborative relationship with parties mutually engaged in efforts to provide better services for students' (ibid., p. 2). Its primary goal is to improve students' reading skills and competence, with a focus on students' strengths and needs and an attention directed to outcomes. Nevertheless, it is not clear how it is 'student-focused' and how interventions are 'individualised' and so far lacks strong evidence on its effectiveness.

Passmore and Brown (2009) presented findings from a multi-school site, three-year longitudinal study in Sandwell Council in the UK to explore how coaching contributes to GCSE students' learning and academic performance. The study confirmed that coaching has potential value as a tool with a non-adult population in supporting educational attainment and examination performance. Nonetheless, the study had no control group when it utilised pure statistical measurements. It focused on one local area and only examined performance in terms of GCSE grades. Therefore it did not offer evidence of any long-term impact of coaching on students' learning capabilities.

For an even younger population, Briggs and Nieuwerburgh (2010) offered a workshop approach to developing peer coaching skills, with a special focus on giving and receiving feedback, in a normal primary school classroom context through different activities that did not seek to address academic areas of curriculum. The researchers predominantly used an ethnographic methodology with pre- and post-responses to the drawing task given to children in Years 5 and 6. However, this study did not present a coherent account to its hypothesis, nor did it indicate how children can transfer these skills to academic studies.

These studies of coaching students on their academic performance and learning motivation suggest that coaching could be an effective tool to support young people's learning. Another factor that seems to contribute to enhancing learning performance is developing mental resilience and coping skills. This point is specified in the next section.

Coaching for students' psychological well-being

The school is increasingly being identified as a context not just for providing education about traditional subjects, but also for assisting young people to develop competences for enhancing well-being, known as 'social-emotional education' (Banerjee, 2010). Well-being is synergistic with better learning (Seligman *et al.*, 2009). Positive emotions have been proven to produce broader attention (Fredrickson, 1998; Bolte et al., 2003; Fredrickson & Branigan, 2005; Rowe *et al.*, 2007), more creative thinking (Isen *et al.*, 1987; Estrada *et al.*, 1994) and more holistic thinking (Isen *et al.*, 1991; Kuhl, 1983, 2000). By building resilience and hope, young people may be better equipped to cope with challenges in later life and deal with emerging self-identity as an adult person (Passmore & Brown, 2009).

A cognitive-behavioural, solution-focused life coaching programme has been applied with an adult population to enhance goal-striving, well-being and hope (Green *et al.*, 2006). The results showed significant increases in goal-striving, well-being and hope, with gains maintained up to 30 weeks later on some variables. This study confirmed that life coaching might help to make a purposeful change

78 An enquiry of educational paradigms

in people's lives and have a long-term impact on psychological positive functioning. Campbell and Gardner conducted a pilot study in 2005 with twelve Year 12 students taking part in a life coaching project delivered by a school counsellor. They found that coaching might be an effective tool to build resilience and well-being in young people and help students cope with the stresses of high school. However, the sample size was too small to draw any significant conclusion.

Life coaching study with students was extended by Green and colleagues (2007) by training teachers to be life coaches and using a larger sample size. The participants were 56 adolescent female students randomly assigned to the coaching group and the control group. Students in the coaching group completed a 10-session life coaching programme, and they demonstrated a statistical increase in cognitive hardness and hope compared to students in the control group. Nonetheless, the study has limitations: students were self-selected participants who were perhaps already highly motivated; academic performance measures were not taken; and the teacher-coaches in the study were trained through only two half-day workshops by a school counsellor. Thus the quality of intervention might be problematic.

The above studies mainly took a workshop or a project-based approach separated from the everyday classroom. Educational researchers and positive psychologists have been considering how to incorporate coaching and positive education into schools and 'teaching' well-being classrooms (Arthur, 2005; Cohen, 2006; Eades, 2005; Duckworth & Seligman, 2005; Seligman *et al.*, 2009) because students' day-to-day interactions and experiences with teachers, peers and coaches are integral to their well-being (Seligman *et al.*, 2009). The promotion of well-being is regarded as an important aspect of schooling (Cohen, 2006). Drawing on evidence-based studies of school-based well-being coaching projects, it is argued that positive education can promote skills and strengths that are valued by most people, produce measurable improvements in students' well-being and behaviours, and facilitate students' engagement in learning and achievement (Seligman *et al.*, 2009). What particularly relates to this book is that the elements of positive psychology, such as resilience, meaning, flow, positive relationships and positive emotions, are strongly connected with students' learning power. Learning how these endeavours have been made to embed positive education into the academic curriculum could help me to think how to incorporate coaching psychology for learning into the classroom.

A call for further research on coaching and learning

Decades ago the words 'mentor' and 'coach' rarely featured in the talk of staff and students in schools. However, the vocabulary of 'coaching' is touched upon by some researchers and increasingly used in the discourse of education (Hargreaves, 2004–2006; Claxton, 2008). The difference between conventional teaching and coaching in the way they shape learning should not be underestimated (Hargreaves, 2005).

Burley and Pomphrey (2011) argued that the discourse in the coaching frameworks for mentoring and coaching in schools 'tends to present more fixed purposes and behaviourist definitions of mentoring and coaching with an emphasis on improvement of individual or institutional practice' (p. 40). I agree with this argument because these coaching endeavours emphasise performance enhancement and public competency that seem to satisfy education policy makers and stakeholders, but they tend to place less emphasis on critical, collaborative reflection on experience and co-construction of new knowledge. Moreover, none of these programmes explicitly demonstrate how students are influenced in their own learning by the coaching their teachers have received. In other words, there is still a gap between coaching and learning in educational contexts: coaches are trained and defined; teachers are coached and sent to different classrooms; teachers practice their understandings from coaching; and students sit in the classrooms and try to learn. There seems to be a lack of shared goals and principles that are continuously reviewed, contested and refined. Another point is that when school coaching programmes try to include a wider school workforce (TDA, 2009), they seem to omit probably the most important force in young people's learning and development: their parents. Although parents are not necessarily situated in the school workforce, they should definitely be engaged in the learning community.

It becomes increasingly apparent that there is a developing trend that coaching researchers try to understand coaching from a learning perspective, and educational researchers try to enhance learning by involving coaching. It seems that these two trends are moving closer to each other in order to build a bridge (see Figure 4.1). However the two ends of the bridge are currently facing some problems in becoming connected.

There are at least two issues that we need to consider. Firstly, if coaching can be an effective tool for enhancing students' learning and academic performance, how does coaching function in the process of knowledge construction, which is integral to learning? Munro (1999) suggested that in educational contexts, coaching could be discriminated from other approaches to instruction or intervention on the basis of 1) who decides the knowledge to be learned; 2) the processes used to learn; and 3) the contexts in which the knowledge is learnt. If we do not deepen our thinking about how coaching brings innovation to the knowledge construction process, then we run the risk of reducing coaching to an instrument for making

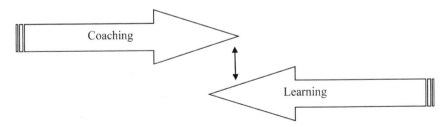

Figure 4.1 The literature gap between coaching and learning

80 An enquiry of educational paradigms

students happier while still passively receiving knowledge in a top-down peda-gogical approach. Secondly, coaching has demonstrated its power in cultivating students' well-being, motivation in learning, and strategic thinking, but there is little research on coaching as a facilitative tool to enhance students' generic learning capabilities, positive learning dispositions, attitudes, values and sense of being a lifelong learner.

To summarise these two issues, there has been a lack of research to systematically look at how coaching makes a difference to the knowledge construction process and learning dispositions development. This book aims to draw coaching and learning theoretically and empirically closer to each other.

Summary

This chapter presents a review of theories and empirical studies about coaching and coaching psychology with particular relevance to learning. It can be concluded that coaching and learning share a considerable overlap in the psychological perspective. However, studies of coaching in the context of formal education are underdeveloped. There is insufficient investigation into coaching for the knowledge construction process and learning disposition development of students. In view of this, I argue for empirical studies that explore the relationship between coaching and learning in a more systematic way and critically reflect on it. More precisely, the studies need to focus on the experiences and psychological processes of both teachers and students, the distinctive process of how coaching is incorporated in the actual learning context, and the possible influences that coaching would have on students' learning. The next part introduces two case studies drawn from my research work in order to investigate how coaching psychology is applied in enquiry-based learning and problem-based learning.

Recommended reading

Costa, A. L., & Garmston, R. J. (2002). *Cognitive coaching: A foundation of renaissance schools*. Norwood, MA: Christopher-Gordon.

Law, H., Ireland, S., & Hussain, Z. (2007). *Psychology of coaching, mentoring & learning*. Chichester: John Wiley & Sons.

Palmer, S. & Whybrow, A. (Eds). (2007). *Handbook of coaching psychology: A guide for practitioners*. Hove: Routledge.

Key points for reflection

- How do psychological theories contribute to the professional understanding and practice of coaching psychology?
- What approaches of coaching psychology that you think are particularly useful for your teaching and facilitation of student learning?

- What kind of coaching or coaching psychology programme you have participated in, and how was it?
- In your opinion, how can we fill the gap between coaching psychology and learning?

References

Allison, S., & Harbour, M. (2009). *The coaching toolkit: A practical guide in your school.* London: Sage.

Arthur, J. (2005). The re-emergence of character education in British education policy. *British Journal of Educational Studies, 53*(3), 239–254.

Auerbach, E. A. (2006). Cognitive coaching. In D. Stober & A. M. Grant (Eds), *Evidence-based coaching handbook.* New York: Wiley.

Banerjee, R. (2010). *Social and emotional aspects of learning in schools: Contributions to improving attainment, behaviour, and attendance.*

Bannink, F. P (2006). *Solution-focused questions: Handbook of solution-focused interviewing.* Amsterdam: Harcourt.

Bannink, F. P. (2007). Solution-focused brief therapy. *Journal of Contemporary Psychotherapy, 37*(2), 87–94.

Beck, A. T. (1976). *Cognitive therapy and the emotional disorders.* New York: International Universities Press.

Beck, J. S. (1995). *Cognitive therapy: Basics and beyond.* New York: Guilford Press.

Biswas-Diener, R., & Dean, B. (2007). *Positive psychology coaching: Putting the science of happiness to work for your clients.* Hoboken, NJ: Wiley.

Bloom, G. (2005). *Blended coaching: Skills and strategies to support principal development.* Thousand Oaks, CA: Corwin Press.

Bloom, G., Castagna, C., & Warren, B. (2003). More than mentors: Principal coaching. *Leadership*, Association of California School Administrators.

Boje, D. M. (1991). Consulting and change in the storytelling organization. *Journal of Organizational Change Management, 4*(3), 7–17.

Bolte, A., Goschke, T., & Kuhl, J. (2003). Emotion and intuition: Effects of positive and negative mood on implicit judgments of semantic coherence. *Psychological Science, 14,* 416–421.

Bolton, M. K. (1999). The role of coaching in student teams: A 'just-in-time' approach to learning. *Journal of Management Education, 23*(3), 233–250.

Briggs, M., & Nieuwerburgh, C. (2010). The development of peer coaching skills in primary school children in years 5 and 6. *Procedia – Social and Behavioral Sciences, 9*(239), 1415–1422.

Burley, S., & Pomphrey, C. (2011). *Mentoring and coaching in schools: Professional learning through collaborative inquiry.* London: Routledge.

Campbell, M. A., & Gardner, S. (2005). A pilot study to assess the effects of life coaching with Year 12 students. In M. Cavanagh, A. Grant, & T. Kemp (Eds), *Evidence-based coaching*, pp. 159–169. Brisbane: Australian Academic Press.

Cantwell, P., & Holmes, S. (1994). Social construction: A paradigm shift for systemic therapy and training. *The Australian and New Zealand Journal of Family Therapy, 15,* 17–26.

82 An enquiry of educational paradigms

Carr, D. (1986). Narrative and the real world: An argument for continuity. *History and Theory, 25*(2), 117–131.

Centre for the Use of Research and Evidence in Education (CUREE). (2004–2005). *Mentoring and coaching for learning: Summary report of the mentoring and coaching CPD capacity building project.* Coventry: CUREE.

Cepeda, L. M., & Davenport, D. S. (2006). Person-centered therapy and solution-focused brief therapy: An integration of present and future awareness. Psychotherapy: Theory, Research, Practice, Training, 43(1), 1–12.

Chafe, W. (1990). Some things that narratives tell us about the mind. In B. K. Britton & A. D. Pellegrini (Eds), *Narrative thought and narrative language* (pp. 79–98). Hillsdale, NJ: Lawrence Erlbaum.

Chaiklin, S. (2003). The zone of proximal development in Vygotsky's analysis of learning and instruction. In A. Kozulin, B. Gindix, V. S. Ageyev, & S. M. Miller (Eds), *Vygotsky's educational theory in cultural context* (pp. 39–63). Cambridge: Cambridge University Press.

Choong, S., & Britton, K. (2007). Character strengths and type: Exploration of covariation. *International Coaching Psychology Review, 2*(1), 9–22.

Claxton, G. (2008). *What's the point of school? Rediscovering the heart of education.* Oxford: Oneworld.

Cohen, J. (2006). Social, emotional, ethical, and academic education: Creating a climate for learning, participation in democracy, and well-being. *Harvard Educational Review, 76,* 201–237.

Costa, A. L., & Garmston, R. J. (2002). *Cognitive coaching: A foundation of renaissance schools.* Norwood, MA: Christopher-Gordon.

Creasey, J., & Paterson, F. (2005). *Leading coaching in schools.* Nottingham, NCSL.

De Shazer, S. (1985). *Keys to solution in brief therapy.* New York: Norton.

Deci, E. L., & Ryan, R. M. (2000). Self-determination theory and the facilitation of intrinsic motivation, social development, and well-being. *American Psychologist, 55,* 68–78.

Department for Education. (2010). *The importance of teaching: The schools white paper.* Retrieved from www.education.gov.uk/publications/eOrderingDownload/CM-7980.pdf

Dilts, R. (2003). *From coach to awakener.* Capitola, CA: Meta Publications.

Drake, D. B. (2003). *How stories change: A narrative analysis of liminal experiences and transitions in identity* (Unpublished doctoral dissertation). Fielding Graduate Institute, Santa Barbara.

Drake, D. B. (2004). *Creating third space: The use of narrative liminality in coaching.* In I. Stein, F. Campone, & L. J. Page (Eds), Proceedings of the second international coaching federation coaching research symposium (pp. 50–59). Quebec City, Canada.

Drake, D. B. (2005). *Narrative coaching: A psychosocial method for working with clients' stories to support transformative results.* Paper presented at the Second Australian Conference on Evidence-Based Coaching, Sydney, Australia.

Drake, D. B. (2007). The art of thinking narratively: Implications for coaching psychology and practice. *Australian Psychologist, 42*(4), 283–294.

Drake, D. B. (2008). Identity, liminality, and development through coaching: An intrapersonal view of intercultural sensitivity. In M. Moral & G. Abbott (Eds), *International business coaching handbook: Successful practices in a changing global environment.* London: Routlege.

Druckman, D., & Bjork, R. A. (Eds). (1991). *In the mind's eye: Enhancing human performance.* Hudson, F. (1999). *The handbook of coaching: A comprehensive resource guide for managers, executives, consultants, and human resource professionals.* San Francisco: Jossey-Bass.

Duckworth, A. L., & Seligman, M. E. P. (2005). Self-discipline outdoes IQ in predicting academic performance of adolescents. *Psychological Science, 16*, 939–944.

Eades, J. M. F. (2005). *Classroom tales: Using storytelling to build emotional, social and academic skills across the primary curriculum.* London: Jessica Kingsley.

Edgerton, N., & Palmer, S. (2005). Space: A psychological model for use within cognitive behavioural coaching, therapy and stress management. *The Coaching Psychologist, 2*(2), 25–31.

Ellis, A., Gordon, J., Neenan, M., & Palmer, S. (1997). *Stress counselling: A rational emotive behaviour approach.* London: Cassell.

Estrada, C. A., Isen, A. M., & Young, M. J. (1994). Positive affect improves creative problem solving and influences reported source of practice satisfaction in physicians. *Motivation and Emotion, 18*, 285–299.

Fillery-Travis, A., & Lane, D. (2006). Does coaching work or are we asking the wrong question? *International Coaching Psychology Review, 1*, 23–36.

Fillery-Travis, A., & Lane, D. (2007). Research: Does coaching work? In S. Palmer & A. Whybrow (Eds), *The handbook of coaching psychology.* Hove: Routledge.

Foster, M. (2001). *Learning our way forward.* Department of Education, Training and Employment, Government of South Australia.

Fredrickson, B. L. (1998). What good are positive emotions? *Review of General Psychiatry, 2*, 300–319.

Fredrickson, B. L., & Branigan, C. (2005). Positive emotions broaden the scope of attention and thought-action repertoires. *Cognitive & Emotion, 19*, 313–332.

Freedman, J., & Combs, G. (1996). *Narrative therapy: The social construction of preferred realities.* New York: Norton.

Gable, S., & Haidt, J. (2005). What (and why) is positive psychology? *Review of General Psychology, 9*(2), 103–110.

Gergen, K. J. (1991). *The saturated self: Dilemmas of identity in contemporary life.* New York: Basic Books.

Gibson, S., & Dembo, M. H. (1984). Teacher efficacy: A construct validation. *Journal of Educational Psychology, 76*, 569–582.

Gottesman, B., & Jennings, J. (1994). *Peer coaching for educators.* Basel: Technomic Publishing.

Graham, F., Rodger, S., & Ziviani, J. (2008). Coaching parents to enable children's participation: An approach for working with parents and their children. *Australian Occupational Therapy Journal, 56*(1), 16–23.

Grant, A. M. (2001). *Towards a psychology of coaching.* Sydney: Coaching Psychology Unit, University of Sydney.

Grant, A. M. (2004). *Workplace, executive and life coaching: An annotated bibliography from the behavioural sciences literature.* Coaching Psychology Unit, University of Sydney, Australia.

Grant, A. M. (2006). An integrative goal-focused approach to executive coaching. In D. Stober & A. M. Grant (Eds), *Evidence-based coaching handbook.* New York: Wiley.

Grant, A. M., & O'Connor, S. A. (2010). The differential effects of solution-focused and problem-focused coaching questions: A pilot study with implications for practice. *Industrial and Commercial Training, 42*(2), 102–111.

84 An enquiry of educational paradigms

Grant, A. M., & Palmer, S. (2002, May). Coaching Psychology. Symposium conducted at the Annual Conference of the Division of Counselling Psychology, British Psychological Society, Torquay.

Green, L. S., Grant, A. M., & Rynsaardt, J. (2007). Evidence-based coaching for senior high school students. *International Coaching Psychology Review, 2*(1), 24–32.

Green, L. S., Oades, L. G., & Grant, A. M. (2006). Cognitive-behavioural, solution-focused life coaching: Enhancing goal striving, well-being, and hope. *The Journal of Positive Psychology, 1*(3), 142–149.

Greene, J. & Grant, A. M. (2003). *Solution-focused coaching.* Harlow: Pearson Education.

Hamman, D., Berthelot, J., Saia, J., & Crowley, E. (2000). Teachers' coaching of learning and its relation to students' strategic learning. *Journal of Educational Psychology, 92*, 342–348.

Hargreaves, D. (2004–2006). *Personalising learning pamphlet* (Series). London: Specialist Schools Trust.

Hargrove, R. A. (1995). *Masterful coaching: Extraordinary results by transforming people and the way they think and work together.* San Diego: Pfeiffer & Company.

Hargrove, R. A. (2008). *Masterful coaching* (3rd Ed.). San Francisco: John Wiley & Sons.

Hart, V., Blattner, J., & Leipsic, A. (2001). Coaching versus therapy: A perspective. *Consulting Psychology Journal: Practice and Research, 53*(4), 229–237.

Hasbrouck, J., & Denton, C. A. (2007). The reading coach's corner: Student-focused coaching: A model for reading coaches. *The Reading Teacher, 60*(7), 690–693.

Hidi, S., & Renninger, K. A. (2006). The four-phase model of interest development. *Educational Psychologist, 41*, 111–127.

Hudson, F. (1999). *The handbook of coaching: A comprehensive resource guide for managers, executives, consultants, and human resource professionals.* San Francisco: Jossey-Bass.

Isen, A. M., Daubman, K. A., & Nowicki, G. P. (1987). Positive affect facilitates creative problem solving. *Journal of Personality and Social Psychology, 52*, 1122–1131.

Isen, A. M., Rosenzweig, A. S., & Young, M. J. (1991). The influence of positive affect on clinical problem solving. *Medical Decision Making, 11*, 221–227.

Ives, Y. (2008). What is coaching? An exploration of conflicting paradigms. *International Journal of Evidence-Based Coaching and Mentoring, 6*(2), 100–113.

Jackson, P., & McKergow, M. (2002). *The solution focus: What works at work.* London: Nicholas Brealey.

James, W. (1892). *The stream of consciousness.* Cleveland & New York: World.

Jane, B., & Peeler, E. (2006, November). *Mentoring: Boosting self-worth, optimising potential.* Paper presented at Conference of the Australian Association for Research in Education, Melbourne.

Joseph, S. (2003). Client-centred psychotherapy: Why the client knows best. *The Psychologist, 16*, 304–307.

Joseph, S. (2006). Person-centred coaching psychology: A meta-theoretical perspective. *International Coaching Psychology Review, 1*(1), 47–54.

Joseph, S., & Worsley, R. (Eds). (2005). *Person-centred psychopathology: A positive psychology of mental health.* Ross on Wye: PCCS Books.

Joyce, B., & Showers, B. (2002). *Designing training and peer coaching: Our need for learning.* Alexandria, VA: Association for Supervision and Curriculum Development.

Kampa-Kokesch, S., & Anderson, M. (2001). Executive coaching: A comprehensive review of the literature. *Consulting Psychology Journal: Practice and Research, 53*(4).

Kauffman, C., & Linley, P. A. (2007). A pragmatic perspective: Putting positive coaching psychology into action. *International Coaching Psychology Review, 2*, 97–102.

Kelly, S. (2007). *The CPD coordinator's toolkit.* London: Paul Chapman Publishing.

Keupp, H. (1999). *Identitatskonstruktinen: das patchwork der identitaten in der spatmoderne.* Reinbek: Rowohlt.

Klockner, K. D., & Hicks, R. E. (2008). My next client: Understanding the big five and positive personality dispositions of those seeking psychological support interventions. *International Coaching Psychology Review, 3*(2), 148–163.

Knight, J. (2008). *Coaching: Approaches and perspectives.* Thousand Oaks, CA: Corwin Press.

Kuhl, J. (1983). Emotion, cognition, and motivation: II. The functional significance of emotions in perception, memory, problem-solving, and overt action, *Sprache & Kognition, 2*, 228–253.

Kuhl, J. (2000). A functional-design approach to motivation and self-regulation: the dynamics of personality systems interactions. In M. Boekaerts, P. R. Pintrich, & M. Zeidner (Eds), *Handbook of self-regulation* (pp. 111–169). San Diego, Academic Press.

Law, H. (2003). Applying psychology in executive coaching programmes for organisations. *The Occupational Psychologist, 49*, 12–19.

Law, H., Ireland, S., & Hussain, Z. (2007). *Psychology of coaching, mentoring & learning.* Chichester: John Wiley & Sons.

Levitt, H. M. (2002). The unsaid in the psychotherapy narrative: Voicing the unvoiced. *Counselling Psychology Quarterly, 15*(4), 333–350.

Linley, P. A., Garcea, N., Hill, J., Minhas, G., Trenier, E., & Willars, J. (2010). Strengthspotting in coaching: Conceptualisation and development of the strengthspotting scale. *International Coaching Psychology Review, 5*(2), 165–176.

Linley, P. A., & Harrington, S. (2006). Strengths coaching: A potential-guided approach to coaching psychology. *International Coaching Psychology Review, 1*(1), 37–45.

Lipstein, R., & Renninger, K. A. (2006). 'Putting things into words': The development of 12–15-year-old students' interest for writing. In S. Hidi & P. Boscolo (Eds), *Motivation to write* (pp. 113–140). Dordrecht, The Netherlands: Kluwer.

Liston-Smith, J. (2008). Appreciative inquiry and solution-focused coaching: Applications of positive psychology in the practice of coaching. *The Coaching Psychologist, 4*(2), 102–105.

Lu, H. (2010). Research on peer coaching in preservice teacher education – A review of literature. *Teaching and Teacher Education, 26*, 748–753.

Maslow, A. H. (1954). *Motivation and personality.* New York: Harper.

Mattingly, C. F. (1998). *Healing dramas and clinic plots: The narrative structure of experience.* Cambridge: Cambridge University Press.

McDermott, I., & Jago, W. (2005). *The coaching bible: The essential handbook.* London: Piatkus Books.

Mercer, N., & Fisher, E. (1993). How do teachers help children to learn? An analysis of teachers' interventions in computer-based activities. *Learning and Instruction, 2*, 339–355.

Munro, J. (1999, November). *Coaching: An educational psychology perspective.* Paper presented at the Combined Colleges Professional Development Day activity on coaching. University of Melbourne.

Neenan, M., & Palmer, S. (2001). Rational emotive behaviour coaching. *Rational Emotive Behaviour Therapist, 9*(1), 34–41.

Oestrich, I. H., & Johansen, F. (2005). *Cognitive coaching*. Stockholm: Liber.

Palmer, S. & Whybrow, A. (Eds). (2007). *Handbook of coaching psychology: A guide for practitioners*. Hove: Routledge.

Palmer, S., & Whybrow, A. (2006). The coaching psychology movement and its development within the British Psychological Society. *International Coaching Psychology Review, 1*(1), 5–11.

Parsloe, E., & Wray, M. (2000). *Coaching and mentoring*. London: Kogan Page.

Passmore, J., & Brown, A. (2009). Coaching non-adult students for enhanced examination performance: A longitudinal study. *Coaching: An International Journal of Theory, Research and Practice, 2*(1), 54–64.

Passmore, J., & Marianetti, O. (2007). The role of mindfulness in coaching. *The Coaching Psychologist, 3*(3), 131–137.

Pearce, W. B. (2007). *Making social worlds: A communication perspective*. Malden, MA: Blackwell Publishers.

Polkinghorne, D. E. (2001). Self and humanistic psychology. In K. J. Schneider, J. F. T. Bugental, & J. F. Pierson (Eds), *The handbook of humanistic psychology: Leading edges in theory, research, and practice*. Thousand Oaks, CA: Sage.

Renninger, K. A., & Hidi, S. (2002). Student interest and achievement: Developmental issues raised by a case study. In A. Wigfield & J. S. Eccles (Eds), *Development of achievement motivation* (pp. 173–195). San Diego, CA: Academic Press.

Rhodes, C., & Beneicke, S. (2002). Coaching, mentoring and peer-networking: Challenges for the management of teacher professional development in schools. *Journal of In-Service Education, 28*(2), 297–310.

Richard, J. T. (1999). Multimodal therapy: A useful model for the executive coach. *Consulting Psychology Journal, 51*(1), 24–30.

Rogers, C. (1956). Client-centred theory. *Journal of Counseling Psychology, 3*(2), 115–120.

Rogers, C. (1963). Psychotherapy today. Or, where do we go from here? *American Journal of Psychotherapy, 17*(1), 5–16.

Ross, J. A. (1992). Teacher efficacy and the effects of coaching on student achievement. *Canadian Journal of Education, 17*(1), 51–65.

Rossi, E. L. (Ed.). (1980). *The nature of hypnosis and suggestion by Milton Erickson* (collected papers). New York: Irvington.

Rossiter, M. (1999). Understanding adult development as narrative. *New Directions for Adult and Continuing Education, 84*, 77–85.

Rowe, G., Hirsh, J. B., Anderson, A. K., & Smith, E. E. (2007). Positive affect increases the breadth of attentional selection, *PNAS Proceedings of the National Academy of Sciences of the United States of America, 104*, 383–388.

Seligman, E. P. (1999). The president's address. *American Psychologist, 54*, 559–562.

Seligman, E. P. (2002). *Authentic happiness: Using the new positive psychology to realize your potential for lasting fulfilment*. New York: Free Press.

Seligman, E. P., & Csikszentmihalyi, M. (2000). Positive psychology: An introduction. *American Psychologist, 55*(1), 5–14.

Seligman, E. P., Ernst, R. M., Gillham, J., Reivich, K., & Linkins, M. (2009). Positive education: Positive psychology and classroom interventions. *Oxford Review of Education, 35*(3), 293–311.

Sheldon, K. M., & King, L. K. (2001). Why positive psychology is necessary. *American Psychologist, 56*, 216–217.

Short, E., Kinman, G., & Baker, S. (2010). Evaluating the impact of a peer coaching intervention on well-being amongst psychology undergraduate students. *International Coaching Psychology Review, 5*(1), 27–35.

Showers, B., & Joyce, B. (1996). The evolution of peer coaching. *Educational Leadership, 53*(6), 12–15.

Simon, J. K., & Berg, I. K. (2002). Solution-focused brief therapy with adolescents. In F. W. Kaslow (Ed.), *Comprehensive handbook of psychotherapy: Interpersonal/ humanistic/ existential* (Vol. 3) (pp. 133–152). New York: John Wiley & Sons.

Stalinski, S. (2003). Developing stronger practitioner certification in coaching-related professions. *International Journal of Evidence-Based Coaching & Mentoring, 1*(1).

Stelter, R. (2009). Coaching as a reflective space in a society of growing diversity – towards a narrative, postmodern paradigm. *International Coaching Psychology Review, 4*(2), 209–219.

Stelter, R., & Law, H. (2010). Coaching – narrative – collaborative practice. *International Coaching Psychology Review, 5*(2), 152–164.

Stevens, R. (2000). Phenomenological approaches to the study of conscious awareness. In M. Velmans (Ed.), *Investigating phenomenal consciousness* (pp. 99–120). Amsterdam/ Philadelphia: John Benjamins.

Stober, D., & Grant, A. M. (2006). Toward a contextual approach to coaching models. In D. Stober & A. M. Grant (Eds), *Evidence-Based Coaching Handbook.* New York: Wiley.

Stojnov, D., & Pavlovic, J. (2010). An invitation to personal construct coaching: From personal construct therapy to personal construct coaching. *International Coaching Psychology Review, 5*(2), 129–139.

Szabo, P., & Meier, D. (2009). *Coaching plain & simple: Solution-focused brief coaching essentials.* New York: Norton.

Tolhurst, J. (2010). *The essential guide to coaching and mentoring* (2nd Ed.). Harlow: Pearson Education.

Training and Development Agency for Schools (TDA). (2008). *Professional standards for qualified teacher status and requirements for initial teacher training.* London: TDA.

Training and Development Agency for Schools (TDA). (2009). *Guidance to accompany the professional standards for qualified teacher status and requirements for initial teacher training.* London: TDA.

Trepper, S. T., Dolan, Y., McCollum E. E., & Nelson, T. (2006). Steve de Shazer and the future of solution-focused therapy. *Journal of Marital and Family Therapy, 32*(2), 133–139.

Van Kessel, L. (2003). *Coaching, a field for professional supervisors?* Retrieved from www.iasag.ch/blog/artikel.van.kessel.supervision.pdf

Visser, C. F., & Butter, R. (2008). *De effectiviteit van oplossingsgericht werken en client-geleide bij coaching en advisering: lessen uit de psychotherapie.* Gedrag & Organisatie.

Walker, S. (2004). The evolution of coaching; patterns, icons & freedom. *International Journal of Evidence Based Coaching & Mentoring, 2*(2), 16–28.

Wells, G. (1999). *Dialogic inquiries in education: Building on the legacy of Vygotsky.* Cambridge University Press.

Wertsch, J. (1985). *Vygotsky and the social formation of mind.* Cambridge, MA: Harvard University Press.

Wertsch, J. (1998). *Mind as action.* New York: Oxford University Press.

Wesson, K., & Boniwell, I. (2007). Flow theory – its application to coaching psychology. *International Coaching Psychology Review, 2*(1), 33–42.

Whitmore, J. (1996). *Coaching for performance*. London: Nicholas Brealey Publishing.

Williams, D. I., & Irving, J. A. (2001). Coaching: An unregulated, unstructured and (potentially) unethical process. *The Occupational Psychologist, 42*, 3–7.

Wise, D., & Jacobo, A. (2010). Towards a framework for leadership coaching. *School Leadership and Management, 30*(2), 159–169.

Zanting, A., & Verloop, N. (2001). Student teachers' beliefs about mentoring and learning to teach during teaching practice. *British Journal Educational Psychology, 71*, 57–80.

Part 2

Empirical case studies of coaching psychology for learning

This part details two empirical studies that are dependent on their local contexts. Together they form an interesting basis for more reflections and investigations. You will read about:

- A participatory study of how coaching psychology could support secondary students in enquiry-based learning in the UK.
- A systems model of coaching psychology for enquiry-based learning.
- A participatory study of how coaching psychology could be combined with problem-based learning to support medical students in China.
- An integrative model of coaching psychology for problem-based learning.
- How to use a mixed methodology of quantitative surveys, semi-structured interviews, narrative interviews and classroom observations in empirical research into coaching psychology in education.

Chapter 5

Coaching psychology for enquiry-based learning (EBL) in secondary education

Introduction

In this chapter, I outline an empirical, participatory enquiry of coaching psychology in enquiry-based learning (EBL) in the context of secondary education. The research project was conducted with a secondary school in South England, lasting from 2010 to 2012. First, I briefly describe the overall research design and the main methodological approaches and procedures. Then I present three types of emerging evidence: the thematic, the narrative and the observational facets of coaching psychology for EBL. These types of evidence cover students' and teachers' experiences and perceptions of coaching and learning, the practical issues in implementing coaching, their learning stories, and the interactions between students and teachers as learning coaches. This chapter not only demonstrates the applicability of coaching psychology to facilitate secondary students' independent learning in EBL, I also hope it could serve as a good example of how to conduct empirical research in the field of coaching psychology and education.

Research design and methodology

I designed the research as an exploratory sequential case study using participatory research methodology. The case study design was expected to capture the complexity and particularity within important circumstances (Stake, 1995), to deal with a variety of evidence using different data collection techniques (Yin, 2003), and to advocate systems thinking and complexity theory in education. It was *exploratory* because there are so many questions associated with coaching psychology for learning that have not been asked before, let alone answered. It was *sequential* because the project entailed three reflective enquiry processes through dynamic prototypes (Bryk *et al.*, 2011), which allowed fast-cycle feedback learning and adaptation for natural development and progressive refinements. It was *participatory* because each process needed people's active, dialectic participation. The students and teachers were involved as co-researchers in the project and co-generators of the research outcomes rather than passive subjects.

92   Empirical case studies

Context and participants

The school (I refer to it as 'N School' in this book) is a mainstream urban state secondary school for students in Year 7 through Year 11 in the New Forest region in the south of England. The sampling strategy was purposeful sampling (Yin, 1993). The school was selected because of its specificity and boundedness: it could be as representative as possible, but also it naturally demonstrated itself as the ideal case. The school participated in a national educational research project, Learning Futures project (2009-2012), and it has gained a significant increase in students' learning power and engagement through developing learning relationships and peer mentoring (Deakin-Crick *et al.*, 2010). The school was trying to redesign their curriculum into a more enquiry-driven, student-centred learning programme and incorporate coaching psychology techniques and strategies in the curriculum. I was fortunate to get access to the school by obtaining the consent of the gatekeeper, the associate head of the school and the co-ordinator of the Learning Futures project. Hence it became my main site of investigation.

There were subsequent choices to make about persons, places, and events, which were embedded cases or mini-cases (Stake, 2005). Year 7 in the school was selected because it is the transitional year from primary school to secondary school. Students in Year 7 would face enormous change in their learning environment, school curriculum, peer groups, teacher-student relationships and their self-development as learners. In addition, early intervention in secondary school might generate a greater impact on students' learning. My research primarily focused on one particular class (coded as '7C1') that attempted to integrate EBL, coaching psychology and parental involvement. The students in this class were coached by two teachers at the same time across the whole length of the project; they would have much more coaching opportunities than other students; and their parents would have the chance to engage in coaching training. Meanwhile, other classes were invited to participate in the course of observation and quantitative investigation for the purpose of comparing 7C1 (with coaching psychology) and other classes (without coaching psychology).

Two history teachers in 7C1 contributed to interviews, classroom observations and the collection of teaching plans in each prototype. These two teachers were the main designers of the Navig8 humanities curriculum, an enquiry-based, collaboratively developed and localised curriculum in the school. They were both specifically trained as coaches by accredited coaching psychologists and external coaching practitioners. They worked intensely to incorporate coaching techniques into their lessons, established what questions to ask and considered how to better support students. From the 30 students who were involved in 7C1, the same six students joined focus groups in each prototype. The recruitment was primarily voluntary, but the teacher's recommendation was also considered. The students were chosen from different enquiry groups in order to have as diverse a coverage in the class as possible. From the six students, three were further chosen for narrative interviews. These three students represented the students of high, medium and low learning power at the beginning of the project, so that their accounts of learning stories would be interesting for me to gain insights in how students with different levels of learning power perceived coaching psychology in their learning and how they viewed themselves as learners.

An overview of the coaching psychology for EBL intervention

There were three prototypes built into the project (the prototypes were sometimes referred to 'phases' by the participants). Initially the themes of interventions were co-designed by the N School and the Learning Futures project team. The steps were repeated for each prototype and data was collected on evidence of change. The steps of interventions for teachers and students are presented in Figure 5.1.

PLAN: Each prototype began with a staff training day when teachers were professionally coached by accredited coaching experts and practitioners. Then the teachers co-designed the EBL curriculum and prepared relevant teaching materials.

DO: The teachers conducted a Hook Day event with students to clarify what the EBL would be, to identify the enquiry questions that the students would be interested in exploring and to divide students into different groups for the purpose of collaborative learning. This event was followed by two weeks of coaching lessons to support and scaffold students' researching and enquiries. During this period of time, students were assigned tasks and required to conduct their own research outside of the school, supported by their peers and parents.

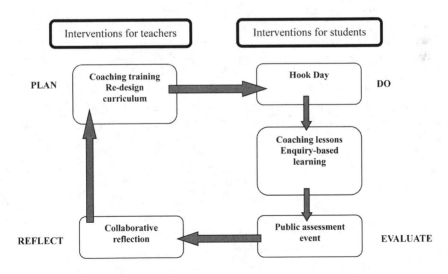

Figure 5.1 Interventions for teachers and students in prototyping

94 Empirical case studies

EVALUATE: Towards the end of each prototype, students were expected to complete their enquiries and present their enquiry outcomes to their teachers, peers, parents and wider communities in a public assessment event.

REFLECT: After the public assessment event for the students, I debriefed the teachers with my observations and findings from interviews, summarised the highlights of findings on the current prototype and made suggestions of curricular or pedagogical adjustments for the purpose of improving the next prototype. The teachers and Learning Futures project team reflected on the process collectively. Future activities were refined and redesigned based on these collective reflections.

Data collection and analysis

I employed mixed methods in data collection and analysis, blending a variety of types of data from multiple resources, and primarily driven by qualitative investigations (QUAL+quan, Hanson *et al.*, 2005). Qualitative methods included semi-structured and narrative interviews, focus groups, observation, and collecting student works and teachers' teaching/learning plans. Quantitative instruments involved 1) Effective Lifelong Learning Inventory (ELLI) surveys, which are a research-validated, self-reported measurement of students' positive learning dispositions on the seven dimensions of learning power; 2) Me and My School student engagement surveys, which are a single scale measuring three aspects of student engagement, including behaviour, cognition and emotional responses to teachers, peers and school learning; and 3) the Learning Futures Engagement surveys, which measure students' engagement with learning beyond the school.

In all three prototypes, the same cohort of teachers and students was invited to participate in semi-structured interviews and focus groups to explore their experiences and practices of coaching psychology for EBL. Unstructured direct observations were conducted in 7C1 and one non-coaching Spanish lesson. The in-depth narrative interviews, taken in an interactive-relational (I: R) approach (Chirban, 1996), were largely limited to the second prototype, given the limitation of time and opportunity. The interviews were carried out on a one-on-one basis using an arts-based projective technique (Bagnoli, 2009). Teachers' teaching plans and students' enquiry works were collected at the end of each prototype. The pre and post quantitative data was collected before and after the three prototypes.

I took an abductive approach in the data analysis, attempting to strike a balance between induction and deduction that recognises the importance of theory as well as the data in the context (Peirce, 1957; Hanson, 1965; Davis, 1972). All the qualitative data was analysed both manually on the transcripts and using QSR Nvivo 8 software for a variety of themes using coding scheme. Braun and Clarke's (2006) thematic analysis framework was adopted for analysing the interview data. Students' narrative accounts were scrutinised by narrative analysis. I created an analytical framework for processing observational data. Considering the prototyping design of the case, I originated a critical thematic analysis approach in order to accurately document any inconsistent or conflicting themes across the three prototypes and rigorously analyse them.

The qualitative evidence: the thematic findings

Five main themes and their sub-themes primarily emerged from the data collected by semi-structured interviews and focus groups (see Table 5.1). Each theme is elaborated and supported by quotations from participants. The qualitative results demonstrate how students and teachers understood coaching psychology and learning, how they experienced coaching in the classroom and what practical issues emerged for implementing coaching in different EBL approaches.

Table 5.1 List of the themes from coaching psychology for EBL research

Theme 1	**Differences between coaching and teaching**
Sub-theme 1a	Non-direct guiding
Sub-theme 1b	Offering freedom of choice
Sub-theme 1c	Extending learning relationships
Theme 2	**Coaching relationships**
Sub-theme 2a	Teachers' mixed roles: Knowledge expert, Learning coach, Mentor, Counsellor
Sub-theme 2b	Adaptation among the roles
Sub-theme 2c	Students' responses to coaching relationships
Theme 3	**The role of coaching in students' learning**
Sub-theme 3a	Optimising learning experiences
Sub-theme 3b	Structuring enquiry-based learning
Sub-theme 3c	Developing learning power
Sub-theme 3d	Fostering confidence and self-efficacy in learning
Sub-theme 3f	Enhancing learning relationships in peers
Theme 4	**Coaching as continuous professional development**
Sub-theme 4a	Exposing current educational problems
Sub-theme 4b	Personal growth as a teacher/coach
Sub-theme 4c	Collaboration with colleagues
Theme 5	**Problems of coaching and potential solutions**
Sub-theme 5a	Fixation on outcomes
Sub-theme 5b	Dilemma in meeting individual needs
Sub-theme 5c	Problem in evaluation
Sub-theme 5d	Quality of coaching relationships
Sub-theme 5e	Negative attitudes of 'researching'
Sub-theme 5f	Gap between theory and practice
Sub-theme 5g	Lack of resources and time
Sub-theme 5h	Decreased interest

I will elaborate on each theme, supported by the inclusion of evidence.

Theme 1: Differences between coaching and teaching

The main difference between teaching and coaching was demonstrated in the instruction styles. Coaching took a less directive approach compared to traditional teaching. A teacher participant stated that '*a teacher obviously would guide students; you give a lot more direction in terms of what they are doing. Whereas I found as a coach, you would be helping and trying to scaffold the conversations to enable them to find a solution independently*'. However, the teacher found '*it's very difficult to get Year 7 round that concept*' that '*rather than offering solutions, you are trying to deliver a pathway through which they could find solutions themselves*'. Sometimes being a coach meant fighting against a teacher's instinct to think about '*how you can intervene to help the kids get to the point without doing it for them*'.

The second distinctive difference between coaching for EBL and teaching in a school subject curriculum was that students were offered freedom of choice in coaching. The majority of students confidently claimed that they were offered freedom to make personal choices in terms of '*the choices of the topics, the content, time and space*'. A student indicated that '*it helps us because it is a fun topic and we can choose what we want to learn and how to learn*'. Students all agreed that the freedom of choice motivated them to learn, and that this was the most important point that made their learning experience positive. Students thought coaching '*takes pressure off you*' because in normal teaching, '*you have to get what teachers ask done*' whilst coaching '*gives you more time and space, your own time instead of teacher's time*'.

The third difference between coaching for EBL and traditional teaching was that coaching tried to extend students' learning relationships. The existing problem with learning relationships in teaching, according to one teacher, was that '*very often there are very few productive relationships within school for our kids*'. The teachers have developed the idea by differentiating learning relationships and social relationships; connecting with parents through letters, forums and coaching events; establishing websites to engage with wider communities; enabling students to contact teachers outside school hours; and encouraging students to be reflective within and outside of the classroom.

Theme 2: Coaching relationships

As one teacher stated, '*coaching for learning in the classroom is more complex than pure coaching*'. It has become obvious that coaching in this context goes beyond simply using coaching skills in teaching. This complexity led to one explanation that emerged from the interviews teachers' different roles in coaching relationships. A coach in the current learning scenario was more towards a professional 'learning facilitator', moving along a continuum of knowledge expert, mentor, coach and counsellor. Teachers have demonstrated their positions as knowledge experts in the students' enquiry process when students needed direct input of information and knowledge in particular disciplines. In the interviews both teacher participants were history teachers, therefore when students asked questions relating to history, the teachers naturally adopted roles as knowledge experts. Teachers became learning coaches when they were deliberately using coaching models, skills, tools and strategies. They took a less controlling manner in the classroom, allowing the students to experiment and make mistakes in their learning. In terms of teachers' understanding of being a coach, they claimed that '*coaching has a goal in sight, helping the students to scaffold how they actually get where they want to be, helping to facilitate their learning, whilst allowing them to steer the course*'. Effective use of questions was highlighted in the scaffolding process. In addition, being a coach means the teacher should obtain basic coaching knowledge and skills as well as the qualities of being a coach. Patience, resilience, collaboration, creativity, listening, risk-taking, open-mindedness, a non-judgemental attitude and adaptability emerged from teachers' accounts. As for the mentor's role, the teachers mentioned that '*students want you to advise: this is what I would do if I were you, if I had that particular problem*'. This was regarded as a mentor's role because it related to more direct guidance and modelling. Also, the mentor's role came in when '*you are providing them with relevant resources through which they are able to succeed and help to scaffold their learning*'. Finally, a counsellor's role was seldom taken up by teachers, but it was an indispensable element on the learning facilitator continuum. It became obvious when students needed emotional support and empathetic listening in the new enquiry experience.

Since teachers had different roles to take in coaching relationships, when and what role to take depended on the teachers' professional judgements of distinctive situations. For example, they took a more or less directive role in helping students to articulate the questions and to make the focus of the enquiry clear. The teachers distinguished different roles in coaching relationships in terms of interactions with students and they generated a metaphor of '*chameleon*' to describe the coach's roles in facilitating EBL. At the beginning it posed a big challenge for the teachers in the classroom – they felt '*exhausted*'. They endorsed '*the courage to fail*' and the development of '*coaching dispositions*', that is, the readiness, will and ability to coach. When the teachers were more familiar with the multiple roles in coaching relationships, rather than consciously focusing on different distinct roles, they felt it was '*an automatic switch between them*'. However, not every teacher enjoyed constantly changing between the roles. Some teachers expressed that they preferred '*being a kind of expert*' and liked '*problem-solving for students*'.

The students' responses to coaching relationships were interesting. In the first prototype, some students were aware that their teachers adopted a coaching approach that was different from the usual teaching method. Students pointed out that a teacher would tell you what to do quite directly and explain how to do it, whereas a coach would give indirect instruction and less explanation. Some students indicated that they were not very comfortable with being coached by their teachers and they felt '*it's a bit strange*' mainly because they had to change

98 Empirical case studies

the way they learned according to how teachers changed the way they taught. Adapting to the role-changing itself became a distraction, taking students' attention away from learning. However, when the students were used to coaching relationships, they were not troubled by the mixed roles as long as they felt supported in their learning.

Theme 3: The role of coaching in students' learning

Coaching seemed to have a positive influence on students' learning experiences and engagement. Generally, students found that coaching was a '*very enjoyable*', positively challenging experience. One student thought coaching was '*not really relevant to us*' at the beginning, then they had positive learning moments that built on positive learning experiences. Students who gave high rates to coaching for EBL said that this kind of learning was '*really good*' and '*interesting*'; they were '*lucky*' to participate in the project; and they could '*work well with group mates*' or '*get well on with the person I worked with*'. Students who gave medium rates thought coaching was '*sometimes all right, sometimes quite fun, but sometimes you can't really think of anything to do*'. This response led to questions about what the actual learning activities were and how the teacher coached students and how this would influence the quality of students' learning experiences. Students who gave low rates found the teachers had been less and less explicit about coaching throughout the three prototypes. This was mainly because teachers gave more detailed expectations and research methods, offered more freedom of choices and more non-direct guidance in the first and second prototype. Teachers noted that they had found positive changes in the students' engagement in learning. In conventional teaching, '*students come like empty vessels and you fill in their heads with information and they go onwards nearly to their assessment*', whilst in coaching lessons, students were '*really challenged and stretched*'. As coaches, they found '*some deep and mutual understanding in terms of coaching or sharing personal experiences*'. This informal, personal way was '*more open and more likely to foster a positive relationship*' between teachers and students.

The teachers agreed that '*enquiry-based learning and coaching for learning are working very well together*' in the sense that they were '*trying to raise the standards of pupils, making them more resilient and independent, and to challenge them*'. The scaffolding of the enquiry process became very important and it needed to achieve a balance between structuring and offering freedom. The teachers mentioned that too much structuring might block students' natural curiosity, because they would rely on teachers to give them enquiry topics rather than generating authentic questions by themselves. However, without breaking down the complex enquiry process and providing any structure, the teachers found students would '*go off the cliff*'. Coaching obviously supported the process of EBL in researching and knowledge construction. Regarding knowledge construction in enquiry, the teachers raised an important question: who is in control of that knowledge? They thought knowledge should be personally constructed. This was achieved by coaching students on '*making connections between the steps they've made*', '*reflecting on what they generally think and feel in a chronological manner*' and '*having more pride in their research and what they have made*'. Therefore students had the ownership of knowledge that they constructed throughout EBL with the support of coaching. Moreover, students might need a balance between coaching and being given the space to do their own research. They only found coaching helpful when they needed it. Since individual learners made their own decisions about whether they needed help, it was a challenging task for teachers to make judgements about when to coach and when not to coach.

Positive changes in students' learning dispositions were noticed: they were more resilient and persistent, more cohesive in group work and better at researching. There was an increasing sense of confidence and pride. Most students mentioned that they had '*a little tiny bit of change*' in their learning power dimensions as *resilience*, *strategic awareness*, and *learning relationships*. The students indicated that they enjoyed and improved their independence in learning – they were more capable of self-directed learning and became less reliant on their teachers. Throughout the three prototypes, there were encouraging signs that students had developed *changing and learning*: they viewed themselves as persons who always want to learn more and learn better. They were open to change and development in the process of learning, and they were less afraid of making mistakes or getting stuck. Coaching also brought benefits such as growth in confidence and self-efficacy during the learning process.

Learning relationships among peers were greatly enhanced, especially when teachers introduced peer critique as the main coaching activity in the classroom. Feedbacks from students were very positive that '*it is the most useful and interesting experience*'. A teacher echoed that '*the students can coach each other. So before, it was very much coming from the teacher, but now they ask each other for help more, so the focus is not always on the teacher being a coach, it's also focusing on pupils coaching each other*'.

Theme 4: Coaching as continuous professional development

By carrying out this innovative coaching practice in real classroom conditions, teachers claimed that they deepened their understanding of existing problems in the current educational culture. One teacher explained that coaching '*is pretty positive . . . it has exposed a massive gap in terms of our provision . . . we are so used to spoon feeding them all the way up through Year 11 – it's about empty vessels to be filled*', and now they would '*focus more and more on the journey, and less just on the final destination*'. This realisation was crucial for teachers to get involved in critical reflection on being a coach and the differences from their previous experience.

The acknowledgement that students need to take responsibility for their own learning prepared teachers for further engagement in continuous professional development with a very different perspective from conventional staff training.

The teachers also thought that their role as coaches continued to grow throughout the process with the student as they were adopting and adapting to different roles more naturally. They viewed themselves as mainly coaches rather than teachers in this project and created a concept of '*ownership of coaching*'. In addition, the teacher suggested that staff in the school could do their own learning profiles '*to know what the result is and think about how they can change or adapt*'.

The teachers actively built relationships with other schools, coaching organisations, communities, and universities for exchanging information and learning from each other. They found it was helpful to have external observers watch and evaluate their coaching practice regularly, not just sporadically. They gained practical experiences and professional learning from various resources and a better understanding of the educational and psychological theories underlining the practice. It was evident that university researchers, coaching practitioners and school teachers have been working closely and effectively to implement coaching psychology in the secondary classroom.

Theme 5: Problems of coaching and potential solutions

Coaching for EBL was not without problems. Apart from limited human resources, training and time, several issues emerged from interviews.

The first concern was that students strongly held a fixed mindset about their enquiry outcomes rather than the learning process because '*the whole education and school system focuses on the end product of learning*'. This represented a big challenge for coaching practice, that it should aim to transform the students' understanding of learning from information absorption and performance orientation to interdependent knowledge construction and a focus on process. The fixation on outcome-orientation of learning caused two major problems. First, some students would react passively to coaching and still expect teachers to pass on knowledge and solutions. Second, students would sacrifice critical curiosity and high intellectual quality in order to move quickly along the process and achieve an outcome. In order to solve the problem, the teachers focused more on the process of enquiry by deliberately prolonging it, inviting more reflections and avoiding mentioning the assessment so that students would not jump into a '*product mode*'. Instead students were encouraged to stay in an '*exploratory mode for a longer period of time*'.

The teachers recognised that implementing coaching is a long-term strategy rather than a quick solution; it aims to enhance learning dispositions that are beneficial for students' lifelong learning and growth as independent learners. However, this does not mean we should forget academic success and the pursuit of good learning outcomes. It is still necessary to ensure that learning outcomes can be shown. Hence in the third prototype teachers coached the students on the process and the outcome by talking them through the expectation of learning outcomes, project management coaching and excellence modelling in how to produce a quality product.

The second concern was how to meet individuals' needs. The students suggested that coaching should take an individual learner's needs into consideration and make coaching more personally relevant to each student. However, it was difficult to coach each individual group or person. The teachers set up a 'Coach's Corner', where each group brought their questions and received coaching for ten minutes in turn. It was effective for a while; but some groups apparently had more questions than other groups and they needed more time. So the Coach's Corner changed its rule: each group could bring their most important questions and receive coaching; if a group thought they did not need coaching at that time, they were free to continue their research.

The third concern is: how do we know whether coaching is successful or not? This was a problem that teachers directly faced in coaching. In the current education system, teachers-as-coaches were still judged by the actual outcomes of their students' learning, which is the criteria for teachers, not for coaches. A sense of safety and value was very important for the teachers as coaches. The teachers felt vulnerable when they faced the ambiguity of evaluating coaching; they were much more comfortable and certain about the criteria of assessing their teaching role if these were direct and straightforward. This difficulty of assessing coaching might make the teachers-as-coaches situate themselves more firmly in a teacher's position.

The fourth concern was that the quality of coaching relationships between students and teachers needed to be enhanced. Some students claimed they did not dare to have an open conversation with their teachers about how coaching could be improved because they were afraid of '*getting the teachers angry*'. There was a particular emphasis on the language that coaches should adopt as well as listening. Students preferred more positive and affirmative language in giving judgemental opinions and making comments as well as indirect guidance during the enquiry process.

The fifth concern was that coaching has posed challenges for teachers in terms of looking at teaching and learning in an exploratory way. Their knowledge of coaching theories in training and actual experiences might not be compatible. This challenge was intensive when practice went on in the classroom, especially when teachers gave freedom to students '*too soon, too much, too early*'. It was suggested that students should start with more tangible content and more structured scaffolding and then move towards more loosely structured coaching and being offered more freedom in personal choices.

Finally, there were limited human resources, reference resources and time in coaching for EBL. And perhaps there was an 'adaptation effect': the students felt coaching was fresh and innovative at the beginning, but there seemed to be a decreased interest in coaching throughout the three prototypes. When the sense of novelty faded away, the students began to '*feel a bit bored*' and they wanted '*normal lessons back*'. This indicates that we need to consider an appropriate level of implementing coaching in school education.

In sum, the findings of the thematic analysis provided strong evidence that coaching was different from the conventional teaching approach. Coaching

102 Empirical case studies

involved different modes of relationships, played a significant role in students' learning and teachers' continuous professional development and was sensitive to the conditions where it was undertaken. The integration and application of coaching in the secondary classroom needed to be improved. I will present the students' learning stories in the next section.

The narrative evidence: students' learning stories

Mark, Nicole and Monica (I use pseudonyms to ensure participants' confidentiality), were invited for narrative interviews at the beginning of the second prototype. They were invited again two months later, at the end of the second prototype, for follow-up narrative interviews to see how they viewed their learning then. These stories are characterised by a connection of increased confidence and learning dispositions, enhanced self-awareness of being a learner, and richer language used by students to describe their learning journeys. Here I select the learning story of one particular student, Nicole, and her drawings, to demonstrate the trustworthy, authentic accounts of how students understood learning and how they viewed themselves as learners throughout coaching for EBL.

'I am not as bossy as I used to be'

Nicole, a young lady of 12 years old, demonstrated her energetic, confident characteristics when she was in the enquiry group that I observed. When she was talking, she was leaning towards the camera, waving her hands cheerfully when she spoke, and turning her body to the person sitting beside her in order to have interaction. However, before the person could respond, she moved her body back to the normal position, or turned to another person if she suddenly changed topic or wanted to talk to someone else. This might indicate that she was positioning herself as the 'centre' of conversations or the 'controller' of topics. These behaviours fit with her description of herself as 'bossy' in her story.

I met Nicole for the first interview in February 2011. She was genuinely interested in and very excited about the narrative interviews when she saw the blank paper and coloured pens on the desk. Without any prompting from me, she began to tell her learning story by describing learning power dimensions using her own metaphors: a monkey as *critical curiosity*, architecture as *creativity*, a jigsaw as *meaning-making*, the TV programme '*Friends*' as *learning relationships* and soldiers in an army as models of *resilience*. I found her metaphor for *changing and learning* especially fascinating:

> For changing and learning, I did a caterpillar changing into a butterfly. I did that because they don't just stay one thing. It's like you picture them turning into other things, and they are still the same thing, but just in a different form.

She drew a house (she called it a 'learning house') and herself in front of the gate. '*I am not already in the house*', she said. I wondered if that meant she did not feel fully engaged in learning at this point. Before I asked, she quickly drew a curvy line, a park and, interestingly, a Tesco supermarket along the curve.

'*Why do you want to draw the road in this shape?*' I asked.

'*Because I think it shows all the twists and turns that I had in my journey,*' she replied instantly.

'*What does it feel like at the top?*' I continued.

She answered: '*It's quite difficult in a way, but it's also fun and challenging. And you want to rise to the challenge and do it as best as you can.*'

I thought she was indeed a very confident girl. '*What does it feel like at the bottom then?*' I asked.

'*At the bottom I'd feel a bit timid, being about to do it . . .*' She turned her eyes away for a few seconds and then looked at me assertively: '*But then again I want to feel I can rise to the challenge and try to make myself better to go to the top*'.

Then I asked her to imagine herself in three positions – 'Where were you?', 'Where are you?', 'Where do you expect yourself to be?' – and how she would feel in these three different positions. She answered:

> *I felt it would be too hard for me and I didn't trust myself. I would find it's too difficult and I would be a mess over it. I wouldn't be able to do anything . . . but now I've done most of it, I think I would be better if I had enough think of it . . . I think I will feel better doing it next time . . . I will be a happy learner and a quick thinker.*

I was curious about the big Tesco in her drawing. Nicole explained:

> *The Tesco indicates a stop, where we can pause and think what we are doing. And then we realise we haven't answered our question yet, so we have to find out answers to that . . . because we always research, research, just carry on researching, and then miss out what the actual question is . . . so we would like to pause and think what we should do. That's a big pause, I did a big Tesco.*

She put many parks with different sizes on the journey indicating different levels of enjoyment and fun in coaching for EBL. She wanted to draw something representing arguments in her learning relationships with peers but she could not think of anything.

'*How about talking mouths?*' I gently offered.

'*Oh yes!*' She immediately put down many mouths along the journey. Meanwhile, she said that she valued quality communication and relationships in learning. She recognised that arguments and conflicts might be caused by individual differences. However, she did not think arguments would help to move the whole group forward to complete the enquiry task. Therefore she learned how to apologise and compromise in order to end an argument with others.

She commented on her coaches using a metaphor of netball:

> *(The teachers) are learning coaches, and they really helped us a lot because if we needed something to be helped out with, then we asked them what we could do to make it better . . . they would give us a strategy . . . it's a bit like netball really. The ball represents us, and the people who are playing represent the places that we need to change.*

She thought that being coached in EBL was a positive experience and she looked forward to continuing the journey. She drew a cup of tea and smiling faces showing relaxation and contentment on completion of the project.

At the end of our first meeting, Nicole presented her learning journey picture like this:

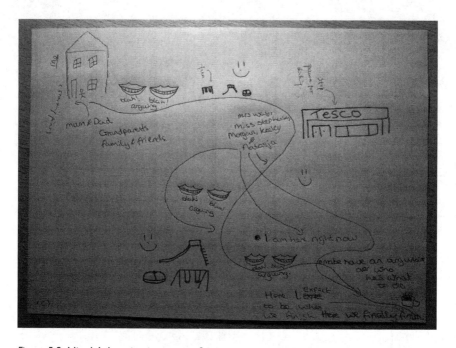

Figure 5.2 Nicole's learning journey at first narrative interview

In April, Nicole and I met again for a second meeting. She seemed to be very pleased about her learning in the last two months and she claimed that '*I have changed as a learner now*'. She said learning power dimensions developed in coaching for EBL:

I have developed creativity, and team work, definitely team work. Resilience helps because we can never give up. Definitely changing and learning. We definitely changed.

This time she made her learning journey a similar shape to the first drawing. The second drawing contained far fewer talking mouths, indicting far fewer arguments in the group. She told me how she and other girls successfully persuaded a boy who was reluctant to do any stage performance to join them for a short drama to present their enquiry outcomes. She thought learning was '*like playing a ball game, and it was fun to play with other people*' with equal status in relationships:

We have fun all the way . . . no one is the boss. I am quite bossy, but I am not the boss now. I think it's better that no one is the boss, otherwise we feel like being a remote control car with someone else's performance. The ideal relationship I think is to have someone you don't work with and work with them, and listen to other people's ideas, work with that as much as you can, and definitely think that you are not the boss.

She told me that the most challenging part of her journey was '*trying to be not so bossy*'. '*It's difficult to appreciate people's knowledge and pretty much take their ideas and not throw them away, and try to work on their ideas and yours*'. She said, '*I sort of made myself the boss the last time because no one wanted to do what I wanted to do*', whereas this time she decided to be '*just a spokesman*': '*I am not as bossy as I used to be, but I still am, and even though I hate to admit it, it is still true.*'

Since she has made a great improvement in *learning relationships*, Nicole highlighted the interdependence and self-awareness of being a learner in a team:

We can learn how good learners we are and how well we can learn with different kinds of people. I think we can learn how we work as individual learners too. We can take individual questions from each of the different people, and we can give our opinion, and we can get other people's opinions. We can learn how well we can judge other people's opinions. I can definitely take that. I can work in groups. I can be more open to more facts and more opinions. I can take in other people's ideas. So I don't just jump and beat. And I don't have to be more dependent on adults and other people. I can be more independent.

I asked how coaching supported her learning, and she replied:

Coaching helped with resilience because coaches can say 'keep going, keep going' like a basketball coach. Coaching definitely helped us to be more independent and work more as a team, and to find out more individual learning abilities.

106 Empirical case studies

For this confident girl, development of learning dispositions was a whole new experience:

> *I think (I developed) a bit about everything because we can all work on different things. We can try and be good at (developing) abilities. Definitely mine is about everything because I am better at something and I am better at others. But I am definitely better or at least good at a little bit of everything.*

She gave me the following picture at the end of our second meeting:

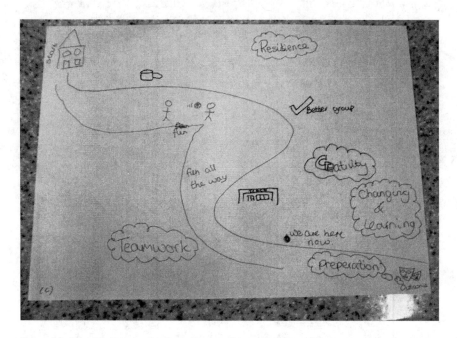

Figure 5.3 Nicole's learning journey at second narrative interview

'*I am a lady cheetah in learning*', she said with eyes shining, '*I have been really quick and quite fierce to everyone.*'

'*. . . but not too much!*' We uttered this at almost the same time, and we had a great laugh.

Due to the limited space of this book, I selected Nicole's story as a representative. Mark's and Monica's stories were fascinating too, showing clear differences between the first and the second interviews. These differences were not only shown in the content of the stories, but also in the richness of the language they used, their tones, their drawings and their interactions with me. I acknowledge their stories as an integrated reflection of their understanding of learning preferences and styles, self-awareness, beliefs and values, attitudes, dispositions and learning identities. At the beginning of the project, the students had quite a vague idea of their learning identities. Throughout the three prototypes, the majority of the students were able to present a general idea of what kind of learner they were and what makes a better learner. In the next section, I will provide observational evidence on how coaching was practically implemented in the learning process and how it looked different from conventional teaching.

The observational evidence: interactions and communication between learning coaches and students

I conducted non-participant, direct classroom observation of twelve coaching lessons in 7C1 in order to look into the practical implementation of coaching in the context of a secondary classroom. The group was separately coached by two teachers for six lessons each. The average length of each lesson was one hour. The longest coaching lesson lasted 3.5 hours. I also observed one Spanish lesson following the traditional school curriculum.

Description of classroom environment

It is important to understand the classroom environment as a social context where coaching lessons took place and how the time and place influenced the activities and interactions. All twelve coaching lessons happened in the two teachers' classrooms, where the students usually take their history lessons. In one teacher's classroom, the layout of seats was in groups, whilst in the other teacher's classroom the seats were in rows. The classrooms were both decorated with samples of students' enquiry work after the first prototype. Six new computers with internet access were installed in each classroom during the second prototype.

Use of tools and coaching materials

An interactive whiteboard, computers and laptops were used in the coaching lessons. In addition to using reference books, dictionaries, textbooks and magazines in the classroom, the students could get access to the school library to find more resources. Each enquiry group was provided with a folder in which students kept sheets about their enquiry questions, mind mapping, group reflection and learning logs.

Communication between teachers and students in coaching

I focused on interpersonal communication and relationships through the use of language, paralanguage and non-verbal communication (NVC) between the teachers and the students.

108 Empirical case studies

The teachers-as-coaches utilised rich verbal and non-verbal language to achieve different purposes in coaching communications. For instance, when they made initial statements or changed topics, they phrased the words in an indirect way rather than speaking in a direct, instructional way. They constantly and flexibly used open questions, paraphrases and summaries on the content and progress of students' enquiries, particularly about the process of interdependent researching and cognitive mind mapping. When students answered questions, the teachers often gave examples in order to prompt more answers and gave immediate feedback by paraphrasing, summarising or using cognitive reflection. The teachers constantly used praise, compliments and assurances such as '*right*' or '*great*'. They repeated students' key words and phrases as a way of showing recognition or agreement and to encourage students to elaborate on their answers. Occasionally, the teachers used humour in order to ease the atmosphere. Direct suggestions and guidance about students' enquiries were given when students asked questions relating to specific knowledge. Direct announcements and clear instructions were given when the teachers assigned tasks or homework. The teachers seemed to assimilate coaching strategies in classroom management and discipline. They used open questions to invite students to reflect on their behaviours rather than simply criticising students for their misconducts. For instance, instead of telling some noisy students to be quiet, the teachers asked '*What would you do if you wanted to hear what I'm saying?*' The students answered, '*Only one person talks at a time*' and '*be quiet*', thus the students knew what behavioural changes they should adopt in the classroom.

In terms of paralanguage, the pitch and tempo of the voice was changed when the teachers intended to change topic or emphasise what they were saying. The female teacher kept her tone of voice soft, gentle and even, with an appropriate volume throughout the conversation, whereas the male teacher used a more dramatic change of his tone in order to draw attention. Both of them used silence in order to give the students time to think and reflect.

Plenty of NVC signals were used by the teachers. When talking to students or asking questions, they maintained direct eye contact with the students. When they intended to close one topic and change to another one, they would stop eye contact briefly, change position and resume eye contact. This could be perceived as expecting the students to be aware of the change of topic. As a sign of attentive and active listening, they used nodding, holding the chin and smiling.

When the teachers were coaching, there were rich, simultaneous language exchanges between the teacher and the enquiry group, the group members who were being coached, and the group members who were not being coached. However, it was very difficult to capture the specific words used by the students due to the fact that different groups were talking at the same time. The discourse in the classroom changed over time. In the first prototype, the students talked only when the teachers asked questions and pointed to a particular student to respond, whilst the rest of the class would remain quiet and listen. This might be similar to the 'question-hand raising-answer' model in most traditional teaching.

In the second prototype, there was a significant change in students' language. They were more enthusiastic and more able to ask critical questions. There was a great deal of verbal exchange among the students themselves, but some of the talk was not about learning. In the third prototype, the focus of language shifted to more learning-oriented talking among students. Except for talking about enquiry projects, the students had less random chatting than they did in the previous two prototypes.

The students' quality of voice varied. There was occasional hesitation when answering questions, but the time interval was not very long. The tempo of the voice did not change much when students were talking to the teachers and their peers. However, students tended to change their tone when they were talking to different people. When they were talking to their peers in the group, their tone tended to be more casual. When they were talking to peers outside of their group, their tone tended to be more distant.

When being coached, the students used eye contact when talking to the teachers. Sometimes there was no eye contact because of thinking, nervousness or attentive listening. Nodding was constantly used as an agreement with or response to the teachers' suggestions. Some students touched their mouth or face when they were answering questions, probably because they were unsure of what they were talking about or because they were expecting other group members' confirmation. Some of the students who were not being coached sat in a close circle with each other and seemed to be absorbed in group work, whereas some students moved position around the classroom and were apparently disengaged from their enquiries.

Student engagement in coaching lessons

The student engagement in 7C1 underwent a gradual and cumulative change. Given the opportunity to take responsibility for planning, monitoring and reflecting on their work through coaching conversations, students were more able to make their own choice of enquiry topics, plan and evaluation. The number of times when students needed direction by their teachers significantly reduced, as did the amount of inactive or off-task behaviours. There was a progressive, positive shift in the learning behaviour of the students. The students became more prepared to be creative in producing ideas. They became increasingly engaged in finding the answers they wanted for themselves and asked the teachers far fewer random questions than usual.

There was also a dramatic increase in cooperation and collaboration among the students within and outside their enquiry groups. Real collaboration took place and students were increasingly articulate about what collaboration involved. They were aware of the different roles that their peers could take in groups. They could actively reflect on their groups' effectiveness with increasing insight. They stayed more focused on the task, became better at resolving conflicts and disagreements, and were more able to invite praise and criticism and request learning resources from peers.

110 Empirical case studies

Although the students were able to take more risks during coaching for EBL, they were still concerned about their learning outcomes and assessment, so they appeared to need monitoring and assurance from teachers as usual. In the third prototype, the students did not ask for much assurance because they felt they were 'on track' given the tightened structure of scaffolding. In general, my observations showed that the 7C1 students gained a greater sense of ownership, responsibility and confidence about their voice in EBL and in their growth as learners. This was an effective way of increasing their engagement in learning.

Comparison of coaching and non-coaching lessons

Compared with my observations in coaching lessons, the non-coaching lesson led by a Spanish language teacher showed a typical top-down, content-oriented pedagogical approach evidenced by the content and teacher–student communication.

The learning tasks in the non-coaching lesson were entirely designed and structured by the teacher. The students were responding to the linear pre-set steps of learning passively, whereas the students in the coaching lessons were responding to the scaffolding of enquiry more actively. The language adopted by the teachers in the coaching lessons was significantly richer than the language used in the non-coaching lesson. In the non-coaching lesson, there were no open questions or any stimulating remarks to encourage students to enquire or explore. The students were quieter and more obedient, and showed concentration on learning activities on the surface. However, if we regard engagement as 'what gets you interested enough to be willing to put in the effort to get better' (Claxton *et al.*, 2011), there was no evidence of deep engagement in learning even when the students demonstrated on-task behaviours. There were significantly fewer discussions and interactions among peers as well as between students and the teacher in the non-coaching lesson.

To conclude, the observational evidence demonstrated that there was an obvious change in students' learning behaviours and engagement in 7C1, highlighting the communication and interactions between the teachers and the students. In addition, the coaching classroom looked different from a teaching classroom. In the next section, I will present the main quantitative findings from the survey questionnaires before and after the interventions.

The quantitative evidence: development of learning power and engagement

The quantitative findings from the analysis indicated that there were changes in students' learning power and engagement. The paired t-tests revealed that there were increases in four learning power dimensions: *critical curiosity, meaning-making, creativity* and *learning relationships*. The Learning Futures engagement scores increased too. Only *meaning-making* showed a significant increase, and this change might be the result of natural cognitive development throughout three EBL projects. Three learning power dimensions, *changing and learning, strategic awareness, resilience*, and Me and My School engagement scores showed decreases, but none of the decreases were significant. It seems that qualitative analysis offered stronger evidence of coaching's potential influence on students' learning.

Summary

This chapter described an empirical study of coaching psychology for EBL in a secondary education setting. The data analysis and collection was a complex nonlinear process, and the students' enquiry approaches evolved as organic processes that occurred naturally. The teachers attached considerable importance to creating coaching conversations with their students in their learning; their role as facilitators was crucial in all phases of the enquiries; their understanding of coaching and learning deepened during the process of experimenting and applying coaching theories to the classroom; and their general experience of coaching was positive and inspiring. Students' focus groups and learning stories demonstrated that there was a strong increase in confidence and self-efficacy, various learning dispositions and learning agency. Direct classroom observations provided clear evidence that coaching emphasised communication and relationships between teachers and students, and coaching lessons were different from traditional subject lessons in various aspects. Nevertheless, there were few significant changes in learning power and engagement evidenced quantitatively. These contradictions are significant to stimulate deeper and more critical thinking that inform a further investigation into the phenomenon. In the next chapter, I offer possible explanations in more detail and present a systems model of Coaching for Learning.

Recommended reading

Denzin, N. K. & Lincoln, Y. S. (Eds). (2005). *The sage handbook of qualitative research* (3rd Ed.) London: Sage.
Yin, R. K. (2003). *Case study research: Design and methods* (3rd Ed.). London: Sage.

Key points for reflection

- How will you design an intervention of coaching for learning in your classroom if you are a secondary school teacher?
- What research methodology you will adopt in order to study coaching for learning?
- What are the key lessons and observations of this study?
- Are there any limitations of this study? What will you do in the future if you are the researcher?

References

Bagnoli, A. (2009). Beyond the standard interview: The use of graphic elicitation and arts-based methods. *Qualitative Research, 9*(5), 547–570.

Braun, V., & Clark, V. (2006). Using thematic analysis in psychology. *Qualitative Research in Psychology, 3*, 77–101.

Bryk, A. S., Gomez, L. M., & Grunow, A. (2011). Getting ideas into action: Building networked improvement communities in education. *Frontiers in Sociology of Social Research, 1*, 127–162.

Chirban, J. T. (1996). *Interview in depth: The interactive-relational approach.* Thousand Oaks: Sage.

Claxton, G., Chambers, M., Powell, G., & Lucas, B. (2011). *The learning powered school: Pioneering 21st century education.* Bristol: TLO Limited.

Davis, W. H. (1972). *Peirce's epistemology.* Martinus Hijhoff: The Hague.

Deakin-Crick, R., Jelfs, H., Ren, K., & Symonds, J. (2010). *Learning futures.* London: Paul Hamlyn Foundation.

Hanson, N. R. (1965). Notes towards a logic of discovery. In R. J. Bernstein (Ed.), *Perspectives on Peirce* (pp. 42–65). New Haven and London: Yale University Press.

Hanson, W. E., Creswell, J. W., Clark, V. L. P., Petska, K. S., & Creswell, J. D. (2005). Mixed methods research designs in counseling psychology. *Journal of Counseling Psychology, 52*, 224–235.

Peirce, C. S. (1957). *Essays in the philosophy of science.* New York: The Liberal Arts Press.

Stake, R. E. (1995). *The art of case study research.* London: Sage.

Stake, R. E. (2005). Qualitative case studies. In N. K. Denzin & Y. S. Lincoln (Eds), *The SAGE handbook of qualitative research* (3rd Ed.) London: Sage.

Yin, R. K. (2003). *Case study research: Design and methods* (3rd Ed.). London: Sage.

Chapter 6

Towards a systems model of Coaching for Learning

Introduction

The previous chapter demonstrates a participatory, exploratory study from which we can tentatively conclude that coaching could facilitate students' enquiry-based learning and enhance their positive learning dispositions in formal secondary education. However, what kind of process this learning exactly involves and how coaching supports this process needs to be further theorised. The analytical synthesis of the findings from the empirical data combined with related theories indicated that the relationship between coaching and learning could be termed 'Coaching for Learning' (Wang, 2013), a participatory complex system that includes a range of interconnected factors regarding the learner and the relationship with the coach. In this chapter, I present a systems model of Coaching for Learning in order to clarify the relationship between coaching and learning in secondary education.

The definition of 'Coaching for Learning'

I propose the following definition of Coaching for Learning (CfL) in order to theorise the relationship between coaching and learning. Coaching for Learning is a participatory system indicating an evolving learning relationship between learning coaches (e.g., teachers, parents or peers) and learners through various modes of coaching relationships. The system involves four key processes in order to enhance the learner's ownership and autonomy, develop positive learning dispositions, scaffold knowledge construction and improve competence and performance. It interrogates context, purpose, processes and performance that lead to intentional learning, change and growth between coaches and learners.

The nature of CfL is multifaceted: it is an intention embedded in a certain worldview, a complex dynamic process, a shared quality relationship and a culture of learning. In theory, CfL is a perspective, a set of principles and beliefs about: 1) how human systems function as a complex, interconnected system nested in our society, a departure from the past metaphor of human systems as machines; 2) how learning happens, bridging personal and public knowledge domains; and

3) how human interaction in a bottom-up pedagogical perspective facilitates learning instead of a completely top-down transmission mode. In practice, CfL can be used as an innovative method to transform students' learning, since coaching has an attendant set of core processes, practices and models that have emerged. In this sense, CfL pragmatically seeks knowledgeable actions and collectively experiments through collaborative dialogues and choices.

The systems model of Coaching for Learning

As can be seen from the empirical findings, coaching has much to offer in the learning process. The question is: how can we organise this information in a way that makes this useful in learning practice? Making explicit the links between coaching and learning and then connecting these links to classroom practice is not easy. One way of integrating this diverse body of knowledge is to develop a visual presentation or model of the various factors related to coaching and learning. Such a model is presented in Figure 6.1. This model may be useful for incorporating coaching and coaching psychology into learning processes in the classroom. It attempts to capture the main processes involved in the facilitative approach to enhance learning and highlights some of the factors that a coach may consider during the CfL engagement.

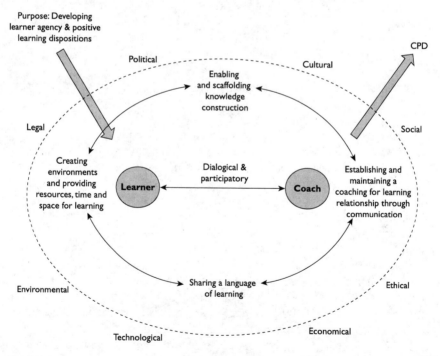

Figure 6.1 The systems model of Coaching for Learning

From a systems approach and participatory perspective, the model of CfL includes a range of interrelated factors internal and external to the learner and to the coach, which shape their interactions and co-learning in place and in time. It demonstrates the core characteristics of a living system with its distinctive participative nature. The system comprises elements regarding contexts, purposes, people, processes and a feedback loop, generated by crystallising and prototyping, for its sustainability.

The context of Coaching for Learning

The context of CfL is presented in Figure 6.2. From the systems model we can see that it is embedded in a wider system. Although the core system may exist within the classroom, with its primary focus on knowledge construction, CfL needs to be extended beyond coaching a student with a sole focus on the arena of the classroom in order to be more effective, generative and lasting. Moreover, the classroom is not a closed system but an open system; in open systems there is a continuing relationship between it and its environment (Carroll, 1996). Teachers and students function within a greater system in which the classroom is only one area; being a teacher or a student is only one role that an individual takes in order to participate in the dynamic system.

The context of CfL therefore occurs in the intersection of the coach's context, the learner's context and the learning context. Individuals in the context co-create

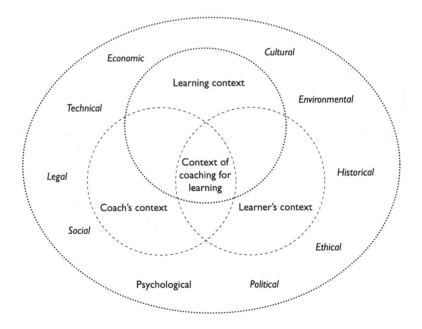

Figure 6.2 The context of Coaching for Learning

116 Empirical case studies

their world with all its meanings, purposes and relationships. This co-creation is dependent on understanding and sharing context (Carroll, 1996). Though the teacher (as a coach) and the student are still the two main roles in the classroom context which construct a learning relationship, the involvement of the wider contexts of these two people is of critical importance in order to extend the learning relationship *inside* a classroom to an *outside* wider learning community (Lave & Wenger, 1991). CfL can never be done merely by one teacher with one student in one classroom; it needs extended collaboration and partnerships in communities, including schools, families and organisations. Each coaching partnership is unique, making its own operating rules, discoveries and journey of progress (McDermott & Jago, 2005).

However, there should be a sense of 'boundary' of CfL. The word 'boundary' is not taken to mean 'limitation' or creating a distance between the system and the 'outside world'. It is a way of understanding boundary that focuses on *how people relate to each other in the system*. This particular system is separated from a number of external entities (such as the coach's personal agenda), and it is enclosed within internal components exclusively focusing on the interactions between the learner and the coach. Thus the boundary is the creation of authentic and professional relationships in which the coach supports the growth, learning and development of the learner. Nevertheless, the boundary is imaginary: what happens 'outside' the system still affects its interrelated elements. The boundary is mainly defined by the purpose, which will be discussed in the next section.

Why: the purpose of Coaching for Learning

The purpose of CfL resonates with the 'learning as a journey' metaphor in Chapter 3. It covers four 'stations': 1) to empower learners' agency and autonomy, enhance their sense of identity and self-awareness, and clarify a sense of ownership and responsibility for their own learning; 2) to develop positive learning dispositions, beliefs and attitudes that are transferable from classroom to different contexts in real world learning and living; 3) to advance knowledge and skills as well as to cultivate knowledge construction and intellectual capabilities; and 4) to enhance authentic performance, competence and achievement.

The main focus of the purposes should be at the fundamental, more personal end of the journey, which should be the learner's agency, identity and positive learning dispositions. Additionally, the purpose of the system should go beyond the idea of 'coaching for the learning journey' because coaching for each station must be further unpacked. The next section elaborates how we can meet these purposes by establishing sustainable processes throughout the learning journey and attuning to different focuses at four stations.

How: the processes of Coaching for Learning

Coaching at four stations

The system of CfL is never presented as a linear process. Teachers-as-coaches view CfL as distinctive emerging dialogues with individual learners rather than following guidelines from coaching manuscripts. I examine CfL at different stations along the learning journey and find that we might expect various aims, focuses, values, roles and methods of coaching in these sub-processes. Table 6.1 illustrates the processes of CfL at four stations.

I need to stress that these processes are a system of communication and improvisation. They are not made up of separate entities; they are not a singular methodology or based on one firmly established way of proceeding. Instead, they are interconnected, generally structured and based on a set of principles following the theoretical background of four stations in the learning journey. The reasons for using coaching vary, and the key steps in the processes can be carried out differently. As a result, no two CfL processes are exactly the same. This notion reflects teaching as a pedagogical design process rather than following a script (see Teaching for Effective Learning Framework, 2010).

The systems model of CfL is paradigmatically grounded in the participatory worldview, but it does not necessarily take the paradigm's methodology in terms of application and implementation in the classroom. The point is to recognise the power of human agency and dialogues as creators of reality and use these concepts to co-create the facilitation processes congruent with the needs of a particular student. Therefore when CfL is applied to classroom practices, it may not appear to follow a procedure of 'Stations 1-2-3-4', but it inevitably touches self-knowledge about personal experiences and identities, public knowledge of curriculum and propositional knowing, as well as performance and practical knowing. The balance among them varies according to an individual student's current circumstances, expectations and needs.

Unpacking the four main processes

There are four main interrelated processes parallel to each other. Each process entails sub-processes and their distinctive elements. Since it is difficult to frame them together in a single model, I will elaborate on each process in turn.

The process of creating learning environments and sources (see Figure 6.3) includes effectively using and updating learning resources and materials (e.g., books, journals, internet); effectively using and updating technological equipment (e.g., interactive whiteboards, computers, laptops, tablets and other ICT equipment); providing timely and constructive feedback; and creating time and space inside as well as outside the classroom for individual study or group collaborative learning.

Table 6.1 Coaching for Learning at four stations

	Station 1 *Agency and identity*	Station 2 *Learning dispositions, values, beliefs and attitudes*	Station 3 *Knowledge, skills and capabilities*	Station 4 *Competence, performance and assessment*
Aim	To coach learners to be reflexive and reflective to understand oneself and one's situation	To facilitate learners to develop positive 'mind habits' and attitudes	To teach skills and capabilities to enable learners to better acquire knowledge and be more efficient through social interactions	To coach learners to enhance competences and improve performance
Expertise of the coach	A co-learner of understanding self or a counsellor in supporting learning about the self	A facilitator in building strengths and resources in critical awareness, positive dispositions and meta-learning	An expert or a mentor who passes on skills and knowledge, a designer and a facilitator of the enquiry-based learning process	A mentor or an examiner who observes, evaluates and offers constructive feedback
Role of the learner	To increase self-awareness and identity as a learner, to foster learner agency and a sense of responsibility	To understand and reflect on their learning power dimensions, and negotiate with the coach on how to improve them as a whole	To engage with others in the process of understanding, developing new insights and co-constructing knowledge	To improve their performance and competences in order to meet public standards and fulfil their role more effectively
Values	Contemplation, self-determination, autonomy, self-knowledge, wisdom, sensitivity, empathy	Communication, collaboration, interaction, interconnectivity, interdependence	Meaning-making and knowledge construction	Accomplishment, measurement, progress, achievement,

	Station 1 *Agency and identity*	Station 2 *Learning dispositions, values, beliefs and attitudes*	Station 3 *Knowledge, skills and capabilities*	Station 4 *Competence, performance and assessment*
Methods of coaching	Using narratives, coaching for reflection, exploring personal stories and experiences	Developing a language of learning, implementing learning power into teaching practice	Guiding, instructing, lecturing, demonstrating, modelling, facilitating collaborative work and group activities	Sharing observations and exploring possibilities, clarifying expectations and standards, feedback
Anticipated outcomes in the classroom	More self-aware and critically aware learners who are more self-motivated and take responsibility for their own learning	More confident and positive learners with enhanced learning power and better learning relationships with teacher and peers	More knowledge and skills gained around certain subjects, the knowledge is meaningful and connected to personal values	Better performance and higher intellectual quality in learning outcomes

120 Empirical case studies

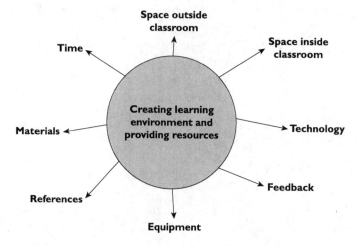

Figure 6.3 Creating environments and providing sources for learning

The process of sharing a language of learning requires a commonly agreed and accepted language to talk about learning (see Figure 6.4). This process includes negotiating purposes and values in learning; clarifying learning goals and expectations; co-identifying and describing learning processes; co-defining meanings of vocabularies of learning power dimensions; supporting students with interpreting learning profiles; and facilitating an individual student's learner identity.

Knowledge construction is the key element that differentiates CfL and coaching from personal growth or executive management. Knowledge is a situational living process, situated and embedded in learning activities. Without contexts and practices, knowledge is reduced to information. Facilitating knowledge construction

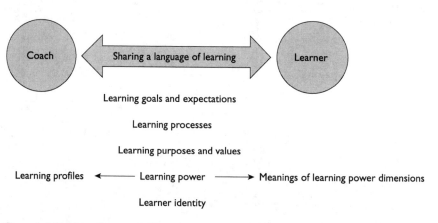

Figure 6.4 Sharing a language of learning

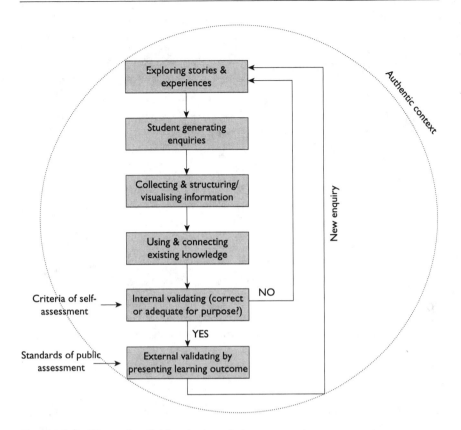

Figure 6.5 Enabling and scaffolding the knowledge construction process

entails an open-ended, formative and dynamic process (see Figure 6.5), which takes a spiral method that covers the following key points: undertaking an enquiry-based learning methodology; designing an authentic context; encouraging generation of meaningful questions as the focus of enquiry; exploring stories and experiences; enabling systematic data gathering; using and connecting an existing body of knowledge; scaffolding mind mapping and researching processes; validating internally and externally and incorporating knowledge into presentation; negotiating assessment criteria; and paying attention to both the process and the product of learning.

The process of building and maintaining a quality coaching relationship (see Figure 6.6) involves establishing effective communication and dialogues between coach and learner. An effective CfL relationship is based on interdependency and trust through the coach actively balancing power and relinquishing control. The communication and dialogues are fundamentally learner-centred, covering the following aspects: co-developing the coaching process and positions; valuing individual voices; providing freedom and choices; responding to learners' needs;

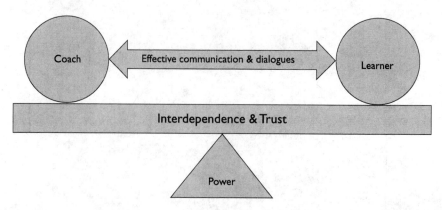

Figure 6.6 Coaching relationship through communication

shifting psychological dynamics; strengthening classroom emotional support; and supporting the management of associated emotions.

Throughout CfL processes, the relationship and communication between coach and learner have been given predominance. Establishing and maintaining a learner-centred relationship through effective communication is the key process in CfL, because it is a shared system as well as individually owned by people who participate in forming, changing and maintaining the system. This is one of the core features that put people at the centre and in every layer of the system. However, overstressing the relationship may lead to dependence and transference, so that the relationship itself becomes a problem. For such practice to be realistic and sustainable, coaches need to become more aware of their relationship with learners as knowledge generators and active participants in their own learning. Power is shared and balanced by both coach and learner; coaching methods become a means to serve the purpose rather than an end in themselves.

Who: people in the system

The teacher and the students are the main two partners involved in the system because they have direct and immediate interactions and conversations in the classroom. Holloway (1995) stressed the centrality of relationship as the context in which tasks are performed: 'the structure and character of the relationship embodies all other factors ... and in turn all other factors are influenced by the relationship ... understanding the relationship is understanding the process' (p. 51). It has been clear from the empirical evidence that teachers adopt different roles. I have categorised these roles as knowledge expert, mentor, coach and counsellor in the previous chapter. The term 'role' was defined as 'the content of a position or the behavioural implications of occupying that position' (Bee & Mitchell, 1984, p. 22). The central meaning here is position-associated *tasks*, which are the behavioural side of roles (Carroll, 1999). Teachers and students take

Table 6.2 Roles and tasks of teachers in Coaching for Learning

Role	Task
Knowledge expert/teacher	To deliver, impart, clarify, inform (knowledge)
Mentor	To provide resources, to instruct (skills), to share experiences, to monitor the process, to evaluate practices
Coach	To support and share (meanings), to scaffold and model the meaning-making process, to facilitate enquiry, to create conditions of self-directed learning
Counsellor	To protect individuals' feelings, to deal with personal issues, to facilitate personal growth

tasks and involve themselves in specific behaviours. Each role sets up a different framework of tasks to be performed, with a different kind of relationship and a different form of communication between teacher and student. Teachers can use a combination of roles when appropriate. These roles are developmental – different roles might be given different weight in different situations; one role could be predominant at one point; and several roles could be taken simultaneously. The roles and tasks are presented in Table 6.2.

The 'role-and-task' model combines roles, tasks, coaching objectives and coaching strategies. The structure is similar to Holloway and Acker's (1986) model of counselling and clinical supervision. However, I need to make two points clear. Firstly, the above framework is to clarify the kind of relationship involved in CfL; it is about the *structure* and *nature* of the relationship, but not the *quality* of the relationship. The second point is that the generic roles and tasks outlined here might not be accepted by all teachers. Furthermore, different teachers might stress different roles. My point is to acknowledge the importance of role/task in order to understand people involved in CfL, but in no way indicate that individuals actually carry out the role/task in the same way.

To extend the argument of who is involved in CfL, we cannot omit the roles of the external, professional coach, students' parents and a wider community in which the classroom learning context acts as a sub-system.

There might be a pattern of enquiry, experimentation, evaluation and reflection that transfers from a professional coach to teachers, and then from teacher to students. The pattern becomes part of the teachers' practice in the classroom and the students' own way of dealing with their learning experiences. Teachers-as-coaches also have a key role in parental liaison and in work with families. It becomes a way of thinking that can cascade through classrooms and families.

In families, parents are potentially important coaches for students, but their roles are less visible than those of teachers. Parents should be actively involved in the CfL system for the following reasons.

124 Empirical case studies

The message of 'parental involvement' in students' learning is not a completely new idea. Many schools have been trying to change the ways they deal with parents and involve them in their children's learning. Research in recent years has made it very clear that parental engagement with their children's learning makes a significant contribution to the achievements of those children and that parental engagement is as important as school in optimising students' learning experiences. Obviously, parents have a powerful influence in shaping their children's characters in ways that are useful for successful learning, for instance, self-regulation, empathy and persistence (Claxton *et al.*, 2011).

Nonetheless, the extent to which parents work together with schools and bridge learning at home and learning at school provokes further discussion. Most schools use traditional ways, such as organising parents' evenings, homework, writing school reports, or having teachers visit an individual student's home. But these approaches send parents the message that 'school deals with everything about learning and then parents get reports on how their children learn at school'. Therefore, parents are still on the receiving end of information instead of being actively involved in their children's learning. This affects most parents' attitudes towards their children's learning: they assume that learning can only happen in schools, as was the way in their generation, and they are comfortable with being detached from their children's learning because 'it is the school's job'. Teachers-as-coaches need to develop effective ways of communicating with parents to ensure that they understand what the school is trying to do, and that what goes on at home and in the wider community complements the approaches adopted at school.

The most basic level of achieving parental engagement is to raise awareness: to communicate with parents about the importance of their roles in children's learning. Of course, all parents are different and their ways of interacting with their children are different, but what schools can do at this level is to genuinely make efforts to engage parents in clear, accessible and welcoming language in order to make parents aware that they are important in their children's learning and that they can do something about it. The next level of engaging parents in their children's learning is looking beyond the basic involvement, which implies a more active and personal level of participation. It is not just about practical arrangements but their mutual vision: what kind of learners they want their children to become and what they can do to facilitate this. It means that schools need to explain to parents what CfL is, what it consists of and why it is so important. It also means developing a shared language that can be understood and used at home to describe their children's learning behaviours and characteristics. Through deep dialogue with their children, parents are able to build home conditions to cultivate effective learning capabilities, dispositions and characters, which offer insight into the development of progression in self-generated home learning and lifelong learning.

Therefore, 'coaching for parents' is an important process in the system of CfL. In the study of CfL in secondary education, a number of parents were coached to be learning facilitators for their children at home. The coaches encouraged parents to appreciate their role in all aspects of their children's learning and living. Playful, meaningful and constructive activities at home are not distractions from learning; instead, they are important forms of learning that children do. Open, sincere and empathetic dialogues with children about their study and life will not threaten parents' authority; instead, they help to establish a positive communicative channel that trust and care can travel through. Coaching parents should particularly focus on how they can interact more purposefully with their children through all forms of communication. The school created an environment in which parents felt they could come and learn together, share the challenges of parenting and talk about their children and their learning issues. They picked up the most important elements in learning power, enquiry-based learning and coaching strategies embedded in the classroom, and then asked themselves how they could experiment with and adopt these ideas in home learning as they thought fit. Moreover, the school website set up a dedicated page about CfL, which provided an opportunity for ongoing conversations after the coaching events. The students' parents were offered a forum on the website to discuss their children's learning. These continual efforts to engage parents in students' learning make potential 'family coaches' more visible, thus further helping the whole participatory, organic system to function in a healthy and sustainable manner.

Evaluating the effectiveness of Coaching for Learning

Go beyond the definition and identification of the processes of CfL and think about the following questions: how can we tell whether CfL really works or not? How can we know that it is not a waste of time and money, and that it really does benefit the learners? How can we measure its impacts on learners and their learning? Where can we get the evidence?

I consider that there should be a systematic way to evaluate the effectiveness of CfL rather than a single method. Moreover, we need to investigate its *developmental* effects rather than merely focusing on one person at one point. My point is based on the following reasons. Firstly, CfL entails a non-singular methodology and it is a complex system aiming at long-term goals. It is difficult to obtain tangible, concrete results quickly. Secondly, the practice of CfL is not aimed directly at raising standards as traditionally defined, but at systematically building transferable learning-related dispositions, expanding the range of valued outcomes to include the development of confidence and capacities to learn, and fostering a sense of ownership and responsibility for learning within individual learners.

For example, the students' learning power dimensions in the participatory study did not increase dramatically; the only significant increase was in the dimension of *meaning-making*. This might sound a fairly disappointing result for those who accentuate pre- and post-intervention in quantitative studies. In this sense, people may question the effectiveness of coaching, and critique that this practice does not work. However, as I have discussed in the previous chapter, the statistical

126 Empirical case studies

data only tells one part of the story, and we should be critical in interpreting its meanings. Moreover, we need to look at other evidence, such as interview data and observations, to see if coaching effects a change in any other aspects of an individual's learning.

Here I suggest a systemic, mixed-method approach to evaluating CfL:

- quantitative: learning power survey or other psychometric tools for assessing positive learning dispositions, school attainment reports, and assessments of meta-cognitive process of knowledge construction, etc.;
- qualitative: personal learning portfolios, interviews with learners and their teachers-as-coaches, narratives, learners' journals, observations of classroom behaviours and practical learning activities.

It is vital to recognise that coaching does not jeopardise students' performance in tests and examinations; indeed, it may even improve them. Therefore, if the attainment and examination results do not go up, it is not a failure. If these results remain the same whilst learning dispositions improve or learner agency develops, then we can read this as a success. If the conventional standards are raised, that is not a surprise, because students who know themselves better as learners are better able to manage and plan their own learning, are more critically engaged in the process of meaning-making and knowledge construction, have more resilience and interdependence in the face of challenges, and do better at exams and tests. Ideally, the impact of coaching prepares students effectively for lifelong learning and real-life learning as well as for examinations and further study.

However the development of learner agency, learning capabilities and dispositions is a long-term goal, whilst the external educational inspectors focus more on actual achievement in the short term. CfL involves a critical and major paradigm shift. Teachers involved in this shift would be exposed to external pressures that potentially make their pedagogical approaches limited. If schools have so much intensive pressure to raise standards, it can be hard for teachers to hold onto the long-term goal. This issue resonates with the findings of the study that teachers have expressed their concerns regarding the gap between the expectations of the current educational system and the practices of CfL. This conflict itself, taking a systems perspective, is exactly where innovation and transformation comes from. We shall discuss it further in Chapter 10.

Features of the systems model of Coaching for Learning

The emerging systems model of CfL demonstrates a number of features of an open system, highlighting *emergence, interrelatedness, adaptation, development* and *sustainability*. The aim is to ensure communication and desirable growth by transforming inputs and adapting to changes when they occur (Flood, 2010).

In systems theory, emergence means the production of pattern or structure that arises from interacting agents according to their own rules. The emergent whole of a system is greater than the sum of its part (Stacey, 1996). The emergent coherence is understood to constitute a whole system, and this emergent whole displays properties that cannot be reduced to the level of individual agents (Stacey, 2005). In this sense, CfL is regarded as an assemblage of interrelated elements comprising a unified whole with emergent properties that have their own regularities (Loveridge, 2009). Therefore, CfL may be thought of as emerging from individuals constituting higher levels as a participatory system with their own regularities, which can be passed over, influenced by and negotiated between each other.

Interrelatedness means that CfL is made up of interrelated parts and most usefully studied as an emergent whole. Since parts or sub-systems comprise people, CfL is concerned with the needs and purposes of both coaches and learners. The whole structure reflects the interrelated nature of its sub-systems, so that it is able to encourage coaches' and learners' participation and involvement, enable democracy and provide conditions for autonomy and agency.

The system is open and adaptive to its environment. Bertalanffy (1968) stated that in an open system the final stage can be reached from various starting conditions and through different processes. This notion is important for understanding CfL, because coaches can work with learners at various levels, begin with different openings and go through multiple processes.

Reeves (2009) acknowledged the necessity of coaching for sustainability: 'only a coaching system that anticipates the need for renewal and works through the psychological and organisational barriers to sustained change will provide enduring results' (p. 18). The feature of sustainability is essential in transformative learning, as argued by Sterling (2003), who posits that the highest level of learning is 'deeply engaging and touches and changes deep levels of values and belief through a process of realisation and re-cognition' (p. 94).

So the question is whether CfL is, or can become, a kind of self-regulating complex system; whether it can be self-aware, self-correcting and self-generating. The whole system focuses on the interactions between internal systems (the individual's structure of interpretation, capacity for self-awareness and self-adaptation, etc.) and external systems (physical learning environment, content of subjects, external assessment criteria, social relationships, etc.). The work of emotional intelligence (Goleman, 1995), to some extent, is associated with internal systems in terms of revealing the importance of being able to be self-aware and monitor feelings and thoughts about feelings. Research shows that by bringing children back to their internal balance, they develop optimal decision-making, communication, creativity, and overall effectiveness, and they move into a more resourceful, intuitive and creative state (Goleman, 1995; Childre & Martin, 1999). This internal relationship with one's self has been explored by Goodman (2002), who defined the self as 'emotional, intellectual or cognitive, physical and sensory selves' that 'create and sustain learning, meaning, purpose and reason' (p. 18).

Empirical case studies

Coaches need to create a trusting and safe environment and relationship for learners to explore, learn and embrace changes, ideally for the development of self-empowerment. So learners need to be appropriately positioned in a place of receptivity, in a state of motivation, balance and congruence. This is where self-determination and sense of agency come into play.

Feedback is essential in maintaining the integrity of the coaching system, not only in the relationship between coaches and learners, but also in the interactions with other systems, such as peers, families and communities. In the coaching relationship it is very important for the coach to model good feedback for the person being coached (Goodman, 2002). However, feedback cannot happen without trust. That is why establishing rapport and connection at the beginning is important, as well as maintaining this trust throughout the coaching process. In the participatory study illustrated in Chapter 5, the teachers and the students already knew each other, which helped them to move to deeper coaching conversations, but they might face a bigger challenge in building a new systems relationship structure that was different from the traditional teacher-student relationship. Both parties might feel uncomfortable and threatened, to the point that they might resist experiencing change. However, they have gained remarkable growth by facing new challenges, altering behaviours and performances, adapting to core innovations and developing necessary competencies.

Summary

This chapter presents the emerging systems model of Coaching for Learning. The evolving, continuously renewed set of relations and processes to facilitate four stations of learning are fundamental to the system. The emergent whole system, situated in the context, comprises 1) the main purposes of cultivating positive learning dispositions and fostering learning agency; 2) the four simultaneous processes of creating the environment, sharing a language of learning, knowledge construction and building a trusting relationship; 3) the people who are anticipated to engage in these processes; 4) the evaluation of the effectiveness when the system is applied in different contexts; and 5) the essential features that make the system interrelated, adaptive, developmental and sustainable.

The interactions and dynamics, the psychological co-dance between people and their communications in the system, are of particular interest to me. This systems perspective highlights the interpersonal relationships and language in the process of CfL. In the next two chapters, I will present another participatory case study of coaching psychology in problem-based learning in medical education and its associated model. Then I will conduct a more detailed investigation as to the psychological and discursive aspects of coaching psychology for learning.

Recommended reading

Lave, J., & Wenger, E. (1991). *Situated learning: Legitimate peripheral participation*. Cambridge: University of Cambridge Press.

McDermott, I., & Jago, W. (2005). *The coaching bible: The essential handbook*. London: Piatkus Books.

Key points for reflection

- What are the key elements of the Coaching for Learning model?
- In what aspects is Coaching for Learning model considered as a 'systems' model?
- What are the key learning/facilitating processes of Coaching for Learning?
- Who are involved in Coaching for Learning and what is the nature of their relationships?

References

Bee, H. L., & Mitchell, S. K. (1984). *The development person* (2nd Ed.). San Francisco: Harper & Row.

Bertalanffy, L. V. (1968). *General system theory: Foundations, development, application*. New York: George Braziller.

Carroll, M. (1996). *Workplace counselling*. London: Sage.

Carroll, M. (1999). Training in the tasks of supervision. In E. Holloway & M. Carroll (Eds), *Training counselling supervisors*. London: Sage.

Childre, D., & Martin, H. (1999). *The HeartMath solution*. San Francisco: Harper.

Claxton, G., Chambers, M., Powell, G., & Lucas, B. (2011). *The learning powered school: Pioneering 21st century education*. Bristol: TLO Limited.

Flood, R. L. (2010). The relationship of 'systems thinking' to action research. *Systemic Practice and Action Research, 23*(4), 269–284.

Goleman, D. (1995). *Emotional intelligence*. New York: Bantam Books.

Goodman, J. C. (2002). *Coaching and systems theory*. Centre for Internal Change. Retrieved from www.internalchange.com/Paper%20on%20coaching%20Systems%20 &%20Choas.pdf

Holloway, E. (1995). *Clinical supervision: A systems approach*. Thousand Oaks, CA: Sage.

Holloway, E., & Acker, M. (1986). *The EPICS (Engagement and Power in Clinical Supervision) model*. University of Oregon Press.

Lave, J., & Wenger, E. (1991). *Situated learning: Legitimate peripheral participation*. Cambridge: University of Cambridge Press.

Loveridge, D. (2009). *Foresight: The art and science of anticipating the future*. New York and London: Routledge.

McDermott, I., & Jago, W. (2005). *The coaching bible: The essential handbook*. London: Piatkus Books.

Reeves, D. B. (2009). Three challenges of web 2.0. *Educational Leadership, 66*(6).

Stacey, R. D. (1996). *Complexity and creativity in organizations*. San Francisco: Berrett-Koehler.

Stacey, R. D. (2005). Organizational identity: The paradox of continuity and potential transformation at the same time. *Group Analysis, 38*(4), 477–494.

Sterling, S. (2003). *Whole systems thinking as a basis for paradigm change in education: Explorations in the context of sustainability* (Unpublished doctorial dissertation). Bath: Centre for Research in Education and the Environment, University of Bath.

Teaching for Effective Learning Framework. (2010). *South Australian Teaching for Effective Learning Framework Guide: A Resource for Developing Quality Teaching and Learning in South Australia.* Department of Education and Children's Services.

Wang, Q. (2013). Towards a systems model of coaching for learning: Empirical lessons from the secondary classroom context. *International Coaching Psychology Review, 8*(1), 35–53.

Chapter 7

Coaching psychology for problem-based learning (PBL) in medical education

Introduction

In Chapter 5 and Chapter 6, I presented an empirical participatory study of coaching psychology for enhancing enquiry-based learning in secondary education. This chapter sets out a different journey: how can coaching psychology be combined with problem-based learning in medical education? What are the impacts of coaching psychology for medical students and teachers? How does coaching psychology contribute to this particular kind of learning? How do medical teachers and students experience this type of medical education? What are their perspectives? More interestingly, the previous empirical case was conducted in the UK, whereas this chapter will focus on an empirical study in Mainland China, which would hopefully inspire readers to investigate cross-cultural and cross-domain features of coaching psychology and learning.

What is problem-based learning in medical education?

In Chapter 3, I discussed the differences between enquiry-based learning and problem-based learning. However, problem-based learning in the context of medical education needs to be explored further in this chapter. Problem-based learning (PBL) is essentially a strategic learning system that represents a major shift in the educational paradigm from teacher-centred to student-centred learning. It aims to enhance collaborative, contextual, integrated, self-directed and reflective learning (Gwee, 2009). Although PBL may take various forms in different institutions, it is generally built on the following principles: relevant, authentic problems form the basis of teaching and learning; students as the central players and active seekers of knowledge; and learning through collaboration and discussions (Norman & Schmidt, 1992). Essential features of PBL include an interdisciplinary approach, authentic activities that are valued in the real world, ill-structured problems, students' collaboration, individually collected information, groups' decision-making process, discussion of principles and goals, and self- and peer-assessment (Savery, 2006). In medical education, PBL provides students with guided experience in the context of complex, authentic patient problems and allows the students to develop content knowledge, thinking strategies, clinical logicality, intrinsic motivation, and effective self-directed and collaborative learning skills (Groves *et al.*, 2005).

As an instructional method widely employed in medical education, PBL has been adopted in Mainland China since the mid-1980s as a means of cultivating students' practical learning capacities and, ultimately, promoting lifelong learning (Kwan, 2005; Ren, 2005; Wang *et al.*, 2010; Wang *et al.*, 2016). Chinese medical schools have been making efforts to explore their own PBL approaches based on their educational conditions, human resources and existing curriculum structures. Most Chinese medical schools select and incorporate some essential features of PBL into their existing curriculum as a hybrid model in which the majority of teaching is done through didactic lectures and practical classes with a small proportion of PBL intermixed (Lian & He, 2013). In addition, there are very few studies of PBL within a visualised model clarifying interrelated factors in the process. Although there are some examples of visualised PBL processes in Chinese medical education (e.g., Li *et al.*, 2011; Liu *et al.*, 2009; Huang *et al.*, 2013), none of these models have psychological underpinnings that are essential for the learning and facilitation involved in PBL. The dynamics between the critical elements of these models are sometimes over-simplified. Currently, the implementation of PBL in relation to medical research in China remains under-explored. This was one of my motivations in conducting an empirical study of coaching psychology and PBL in the Chinese context.

PBL tutoring and facilitation

From an instructive perspective, PBL emphasises the importance of understanding not only content but also disciplinary epistemologies and investigative strategies through collaborative problem solving and sense making, reflecting on experiences, developing evidence-based explanations, communicating ideas, enhancing discipline-specific reasoning skills and engaging in self-directed enquiry (Hmelo-Silver *et al.*, 2007). To successfully use PBL, students must take responsibility for the learning process. However, for many students, this does not occur naturally or easily (English & Kitsantas, 2013). Previous studies have shown that PBL fosters the development of self-directed, lifelong learning *as long as students are supported and guided* (Miflin *et al.*, 2000). Therefore, PBL tutoring or facilitation, as a supporting system, is of crucial importance to the effective functioning of PBL. This supporting system primarily requires an understanding of the learning process to create a supportive learning environment that encourages active participation by all members and continuously monitors the quality of learning. The system involves a rigorous, structured and flexible approach delivered by PBL tutors (Barrows & Tamblyn, 1980; Evenson & Hmelo-Silver, 2000). However, the literature varies widely on the characteristics of effective PBL tutors, especially on the tutor's role as a content expert or/and a process expert. For example, Barrows and Tamblyn believed that the PBL tutor's role should be facilitative and have expertise in group facilitation (i.e., process expertise), rather than be didactic and have expertise in a subject area (i.e., content expertise). Meanwhile, other scholars argue that the most effective tutors are those with both clinical content knowledge and the ability to facilitate the learning process and to empathise with students' circumstances (De Grave *et al.*, 1999; Papinczak *et al.*, 2009). The sophisticated role of the PBL tutor indicates striking the right balance between process facilitation and information delivery, a balance that alters at different points in the PBL process (Edelson, 2001).

PBL tutors are required to acquire a mixture of direct and non-directive facilitation techniques built on humanistic attitudes of education that support significant, meaningful and experiential learning (Rogers, 1986; Barrows, 1986). The directive facilitation approach is important, given the complex nature of PBL; for example, a tutor may provide direct instruction on a just-in-time basis when students are experiencing difficulties (Hmelo-Silver, 2004).

How coaching psychology is related to PBL

The non-directive facilitative approach in PBL is particularly related to the perspective of coaching psychology. I believe that the extensive studies on coaching and coaching psychology have invigorated the domain of PBL facilitation. As defined in Chapter 4, coaching psychology focuses on the enhancement of individuals' well-being, goal attainment and performance in personal life and the domain of work. Coaching can be seen as a process of human development that involves focused interaction between the coach and the learner, and the use of appropriate strategies, tools and techniques, and the process should be underpinned by models grounded in established learning theories or psychological approaches. In the field of education, coaching is regarded as a learning methodology, although sometimes the boundaries are blurred (Law, 2013). The use of coaching psychology for learning emphasises personal involvement, careful listening, acceptance, empathy and reflection to create a non-threatening and non-judgemental environment where learners feel free to delve into their own experiences and seek answers to their own problems (Wang, 2013), and these elements are all important for PBL.

The effect of coaching psychology implemented in enquiry-based learning could shed light on the domain of PBL. Coaching psychologists believe that knowledge needs to be personally appropriated and that this goal can be achieved through a specific type of encounter between the coach and the learners. The responsibility for solving the problems and learning rests with the learners rather than with the coach. As evidenced in Chapter 6, incorporating coaching psychology into an enquiry-based learning process is beneficial in terms of optimising students' learning experience, scaffolding the enquiry process, developing positive learning dispositions, and fostering students' learning relationships, autonomy, self-awareness and learning agency. In PBL, coaching psychology is particularly concerned with how tutors and students establish and maintain a dialogical and participatory relationship through effective communication, so that they explore real-case clinical problems, construct knowledge, search for solutions, and develop positive learning dispositions and self-determination in learning as in enquiry-based learning. Actually, although the literature on coaching in PBL is limited, some researchers have touched on the subject. The term 'coaching' has been mentioned by a few studies in facilitating cognitive development, such as critical thinking or clinical logicality in the PBL process. For instance, Barrows and Tamblyn (1980), in their classic book *Problem-based learning: An approach to medical education*, offered their vision of a PBL tutor as a meta-cognitive coach and mentor. Maudsley (1999) noted that the PBL tutor becomes both the steward of the group process and the meta-cognitive coach by guiding and supporting students' learning. Margetson (1994) and Papinczak *et al.* (2009) suggested that PBL tutors are expected to manage increasingly diverse and ambiguous roles, defined as mentor, coach, model and guide. In addition, it is anticipated that the PBL tutor should function as a group facilitator to support students' self-directed, active learning and foster critical thinking skills and lifelong learning habits rather than merely convey knowledge (Das *et al.*, 2002; Gilkison, 2004). The tutor's role is to coach students only when appropriate to ensure that they make optimal use of the learning opportunities and then withdraw as students develop expertise in the process while continuing to monitor the quality of learning (Wang & Millward, 2014).

The commonalities between coaching psychology and PBL

Coaching psychology and PBL may differ in various aspects, in that one is a sub-discipline in the field of psychology and the other is a learning methodology. For example, coaching psychology considers the qualities and characteristics of coaches from a humanistic perspective, whereas in PBL, tutors' personal qualities are not considered to be a main factor. However, there are several common threads running through the review of PBL and coaching psychology.

Philosophically, they are both grounded in social constructionism, which is concerned with how learners construct new knowledge and build their own mental structures through social interaction with other people and their environment. They both indicate that inter-subjectivity through discussion and participation is essential in socially generated and shared knowledge. Theoretically, coaching psychology and PBL both explicitly stress the developmental, situated nature of the learning process and learners' meaning-making and reflection based on their self-directedness and self-determination. In practice, they both emphasise experiential learning, which refers to using an authentic method of achieving understanding through confronting problems and exploring solutions in real learning contexts. Furthermore, they both acknowledge the importance of learning facilitators, i.e., coaches, tutors or mentors, who play an essential role in supporting learners in their own learning and development. Therefore, I posit that PBL and coaching psychology share an affinity in terms of learning facilitation.

The (possible) differences between **PBL** tutoring and **PBL** coaching

Although there is some literature on the relation between coaching and PBL facilitation and commonalities between coaching psychology and PBL in various aspects, I consider that coaching may not be intrinsic to the PBL process, and that it has been overlooked particularly in the context of Chinese medical education. A few possible distinctions could be made between PBL tutoring as we usually know it and PBL coaching. First, PBL coaching includes the coach's personal qualities from a humanistic perspective into its process, stressing the coach's authenticity, congruence, and unconditional positive regard toward learners. In PBL tutoring, medical teachers do not usually receive special training on this aspect. Second, PBL coaching explicitly considers empathy, care and medical humanity as one of the core learning goals in medical education. It requires the coach to provide good modelling of empathetic attitudes and behaviours, and display effective communication with learners in a non-didactic way. In comparison, PBL tutoring may concentrate more on solving clinical problems and overlook humanistic issues that are related to the patients. Third, PBL coaching pays particular attention to the emotional and motivational aspects of learners. Whilst addressing cognitive scaffolding, critical thinking and solution orientation as in PBL tutoring, PBL coaching involves emotional scaffolding to establish rapport, trust and a sustainable nurturing relationship with learners. In addition, PBL coaching encourages learners to 'own' the problems, to find personal connections with and meaning in the cases, and to construct stories about the problems and patients, so that intrinsic motivation is enhanced. Finally, although PBL tutoring and PBL coaching both involve drawing from students' own resources and requiring them to come up with their own solutions, PBL coaching emphasises the flexible use of various coaching skills, such as active listening, open questions, probing, summarising and reflecting, to deal with learners' cognitive, emotional, motivational and social issues.

The nature of PBL is moving towards a *learning design* and *a facilitation system*, which is the core of coaching psychology for learning (Wang, 2013). In the next section, I will present an empirical study that aims to explore a new framework that integrates essential features of current PBL and the perspective of coaching psychology in the context of medical education. The study mainly employed a participatory research approach, and the data was analysed qualitatively. In the first phase of the study, a systematic visual representation of the PBL and coaching psychology processes was co-constructed by researchers, PBL tutors and medical students, depending on the local context. In the second phase of the study, a group of medical teachers and students pioneered the new model in their PBL tutorial settings. Teachers' and students' experiences of PBL coaching were explored, described and discussed. The terms 'medical teachers' and 'tutors' are used interchangeably in the study.

Research methodology: participatory and phenomenological

The overall study design was informed by a research methodology based on a participatory inquiry paradigm (Heron & Reason, 1997). Participatory research is 'an orientation to inquiry' and can be regarded as a methodology that argues in favour of the significance and usefulness of involving research partners in a knowledge-production process that is reflexive, flexible and iterative (Reason & Bradbury, 2008). Participatory research methods may not be fundamentally distinct from other empirical social research approaches and they are linked closely to qualitative methods (Bergold & Thomas, 2012). The key element of participatory research is not the methods; rather, it is the attitude of researchers, which in turn determines how, by, and for whom research is conceptualised and conducted. The most important distinction between participatory research and other research methodologies is the location of power at the various stages of the research process (Cornwell & Jewkes, 1995). Rooted in common principles of action research and participatory action research, participatory research emphasises listening, observing, feedback, interaction and open dialogue to establish a non-hierarchical learning community that assumes a reciprocity of influence. Through a process of mutual learning that takes place throughout the research process rather than at distinct stages, participants are included in the research as owners of their own knowledge and empowered to take action (Rahman & Fals-Borda, 1991).

In the first phase of this study, we wanted to engage everyone and construct an integrative framework of coaching psychology and PBL, trying to define PBL coaching as a new facilitative method in medical education. Therefore, the application of participatory methodologies was collaborative and consultative. We formed an interesting combination in terms of professions: the medical teachers and students had experience in PBL in medical education but did not know about coaching psychology, whilst the research team (four research assistants and myself) were qualified as educational psychologists and coaching psychologists but did not experience PBL in medical education. Therefore, researchers and participants were regarded as learning partners and active contributors. The participants were capable of identifying their own problems, analysing their own situation and designing their own solutions, and the role of researchers was modified from directors to facilitators or catalysts, creating spaces where participants could be empowered to engage in the research process. Then there was movement towards relinquishing control and developing participants' ownership of the research question and the information that was generated, analysed, represented and acted upon in the future.

In the second phase of the study, medical teachers and students implemented PBL coaching in their existing curriculum for one semester. We then asked the principal question: what are medical teachers' and students' experiences and perspectives of PBL coaching? We employed interpretative phenomenological analysis (IPA) to investigate this question. IPA is a qualitative research methodology that is specifically dedicated to the detailed examination of personal meaning and lived experience (Smith & Osborn, 2003). We wanted to explore the realistic accounts of individual teachers' and students' lived experience of PBL coaching, and the meanings that particular experiences, events and states hold for participants. Like small-scale participatory research, IPA is modest in terms of its scope, and it is not interested in generalising an objective statement of event itself to a wide population. It is more concerned with an individual's personal perception of an object or event, and the specifics of an individual's constructed world (Eatough & Smith, 2008). However, IPA should not be simpled as a series of descriptions of participants' experiences presented in the interview transcripts. Instead, it acknowledges the engagement and the reflexive role of researchers in the interpretation of and interaction with the participants' texts (Smith & Osborn, 2003; Smith *et al.*, 2009), thus rendering the analytical process dialectical and participatory.

Context of the study

The research was conducted at the medical school of Tongji University in China in the academic year 2014–2015. At this medical school, a systematic programme has been developed integrating problem-, lecture-, clinical- and competence-based learning at undergraduate level. The undergraduate medical education programme usually lasts five years and leads to a bachelor's degree (commonly called a 'five-year programme'). The undergraduate programme also formed a part of the combined programme, which lasts seven years and leads to a master's degree (commonly called a 'seven-year programme'). In these two programmes, the curriculum in the first four years is exactly the same, consisting of discipline-based modules, such as basic science, biochemistry, immunology, molecules, pharmacology, genetics, respiratory, Chinese medicine and so on. Each year consists of four modules that last eight weeks each. Modules are structured on the basis of lectures, PBL sessions, laboratory practice and evidence-based medicine. PBL is included primarily in the second and third year, and each module includes two PBL scenarios/problem cases. At the beginning of the second year, students are introduced to the concept, the process, the roles of learners and tutors, and the assessment process of PBL. The PBL tutors, mainly from the clinical science faculty, attend a week's training on PBL tutoring prior to the sessions. The teaching faculty in the medical school was interested in incorporating coaching psychology into their existing PBL approach, therefore we established a participatory research team to co-design a psychological model of PBL coaching and implement it in the medical education setting.

First phase of the study

Participants

In the first phase, four research assistants, myself and ten participants from the medical school were involved. Participants included four second year medical

138 Empirical case studies

students (two females and two males) who had nearly finished their first PBL module at the medical school; four final year medical students (three females and one male) who had finished a series of PBL modules during their university education; and two respiratory doctors (one female and one male) who were professionally trained as accredited PBL tutors with a minimum of three years of PBL experience. They participated in the study voluntarily and completed the entire research process of co-constructing the integrative model of PBL coaching.

Research procedure

This phase of the study consisted of four workshops held from October 2014 to January 2015. During the workshops, our research team and the participants were divided into two groups, each with a mix of medical teachers, students and researchers. The main learning points were summarised at the end of each workshop to aid personal reflection, provide continuity and guide participants towards the next workshop.

The first workshop began with an introductory session of ice-breaking activities so that we got to know each other in the team, developed rapport and team spirit, and formed common goals in the study. The introductory session was followed by a discussion of the existing PBL curriculum in the medical school. Then I introduced the main concepts of coaching psychology and explained how it is related to PBL and other kinds of learning in a broader sense.

In the second workshop, we brainstormed and further explored the possibility of adopting and incorporating coaching psychology into the PBL curriculum by specifying what could be changed from a coaching perspective, what psychological underpinnings were there and how we could blend features of coaching into PBL. As the outcome of this workshop, we generated three different drafts of the integrated model of coaching psychology and PBL.

The third workshop focused on reviewing the structures of the draft models, investigating the advantages and the limitations of the draft models, extracting the essential elements in PBL coaching, modifying and refining the drafts, and advancing the discussion towards a more integrated model.

The final workshop concentrated on making implementation plans of the model and practising key coaching skills and techniques (e.g., active listening, open questions and evocating) that would be needed in the application. At the end of the workshop, participants were asked to provide their feedback and suggestions. The feedback was generally very positive. Participants reported a better understanding of PBL and coaching psychology, mastery of coaching skills and techniques, and increased confidence in the implementation of the new model. The participants stated that they felt creative and energetic, and highly engaged and motivated in the group discussion and collaborative creation of the model. The participatory research approach seemed to provide a friendly, open and safe learning environment that allowed people to share opinions and challenged them to engage in deep thinking.

Data collection and analysis

Data were primarily collected through qualitative methods. We video-recorded our participatory observation of participants' conversations, behaviours and interactional patterns in each workshop. We conducted and video-recorded four focus groups and eight semi-structured interviews, collected participants' notes, posters, PPT, other relevant documents and our reflective journals. These methods were complemented by the collection of some descriptive quantitative data gathered from the evaluation forms at the end of the study. Of note, some of the data collection and analysis processes were interactive and continuous in a spiral form that enabled us to reflect on the previous analytical results and alter actions in the next phase of data collection.

The data analysis process was inspired by Glaser and Strauss' (1967) grounded theory and Braun and Clark's (2006) thematic analysis method with the purpose of developing a model. The research assistants and I independently coded interviews, documents and observational data after each workshop, performed thematic content analysis, discussed disagreement, and reached consensus on the overall analysis. We then sent our preliminary findings to participants, invited them to offer their opinions and included the feedback sessions as an integral part of the data analysis process. The model was drafted, discussed, modified and shared with participants. In this way, we not only triangulated the sources and methods of data analysis but also deepened our understanding as researchers through the diversity of our opinions and experiences. The outcome of the first phase of the study was an integrated model of coaching psychology and PBL (i.e., CPBL model) to support medical teachers to conduct PBL coaching with their students more professionally and in a more structured way. The model will be presented and discussed in the next chapter.

Second phase of the study

Participants and the implementation

In the second phase of the study, in order to try the CPBL model on a small scale, the faculty decided to incorporate coaching only in the respiratory module in the semester from April to July 2015. One hundred undergraduate students from the five-year programme (68%) and the seven-year programme (32%) took the module. All the students were in their third year, majoring in clinical medicine. They had taken various PBL modules in their second year. Only one student, who was an exchange international student from Pakistan, had never taken a PBL course. Eight students had attended the course on coaching psychology. For most students, it was the first time that they would be instructed in a coaching approach. Six respiratory doctors functioned as coaches in the PBL session. Two of them were professionally trained as PBL facilitators/tutors in the US, one in Taiwan, and other three were locally trained in the medical school of Tongji University. All of them had at least two years' experience of PBL tutoring.

140   Empirical case studies

The faculty launched a four-day training course on PBL coaching that covered the philosophy, the process, the role of coaches and learners, and the essential skills of coaching, delivered by myself. All six teachers have taken the PBL coaching training course and they had acquired coaching experience and skills to varying levels.

In the current PBL sessions, 15 to 18 students worked together with a tutor and there were six parallel groups. There were two PBL scenarios, and each was processed in three sessions (two hours per session) over three weeks. During the sessions, tutors were consciously interacting with students in a coaching approach and students were expected to work collaboratively on the scenarios. Between the sessions, students were expected to study independently and interdependently toward their learning objectives as defined in the previous session. They reported an average of five hours' self-directed learning and three hours' collaborative learning per week throughout the sessions.

Participants in IPA study

Students and tutors were informed about the IPA study and invited to participate in the interviews. Twenty students (Mean age = 20.9, F = 11, M = 9) and five tutors (Mean age = 37.2, F = 3, M = 2) voluntarily joined in the study. They were numbered in the order of signing up for the interviews. Only one tutor declined the interview invitation, due to urgent clinical work. Among the student participants, two female students and one male student had taken the coaching training course. All tutor participants had taken the coaching training course. The students were from different PBL groups coached by different tutors.

Data collection and analysis

Prior to the formal interviews, we conducted pilot interviews and developed a 'prompt sheet' with a few main points for discussion. For example, 'How do you perceive yourself as a learner/tutor in PBL coaching?', 'What do you think of PBL coaching?', 'Is PBL coaching different from the PBL tutoring that you have conducted/taken before? If so, what are the main differences?', 'How does PBL coaching impact on your tutoring/learning?', 'What issues that you would like to raise about the current PBL sessions?' The sheet was merely the basis for a conversation; it was not intended to be prescriptive and certainly not limiting in the sense of overriding the expressed interests of the participants. Twenty-five interviews were conducted in Chinese, each lasting from 30 to 55 minutes (with an average length of 45 minutes). All the interviews were audio-recorded, then transcribed into Chinese texts and translated into English with meticulous accuracy.

Four data analysts, including three research assistants and myself, independently reviewed the transcripts and conducted data analysis according to an iterative four-stage scheme developed by Biggerstaff and Thompson (2008). Stage 1 involved the first encounter with the texts. We attempted to suspend presuppositions and judgements when reading the texts and focus on what was actually presented in the transcripts. We made notes of thoughts, observations and reflections that occurred while engaging with the text. At Stage 2, we moved on to re-read the transcripts and identified preliminary themes that captured the essential features of the interviews. We also looked for possible connections between themes at this stage. Occasional disconfirmatory narratives were identified in some participants and such dissonance prompted us to revisit earlier transcripts in case something vital had been missed or misunderstood. At Stage 3, we grouped related themes together as clusters or concepts, and this provided an overall structure indicating a hierarchical relationship between the themes. The final stage involved tabulating themes in a summary table with quotations that best captured the essence of the participants' thoughts and feelings about their PBL coaching and learning experiences. The scheme was applied to all the interview data until we had achieved a consolidated list of categories from the cyclical analysis. The results will be presented and discussed in the next chapter.

Reflexive statement

As Creswell (2003) said, 'one cannot escape the personal interpretation brought to the qualitative analyses'. We inevitably interpreted the data through our own unique lenses, and created the meaning of participants' experiences using the stored past knowledge and long-held assumptions that we brought to the new research setting. For example, how PBL approaches have developed in China and how Chinese learners usually perceive medical education might have a great impact on how we situated and interpreted participants' responses from a socio-cultural perspective. In this study, we were aware that the appropriate perspective of analysis did not come automatically – we must constantly consult the participants, their texts and other possible theoretical approaches in order to arrive at an explicit awareness of the phenomenon and settle on a proper angle (Giorgi & Giorgi, 2008). We were cautious about the potential influence of our role of researchers on the process of construction and application of the PBL coaching model. We took a reflexive position in understanding what the participants actually said about their opinions and experiences rather than giving them hints about what we wanted to hear. After each session and interview, we wrote journals reflecting initial impressions, immediate observations and interactions with the participants. The notes evolved throughout the research process, covering our reactions, positions, thoughts and affections, so that we could conceptualise and systematically present what the participants had said, and articulate and clarify the findings that emerged from the data. The reflective journals were kept until the completion of the study. Afterwards, we held individual meetings with each participant to confirm that the findings accurately reflected their thoughts and experiences.

Summary

In this chapter, we have told a different story of coaching psychology in learning, that is, how it could contribute to PBL in medical education. We again adopted participatory methodology to combine research goals and action goals, because they contributed to establishing a learning community and generating valid data. The study engaged all members equally as co-researchers and enabled the creation, development and modification of a new model for medical education as the result of collective wisdom. The collaborative endeavour between researchers, PBL tutors and medical students could help medical education researchers understand the nature of PBL and coaching psychology, and make more effort to better implement it. In the next chapter, I will present the integrated model of coaching psychology and PBL as well as medical tutors' and students' perceptions of PBL coaching.

Recommended reading

Barrows, H. S., & Tamblyn, R. M. (1980). *Problem-based learning: An approach to medical education*. Springfield, IL: Springer.

Evenson, D. H., & Hmelo-Silver, C. E. (2000). *Problem-based learning: A research perspective on learning interactions*. Mahwah, NJ: Lawrence Erlbaum Associates.

Smith, J. A., Flowers, P., & Larkin, M. (2009). *Interpretive phenomenological analysis*. London: Sage.

Key points for reflection

*   How would you design an intervention of coaching psychology for problem-based learning if you were a medical teacher?
*   What research methodology would you adopt in order to study coaching psychology for problem-based learning?
*   What are the key lessons and observations that we can learn from this study?
*   Are there any limitations of this study? What will you do in the future if you are the researcher?

References

Barrows, H. S. (1986). A taxonomy of problem-based learning methods. *Medical Education, 20*(6), 481–486.

Barrows, H. S., & Tamblyn, R. M. (1980). *Problem-based learning: An approach to medical education*. Springfild, IL: Springer.

Bergold, J., & Thomas, S. (2012). Participatory research methods: A methodological approach in motion. *Forum: Qualitative Social Research, 13*(1).

Biggerstaff, D., & Thompson, A. R. (2008). Interpretative phenomenological analysis (IPA): a qualitative methodology for choice in healthcare research. *Qualitative Research in Psychology, 5*(3), 214–224.

Braun, V., & Clark, V. (2006). Using thematic analysis in psychology. *Qualitative Research in Psychology, 3*, 77–101.

Cornwall, A., & Jewkes, R. (1995). What is participatory research? *Social Science & Medicine, 41*(12), 1667–1676.

Creswell, J. (2003). *Research design: qualitative quantitative and mixed methods approaches*. London: Sage.

Das, M., Mpofu, D. J., Hasan, M. Y., & Stewart, T. S. (2002). Student perceptions of tutor skills in problem-based learning tutorials. *Medical Education, 36*(3), 272–278.

De Grave, W. S., Dolmans, D. H. J. M., & Vleuten, C. P. M. V. D. (1999). Profiles of effective tutors in problem-based learning: scaffolding student learning. *Medical Education, 33*(12), 901–906.

Eatough, V., & Smith, J. A. (2008). Interpretative phenomenological analysis. In C. Willig & W. Stainton-Rogers (Eds), *The SAGE handbook of qualitative research in psychology*. London: Sage.

Edelson, D. C. (2001). Learning-for-use: A framework for integration content and process learning in the design of inquiry activities. *Journal of Research in Science Teaching, 8*, 355–385.

English, M. C., & Kitsantas, A. (2013). Supporting student self-regulated learning in problem-and project-based learning. *Interdisciplinary Journal of Problem-based Learning, 7*(2), 128–150.

Evenson, D. H., & Hmelo-Silver, C. E. (2000). *Problem-based learning: A research perspective on learning interactions*. Mahwah, NJ: Lawrence Erlbaum Associates.

Gilkison, A. (2004). Problem-based learning tutor expertise: the need for different questions. *Medical Education, 38*(9), 921–926.

Giorgi, A. P., & Giorgi, B. (2008). Phenomenological psychology. In C. Willig & W. Stainton-Rogers (Eds) *The SAGE handbook of qualitative research in psychology*. London: Sage; 2008.

Glaser, B., & Strauss, A. (1967). *The discovery of grounded theory*. Chicago, IL: Aldine.

Groves, M., Régo, P., & O'Rourke, P. (2005). Tutoring in problem-based learning medical curricula: the influence of tutor background and style on effectiveness. *BMC Medical Education, 5*(1), 20.

Gwee M. C. E. (2009). Problem-based learning: A strategic learning system design for the education of healthcare professionals in the 21st century. *Kaohsiung Journal of Medical Sciences, 25*, 231–239.

Heron, J., & Reason, P. (1997). A participatory inquiry paradigm. *Qualitative Inquiry, 3*(3), 274–294.

Hmelo-Silver, C. E. (2004). Problem-based learning: what and how do students learn? *Educational Psychology Review, 16*(3), 235–266.

Hmelo-Silver, C. E., Duncan, R. G., & Chinn, C. A. (2007). Scaffolding and achievement in problem-based and inquiry learning: a response to Kirschner, Sweller, and Clark (2006). *Educational Psychologist, 42*(2), 99–107.

Huang, Y. M., Zhao, Y. H., Wang, X. N., & Zhang, H. (2013). Expanding application of PBL model and practicing exploration of PBL model. *Journal of Medical Informatics, 34*(4), 84–88.

Kwan, C. Y. (2005). Learning of medical pharmacology via innovation: A personal experience at McMaster and in Asia. *Acta Pharmacol Sin, 25*, 1186–1194.

Law, H. (2013). *The psychology of coaching, mentoring and learning* (2nd Ed.). Chichester: John Wiley & Sons.

Li, J., Lu, S., Song, H., Zhang, Q., Zheng, H., & Qin, C. (2011). Exploring the application of medical PBL from students' perspective. *Heilongjiang Medical Pharmacy, 34*(5), 75–76.

Lian, J., & He, F. (2013). Improved performance of students instructed in a hybrid PBL format. *Biochem Mol Biol Educ, 41*(1), 5–10.

Liu, W., Sun, Z., Xue, Y., Gao, F., Chen, S., Yang, Z., & Zhao, Y. (2009). Constructing PBL model in imitating clinical nursing education. *Chinese Higher Medical Education, 9*, 89–91.

Margetson, D. (1994). Current educational reform and the significance of problem-based learning. *Studies in Higher Education, 19*, 5–19.

Maudsley, G. (1999). Roles and responsibilities of the problem based learning tutor in the undergraduate medical curriculum. *British Medical Journal, 318*(7184), 657–661.

Miflin, B. M., Campbell, C. B., & Price, D. A. (2000). A conceptual framework to guide the development of self-directed, lifelong learning in problem-based medical curricula. *Medical Education, 34*(4), 299–306.

Norman, G. R., & Schmidt, H. G. (1992). The psychological basis of problem-based learning: a review of the evidence. *Academic Medicine Journal of the Association of American Medical Colleges, 67*(9), 557–65.

Papinczak, T., Tunny, T., & Young, L. (2009). Conducting the symphony: a qualitative study of facilitation in problem-based learning tutorials. *Medical Education, 43*(4), 377–383.

Rahman, M. A., & Fals-Borda, O. A. (Eds). (1991). A self-review of par. In *Action and knowledge: Breaking the monopoly with participatory action research.* London: Intermediate Technology Publications.

Reason, P., & Bradbury, H. (2008). *The SAGE handbook of action research: Participatory inquiry and practice.* London: Sage.

Ren, Y. (2005). Exploring problem-based learning in the context of Chinese culture. *Modern Educational Technology, 15*(2), 45–48.

Rogers, C. G. (1986). On the development of the person-centered approach: What is essential . . .? *Person-Centered Review, 1*(3), 257–259.

Savery J. R. (2006). Overview of problem-based learning: Definitions and distinctions. *Interdisciplinary Journal of Problem-based Learning, 1*(1), 9–20.

Smith, J. A., Flowers, P., & Larkin, M. (2009). *Interpretive phenomenological analysis.* London: Sage.

Smith, J. A., & Osborn, M. (2003). Interpretative phenomenological analysis. In J. A. Smith (Ed.), *Qualitative psychology: a practical guide to research methods.* London: Sage.

Wang, J., Zhang, W., Qin, L., Zhao, J., Zhang, S., & Gu, J., *et al.* (2010). Problem-based learning in regional anatomy education at Peking University. *Anatomical Sciences Education, 3*(3), 121–126.

Wang, Q. (2013). Towards a systems model of coaching for learning: Empirical lessons from the secondary classroom context. *International Coaching Psychology Review, 8*(1), 35–53.

Wang, Q., Li, H., Pang, W., Liang, S., & Su, Y. (2016). Developing an integrated framework of problem-based learning and coaching psychology for medical education: a participatory research. *BMC Medical Education, 16*(1), 2.

Wang, Q., & Millward, I. (2014). Developing a unified psychological model of coaching and mentoring in supporting the learning and development of adolescents. *International Journal of Evidence Based Coaching & Mentoring, 12*(2), 91–108.

Chapter 8

PBL coaching

Towards an integrative model of CPBL

Introduction

In the last chapter, I discussed the possible links between coaching psychology and PBL in medical education, suggested the idea of PBL coaching, and presented the methodological part of an empirical participatory study conducted in Mainland China. In this study, medical teachers and students were recruited as participants to co-create a model integrating coaching psychology and PBL approaches, and to implement it in real medical education settings. This unorthodox approach fundamentally changed the role of participants from subjects of psychological studies to co-owners of the research process and product. A phenomenological investigation revealed how participants perceived PBL coaching and elucidated what we could learn from the research. In this chapter, I will illustrate the model integrating PBL and coaching psychology, the CPBL model, present the key findings that emerged from the IPA study, and provide a synthesised discussion on the particular contributions that coaching makes to the PBL process.

The CPBL model

In the first phase of the study, participants discovered the meaning of coaching psychology and PBL experience, inquired into the roots of the preconceptions of PBL in Chinese medical education and formulated a new pedagogical framework through a series of democratic and transformative meaning-making processes. The model shares some common key elements of PBL with other established models that we have reviewed. However, the model has a number of innovative aspects, particularly in the Chinese medical educational context, and it appears to reflect a general, comprehensive medical education approach facilitated by a coaching perspective rather than merely a tutorial process. Coaching psychology brings a number of contributions to the existing PBL approach, as indicated by the CPBL model (see Figure 8.1).

Empirical case studies

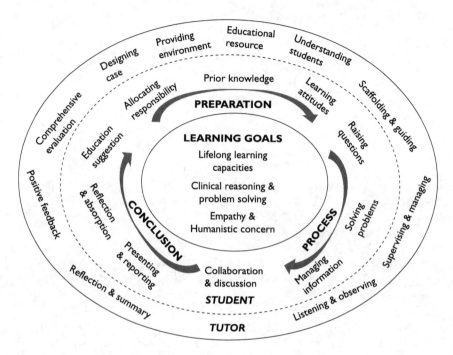

Figure 8.1 The CPBL model for PBL coaching

I explicitly address the following four points:

1. The new model regards empathy and medical humanity as key learning goals in PBL tutorials.
2. PBL coaching emphasises not only the cognitive scaffolding mentioned in the earlier PBL research but also the emotional scaffolding which was often overlooked by previous studies.
3. The new model recognises the multiplicity of roles that tutors adopt during the PBL tutorial and gives more weight to the balance between the roles of knowledge experts and academic coaches.
4. PBL coaching addresses mutual feedback and communication between tutors and students in a democratic, collaborative learning environment.

These ideas have been covered in some specific PBL approaches adopted in various institutions. However, the results and the feedback from the participants highlighted that Chinese medical tutors and administrative committees in the medical schools have not paid much attention to these points or have done so only at a superficial level. These four points are essential for supporting medical teachers' and students' personal and professional development.

The structure of the CPBL model

The CPBL model consists of the learning goals at the centre, the main activities undertaken by tutors and students, and three phases: *Preparation, Process* and *Conclusion*, which lead to the next learning cycle. We propose that dynamic, reciprocal interconnections exist among students, tutors, PBL activities and learning goals. Given the nature of these interrelationships, each phase of PBL represents opportunities for both students and tutors to develop specific learning capacities. Therefore, the model describes a structure in which students and tutors can focus their efforts on achieving learning goals through a series of learning and facilitating activities.

The learning goals include 1) lifelong learning capacities and positive learning dispositions, such as collaborative learning ability, communication skills, leadership, creativity and resilience. 2) Reasoning and problem-solving abilities that are particularly required in clinical settings, including understanding symptoms, identifying problems, managing knowledge and information from different resources, systematic investigation, and actively seeking appropriate solutions. 3) Empathy and humanistic concern that involve demonstrating a patient-centred attitude, providing professional attention, care and warmth, responding to the needs of the individual patient, being authentic and congruent in professional work, and managing communication and ethical issues with patients and their families.

The student and tutor circles are represented by broken lines that indicate that there are no barriers between students, tutors and the wider educational context. PBL activities performed by students and tutors have mutual influence on each other. The tutor circle seems to wrap the student circle, representing that a tutor should always facilitate and support the development of students while both groups aim to achieve shared learning goals. A tutor always metaphorically 'embraces' students, who are encouraged to take responsibility for and develop ownership of the PBL process.

In the Preparation phase, students and tutors need to complete necessary PBL launch tasks. This first requires the course team to redesign the PBL curriculum by radically changing the content and providing a staff development programme that introduces tutors to the messages of coaching psychology. In this phase, the tutor should initiate certain activities, including designing cases, providing a supportive learning environment, identifying and preparing necessary learning resources and technical equipment, and understanding students' level of learning and, ideally, their individual background. Student activities include developing positive attitudes and a sense of preparedness for learning, building on prior knowledge that will serve as the basis of further intellectual development, and allocating roles in learning groups.

The Process phase includes students' iterative cycle of raising and answering questions, managing resources and information, and collaborating and discussing

148 Empirical case studies

the problems. These activities should be facilitated by the tutor's appropriate scaffolding and guidance, monitoring the process towards the goals, managing group dynamics, listening to students' voices and observing students' performance. In this phase, students engage in complex learning tasks and explore their own path to solving the problems. To support students through this phase, the tutor mainly plays the role of a coach and a group facilitator. These two roles indicate the important incorporation of coaching psychology in PBL. The coach's role consists of scaffolding the learning process by using various learning materials, intentionally eliciting students' articulation of thoughts and reasoning, modelling higher-order cognitive skills, using group coaching techniques to ensure students' active participation in discussions, and linking the collective activities to the learning goals.

During the Conclusion phase, the students share their solutions; discuss their rationale and present their learning outcomes orally to teachers and other students; reflect on the new knowledge, conceptual understanding and overall learning experience; conduct peer- and self-assessment; and provide suggestions for improving the PBL curriculum in relation to the learning goals and expectations. In this phase, the tutor's role is to conduct comprehensive assessments (both summative and formative) of students' performance, provide positive and encouraging feedback, summarise the key learning points and reflect on what has been working well and what might be done differently in the future. It is important to note that although this phase starts with students' learning performance and assessment, it focuses on ongoing reflection and feedback, which are critical in shaping the future course of actions.

The features of the CPBL model

Empathy as a key learning goal

The CPBL model explicitly considers empathy and humanistic concerns as one of the learning goals in medical education. Empathy is recognised as a central element in achieving positive health care outcomes (Halpern, 2003; Hojat *et al.*, 2011) and as a professional skill that a 'good doctor' possesses (GMC, 2009). Nevertheless, the development of empathy is not explicitly included in the Chinese medical PBL curriculum. In the CPBL model, we adopt a three-factor model of medical empathy that consists of 'perspective taking', 'compassionate care' and 'standing in the patient's shoes' (Hojat *et al.*, 2011; Kataoka *et al.* 2009). We add 'skilful communication' as the fourth factor because the three factors listed above are expressed through effective communication between doctors and patients. We believe that empathy cannot be directly *taught* in the classroom. Rather, empathy could be *coached* in a learner-centred, non-didactic way. One phenomenological enquiry on empathy suggested that one way to enhance medical students' empathetic skills is to model these skills during medical school (Tavakol *et al.*, 2012). By displaying a willingness to listen, connect, care and engage in other empathetic behaviours towards students, the tutor could make coaching a role-modelling process that leads to students' awareness of building rapport with patients and satisfying their psychological and affective needs in clinical practice. In addition, students should be given time and space to observe, acquire and demonstrate an empathetic disposition.

Authentic learning experience

The CPBL model highly values and promotes an *authentic learning experience* when students enquire into problems. Authenticity is connected with its dynamic and educative character as well as its capacity to promote enquiry skills, provide a sense of freedom and form a self-directive purpose (Dewey, 1938; Rogers, 1951). In addition, the authentic problem-solving experience is embedded in meaningful contexts because real-world practice is more suffused with complex and ill-structured problems (McCaughan, 2013; Pierrakos *et al.*, 2010). The authentic experience should be defined and owned by the students themselves. The tutor could enhance this kind of experience by preparing an appropriate problem scenario, allowing students to have a voice and choice in conducting the enquiry strategically, understanding each student's learning needs, facilitating dialogues among small groups, stimulating students to integrate new learning content with previous knowledge and encouraging students to step out of their comfort zone (English & Kitsantas, 2013).

Three modes in learning-centred coaching

The CPBL model indicates a learning-centred coaching process that is similar to what Gyori (2013) called a 'three-mode process of mentorship'. It consists of bottom-up (modelling and scaffolding), lateral (collaborating and engaging) and top-down (organising and supervising) processes for sharing autonomy and participating in deep learning. Regarding the bottom-up process, the tutor needs to demonstrate how to perform clinical problem solving through behaviour modelling (Bandura, 1977) and scaffold the learning tasks to foster students' meta-cognitive capabilities. The lateral process allows co-learning between the tutor and the students to emerge organically in a highly collaborative environment. The top-down process concerns promoting students' self-directed learning to generate more questions, reach for the answers and discover the answers through a process of systematic inquiry as well as maintaining important professional standards. These three processes are interrelated in the model. For instance, when working with students, the tutor models effective collaboration and simultaneously supervises the process of collaboration in which they are participating.

Cognitive and emotional scaffolding

Scaffolding refers to the temporary support provided to learners (by another person who might be more capable) to complete a task that they would not be able

150 Empirical case studies

to complete independently and to facilitate the learners' zone of proximal development (Vygotsky, 1978). Scaffolding should be gradually withdrawn as the students become increasingly competent and responsible for their own learning (King, 1997; Wood *et al.*, 1976; van de Pol *et al.*, 2010). Cognitive and emotional scaffolding is at the heart of coaching psychology for learning (Wang, 2013). In the CPBL model, the tutor should acquire the basic attitudes, beliefs, characteristics and skills necessary for any PBL curriculum, such as supporting meta-cognitive development and strategic and reflective questioning, modulating the level of challenge of the learning to meet student requirements, and monitoring students' educational progress and group dynamics (Barrows, 1988; Barrows & Wee, 2007; Hmelo-Silver & Barrows, 2006).

From a cognitive perspective, students need to integrate, possess and apply a large amount of domain knowledge during the problem-solving process. Thus, students' cognitive loads are expected to increase over the course of PBL (Pierrakos *et al.*, 2010). Cognitive scaffolding can reduce cognitive loads by transforming difficult and complex problems into more manageable and accessible tasks, providing predictable ways to move through activity structures, restricting the options available to the learners and setting social norms for participation and the use of resources (Leinhardt & Steele, 2005; Quintana *et al.*, 2004). Moreover, the tutor uses cognitive scaffolding to help students acquire disciplinary ways of thinking and acting, support mindful and productive engagement with the learning processes, model questions that students need to be asking themselves, provide a framework for students to construct knowledge independently, offer explanations when needed, and problematise important aspects of students' work to enable them to engage with key disciplinary strategies (Collins *et al.*, 1989; Reiser, 2004; Rogoff, 1990; Veronese *et al.*, 2013). It is associated with coaching dialogues for assessing the level of students' thinking and moving it through a systematic series of questions (Pithers & Soden, 2000).

Emotional scaffolding is important for guiding students through the frustration, lack of confidence, emotional issues and teamwork problems that they might experience during PBL (Gonzales & Dejarnette, 2015). There is a focus on the nondirective facilitation of emotional scaffolding regarding self-determination and actualisation tendency (Rogers, 1942). The students involved in PBL are considered the experts on their own affective needs, and the tutor is considered an expert only on maintaining the attitudinal conditions and managing rapport in the relationship with the students, rather than an expert on the students or how the students should learn (Brodley, 1986; Pope, 1981; Zimmerman, 2000; Robinson *et al.*, 2014). Emotional scaffolding includes being a friend, a colleague, a mentor, a coach, a role model or a counsellor to the students (McLean, 2003). The tutor's responsibility is to use active and empathetic listening, understand students' available educational and social backgrounds, respect and value students' viewpoints with a non-judgemental attitude, demonstrate outstanding communication skills and hold beliefs consistent with the humanistic approach.

The tutor's role as a knowledge expert and group facilitator

This model emphasises that the tutor needs to act as a coach, playing a balanced role as an expert in both the subject matter and in facilitating students' learning process. The tutor should demonstrate social congruence to communicate informally and empathetically with students, create a learning environment that encourages the open exchange of thoughts, thus affecting group functioning and student achievement (Chng *et al.*, 2015; Schmidt & Moust, 1995; Yew & Yong, 2014). It is found that tutors with subject content expertise are more inclined to play a directive role in the tutorial process (Silver & Wilkerson, 1991). Although content experts have positive effects on student learning, it may be beneficial for these experts to develop knowledge of *when* and *how* to use this expertise to facilitate learning. Most Chinese PBL tutors are doctors or clinicians in a specific area. They are content experts in certain fields but have very limited training in educational psychology, learning facilitation and coaching psychology. Therefore, the development of a broad range of knowledge and strategies, including coaching, to stimulate student learning and encourage optimal group functioning should be a major focus of tutor recruitment and training.

Mutual feedback between the tutor and the students

The CPBL model emphasises mutual feedback between the tutor and the students. The ongoing feedback can be categorised into two types: specific feedback and general feedback. Specific feedback refers to asking clear and focused questions to prompt thinking instead of providing direct guidance or correcting errors, offering suggestions and pointing the students to a specific resource for additional information about certain concepts. This kind of feedback requires the tutor to observe students' level of understanding and respond accordingly in a student-centred environment (Ertmer & Simon, 2006; Saye & Brush, 2002). General feedback needs to be non-threatening and mastery-oriented to enhance self-directed learning, a sense of agency and ownership over learning (Greene & Azevedo, 2007; Polman, 2004). This type of feedback is provided to empower students with intellectual responsibility (Barron *et al.*, 1998) and improve their self-efficacy beliefs (Bandura, 1997). Students could evaluate the tutor's performance, but such evaluation should be carried out with caution because less experienced tutors may engage in behaviours aimed at pleasing students. Because the tutor's and the students' expectations may differ, the tutor's roles and duties must be made explicit to both parties from the outset (McLean, 2003). Feedback cannot be given without mutual trust between the tutor and the students. Therefore, it is important to establish rapport and connection at the beginning of the process and to maintain this trust throughout the PBL coaching process (Robinson *et al.*, 2014).

152 Empirical case studies

The phenomenological findings

As stated in Chapter 7, the IPA study investigated the medical teachers' and students' experiences and views of PBL coaching, using the CPBL model in their medical education and training for one semester. We identified six main themes with sub-themes that uncovered the multifaceted nature of PBL coaching (see Table 8.1). Theme 1 and Theme 2 together refer to a similar mindset shared by PBL coaching and PBL tutoring to support students' self-directed learning. Theme 3 and Theme 4 uncover the characteristics of coaching relationships between tutors and students, the learning dynamics among students themselves, and the coaching skills needed to ensure the healthy functioning of PBL groups. Theme 5 and Theme 6 address that coaching accentuates enhancing students' emotional, psychological and empathetic aspects in medical education, although it may face several practical challenges in implementation. To provide an insight into the themes, extracts were selected on the basis of being representative and interesting illustrations of each of the main themes.

Theme 1: Mindsets of coaching and learning

Students and tutors commented on their general impressions of the PBL coaching process that reflected their basic mindsets of coaching and learning. Three sub-themes became apparent: a perceived positive attitude to coaching, some resistance to change and a preference for mixing lecturing and coaching.

Table 8.1 The themes in students' and tutors' experiences of PBL coaching

Main theme	Sub-ordinate theme
1. Mindsets of coaching and learning	• Positive attitude of coaching • Resistance to change • Mixture of lecturing and coaching
2. Development of learning dispositions and capacities	• Lifelong learning dispositions • Higher-order learning capacities • Professional abilities in medical/clinical settings
3. Student group collaboration	• Group dynamics • Tutor facilitation in group work • The special role of student Chair
4. Coaching relationship	• Multi-faceted relationship • Mutual feedback
5. Personal and professional development	• Psychological health and well-being • Medical humanity and empathy • Professional identity
6. Challenges and difficulties in the implementation of CPBL model	• Limited time and resources • Ambiguous criteria of assessment • Insufficiently skilled facilitators

The tutors showed a positive attitude toward PBL coaching and most student participants seemed to embrace the idea of coaching. They agreed that instruction and guidance was essential, and that direct telling should be avoided:

This [PBL coaching] method guided students to learn actively. We emphasised inspiring and illuminating questions, and we encourage students and positively guide them to think. This is what we lack in our educational system. When I was teaching the students following a traditional method in the ward, they seemed to be lost immediately. But this year when I was coaching, I felt that the students were quite capable, completely different from the previous students. (T5)

However, there was a strong influence of traditional teaching and learning on their actual behaviours in the PBL coaching process. Some participants were familiar and comfortable with didactic lecturing and knowledge transmission. Most participants mentioned that it was difficult to change the conventional mindset immediately and that there should be a transitional period. A mixture of coaching and traditional lecture-based learning seemed to be an ideal implementation in the current PBL environment. The point is to guide the students' thinking process in a timely manner and encourage them to critically think about 'clinical facts' rather than merely transmit inert knowledge:

A senior tutor told us that talking too much or talking too little is equally inappropriate. My experience is that there should be some talking . . . I think we need to lead the thinking process. So I don't think that talking less is more. We need to talk to scaffold student thinking. Maybe I should do a bit of coaching and a bit of lecturing, trying to mix them in a way that fit the students' needs. (T4)

Theme 2: Development of learning dispositions and capacities

The students and tutors expressed that they developed a variety of learning attitudes and higher-order capacities throughout PBL coaching. These included a number of positive lifelong learning dispositions such as learning agency, self-directedness in learning, self-reliance and independence, and creativity.

When we faced a completely new case, we needed to imagine openly and bravely what kind of disease it could be from available information. It inspired us to develop imagination and creativity . . . We analysed the case little by little, and it was an exercise for our logical thinking and how to use the learned knowledge. (F4)

Most students mentioned that they developed specific intellectual and cognitive capacities such as logical thinking, critical thinking, effective use of current knowledge and information management, facilitated by PBL coaching. These learning capacities might underlie a number of distinctive higher-order learning capacities. Moreover, the students reported the development of professional skills such as clinical reasoning ability and diagnostic ability. These included critical evaluation and selection of information resources and identifying the disease mechanism based on available information.

> *When we faced a completely unfamiliar case, and we hadn't learned it before, we might generate all kinds of hypotheses ... Then the tutors would demonstrate a way of thinking, like how to search for evidence from symptoms, examinations or other information relevant to the disease. It's like teaching us how to fish rather than giving us the fish. I felt that tutors not only supported us, they gave us a model of logical thinking, which was quite important. (F6)*

The tutors resonated that information management was of critical importance to clinical criticality. Most of them thought that the provision of reliable resources for the students was mainly the tutors' responsibility. However, one tutor disagreed and held a strong opinion that students should independently search for clinical information that is relevant to problem solving. This reflected tutors' different levels of cultivating self-directedness in students.

Theme 3: Student group collaboration

The students were encouraged to attend to the collaborative process through interdependent learning within the group. The theme of student group collaboration highlights the complexity of students' teamwork in PBL coaching. Three sub-themes were identified: group dynamics, tutors' group facilitation and the special role of the student Chair.

Most participants enjoyed a sense of belongingness and relatedness in PBL groups. They gradually developed team spirit once their voice was heard, although the collaborative learning experience was not a smooth journey. The challenges were perceived as opportunities for developing interpersonal communication skills. Extroverts, such as outgoing, active students, were generally preferred in groups for initiating discussions and reinvigorating learning atmosphere by openly sharing their opinions. However, extroverts would seem to be more powerful and dominant in the group, and sometimes they overlooked the influence of their behaviour on others. An over-dominance of conversation and complex power relationships were perceived as problematic by some students. Although the students were all in their third year in medical school, majoring in clinical medicine, they exhibited individual differences in gender, educational background before university, personality traits and expertise. Students from different programmes (five-year or seven-year programme) seemed to have difficulty in forming learning alliances, which might require more balanced dynamic and mutual understanding in the team.

The tutors' coaching was found crucial in monitoring, managing and regulating the group dynamics by providing observational information and necessary intervention. When students were not aware of how their behaviours and attitudes influenced the rest of the group, the tutors would intervene in the process. Participants agreed that tutors should take less control over the flow of group discussion and allow the students to work through the process themselves. Tutors should relinquish control but continue consistent observation and monitoring.

> .*The tutor should be instructors of the field. The main discussion should be led by the students themselves, and then the students could arrange some activities around certain topics. If the discussion misses the point, or there is a big mistake in the direction, the tutors should correct the students. And the tutors should observe each student to help them or correct their mistakes. (M5)*

In each group, there was a student Chair, elected by the group members, who played a leading role in making the overall arrangements of the group work, organising the information collected and the questions generated by the members, allocating learning materials and managing the discussion process. The Chair was elected again when the second PBL scenario started. Being the student Chair was reported to be a different experience from being a group member. The Chair shouldered more responsibilities and took a more active role in collaborative learning. They demonstrated positive attitudes in terms of capacity development and knowledge building. Meanwhile, some students might feel vulnerable in taking up this role, because being the Chair indicated that the students would exert more pressure, especially when the role was not self-selected. Moreover, being the Chair indicated that the students might undertake more information management and problem-solving tasks when other group members did not complete their share of work responsibly.

Theme 4: Coaching relationship

The participants noted that a satisfactory coaching relationship was established, maintained and developed by the joint efforts of both students and tutors through-out the learning-facilitating process. The learning relationship between students and tutors was complicated and multifaceted. At the beginning, it involved a clear apprenticeship as the tutors mentored the students on the principles of the course and offered more guidance. The relationship evolved towards a more equal relationship as students increasingly became adept and self-directed learners. Tutors were not necessarily playing a more authoritative role in the coaching relationship. The quality of the tutor-student relationship seemed to play an important role in the learning process. Students' readiness and openness to coaching depended on their preference of tutors to some extent. In addition, it was suggested that particular tutors should consistently work with one group of students because the tutors and students became more familiar with each other and adapted to different learning styles and habits throughout the course.

> *The tutor's role in this course was definitely different from the role in big lectures. In lectures tutors are the main players. In this course, I think tutors were facilitators to students. Students were the learning agents. We just helped them, gave hints, and answered their questions when they didn't know. (T3)*
> *The tutors were like coaches to some extent. They would coach you what you can do, but they wouldn't tell you directly how to do it. (M6)*

The students and tutors were invited to provide feedback to each other in the last session, which was considered important for fostering the coaching relationship. The tutors sometimes gave feedback to students in the process of learning. A feedback form was designed by the administrative committee for students to provide their opinions on the overall quality of the course. However, the form was reported to be a disappointing tool. It only asked a few closed questions and listed evaluative scales. The problem of mutual feedback was constantly noted by students and tutors. It was suggested that there was a need for a more effective and authentic form of feedback.

Theme 5: Personal and professional development

This theme centred on the development of the learner as a whole person, which involved students' psychological well-being, education in medical humanity and empathy, and the continued cultivation of professional identities for both students and tutors. The tutors provided students with emotional scaffolding by understanding their personal learning styles, creating a harmonious and engaging learning atmosphere, and demonstrating warm regard towards individual students.

> *I felt supportive in coaching . . . it was psychologically safe and open for me to discuss issues, not only the medical problems but also my own problems with understanding certain knowledge or with presentations in public. (F1)*

The enhancement of psychological health and well-being was mostly achieved by tutors' attentive listening, open questioning, motivational interviewing, using humour and other coaching skills. Interestingly, one tutor coached the students with stress management skills and helped them to be psychologically resilient and better prepared for their medical career.

> *I sometimes tell [the students] my experience of coping with stress, like relaxation skills, thinking things in a brighter way . . . As you know, working as a doctor is a huge pressure. We are responsible for the patients, and we are responsible for many other people, and ourselves . . . We are very, very busy people. When I am working in the ward, I cannot find time even for drinking*

water or going to toilet . . . Anyway, I tell the students what they will face when they become real doctors, and how to deal with the difficulties using my own experiences. I don't want them to be afraid . . . And coaching the students how to cope with stress is not something we usually do in PBL. (T4)

The majority of respondents noted that there was a stronger sense of medical humanity and empathy in PBL coaching. The tutors modelled interpersonal communication skills and demonstrated humanistic concerns in clinical practice, which greatly helped the students to develop an awareness of humanistic consideration, empathy, sensitivity to clinical issues and a holistic view of patients.

In one case, the doctors went to the patient's home to observe his living environment. It was one part of collecting the disease history. The tutors told us that doctors are not machines to offer treatment. We need to communicate with patients and attend to their life. We should consider individual patient's condition more holistically. What we are facing is not a pile of physical examination results and papers, but a real patient, a human being. We should pay attention to him or her as a whole person. I felt humanistic consideration and empathy were really important throughout coaching. (F7)

The students reported that they were connected with an authentic sense of professional identity. It related to their deepened understanding of what kind of doctors they would become and what they could contribute to the clinical environment. Role playing was considered a powerful coaching method for fostering professional identity.

Role playing was very useful. I had this idea spontaneously. You let the students take a real doctor's role and they became immediately engaged and had very strong motivation. They hope to be young doctors who can help their friends, families and other people . . . And you encourage them to be real doctors in the future to treat diseases described in the cases and help patients to relieve the pain. They felt like really adopting their roles as doctors. Becoming good doctors takes generations after generations. I hope they would do a better job than us. (T4)

Theme 6: Challenges and difficulties in the implementation of the CPBL model

A number of barriers to implementing the CPBL model in the current medical educational setting were noted by the participants. The most frequent ones included limited time and resources, ambiguous assessment criteria of and insufficiently skilled facilitators. Most participants were concerned that PBL coaching might take up too much time in training and preparation. In order to implement the CPBL model successfully, medical teachers need to receive systematic training on

158 Empirical case studies

PBL coaching, which normally takes one to two weeks. Another main challenge was that the assessment criteria for both student attainment and tutor effectiveness were unclear.

> *It seemed that there was no criteria of how we did in coaching: whether we were good coaches or not; whether we were coaching students in the right way. We need more professional guidance and evaluation in coaching. (T4)*

The students were also not sure how they would be assessed in terms of learning. Most of them wanted to know the specific criteria for each aspect (e.g., exam scores, learning capacity, learning disposition) so that they would know where to improve themselves. However, one student claimed that knowing the assessment criteria at the beginning of the course might endanger their intrinsic motivation in learning. Finally, the tutors recognised that coaching was a potentially effective facilitation paradigm but that their coaching skills seemed to be inadequate. Deciding when to intervene was perceived as a common difficulty. Sufficient training in coaching and more experience were suggested in order to enhance the quality of intervention.

Synthesised discussion

In this section, I synthesise the model and the themes to address considerable similarities between PBL coaching and PBL tutoring as well as the particular contributions that coaching makes to the existing PBL curriculum.

Coaching to support student self-directed and self-regulated learning

It is apparent in participants' comments that PBL coaching, like PBL tutoring, aims to foster students' capacity for self-directed and self-regulated learning. One of the distinguishing features and attractions of PBL in medical education is the potential to foster self-directed learning as a lifelong habit (Hmelo-Silver, 2000, 2004; Levett-Jones, 2005). In order for the student-centred approach to be realised, students must make the shift to their new roles as active learners and develop self-regulation and self-discipline in learning. This notion is reflected in the theory of andragogy (Knowles, 1970; Knowles *et al.*, 1998) that adult learners are self-directed and goal-oriented. In PBL, students become responsible for their own learning, which necessitates reflective, critical thinking about what is being learned (Bereiter & Scardamalia, 1989). Self-directed and self-regulated learning is commonly associated with intrinsic motivation, which occurs when students work on a task motivated by their own interest, challenges and sense of satisfaction, and when their needs of autonomy, competence and relatedness are met (Zimmerman, 2002). We found that students could perform extrinsically motivated actions with an attitude of willingness that reflected an inner acceptance of the value or utility of tasks. Thus two kinds of motivation are also important for self-directed and self-regulated learning on two external regulatory levels: identified regulation and integrated regulation (Ryan & Deci, 2000). When students consciously value learning actions as having personal importance (e.g., engaging in collaborative discussion was important for a sense of belongingness to the team), they identify and internalise views of others in relation to the actions. Where learning actions are congruent with students' identities and synthesised with the self (e.g., the professional identity of being a good doctor), then the actions are regulated in an integrated way. These two kinds of actions are still viewed as extrinsically motivated because they are performed to achieve particular outcomes rather than because they are experienced as inherently interesting and enjoyable. However, we consider that these two types of motivation may be more pervasive than 'purely' intrinsic motivation in formal educational settings as students are required to achieve certain learning outcomes evaluated by various forms of assessment, whether formative or summative. As Evensen (2000) proposed, self-directed learning may be an individual characteristic that changes over time, for better or worse. The point here is that a coaching approach can potentially foster identified and integrated motivations, internalise the responsibility and sense of value for extrinsic goals as well as intrinsic motivation in order to catalyse students' self-directedness and self-determination in learning. Tutors can provide intentional support by consciously cultivating behaviours, goals, beliefs and strategies that lead to self-directed and self-regulated learning and by establishing a dynamic, reciprocal coaching relationship with students.

The coaching relationship between the tutor and learners

The dynamics of the coaching relationship may be different from the overtly hierarchical relationship that is frequently associated with teaching or lecturing in clinical settings. The coaching process is co-created moment by moment as the tutor and students work together in a supportive manner and style of communication (Whitmore, 2009). There is a gradual transition towards the coaching relationship, as noted in the study. At the beginning, the tutor takes a leading role in launching the problem and offers more direct guidance, then provides ongoing monitoring and observation of guided collaborative inquiries and solution creation in student groups. Finally, the tutor carefully reduces the amount of direction as the students become more experienced learners. In this aspect, PBL coaching may not be significantly different from PBL tutoring, where the tutor also provides students with appropriate structure, scaffolding and guidance, so that students simultaneously begin to develop self-directed and self-regulated learning skills and knowledge construction through problem solving. Where PBL coaching might differ from PBL tutoring is that coaching expressively stresses the quality of the coaching relationship between students and tutors, interpersonal communication ability and the personal qualities of coaches (Wang *et al.*, 2016). How students perceive the quality of the relationships with their tutors could determine whether

160 Empirical case studies

they feel sufficiently open to the challenges in PBL. The tutor's interpersonal communication skills are a critical element in managing group dynamics and modelling effective interactions for students, which may be contrary to the findings of Van Berkel & Dolmans' (2006) study that the tutor's interpersonal behaviour and stimulation of contextual learning did not significantly contribute to better group functioning. The tutor's personality, friendliness, approachability and social congruence are also essential in forming a learning partnership in PBL coaching. This is related to the notion of genuineness, congruence or authenticity from a humanistic perspective of coaching (Stober, 2006). Nonetheless, the limited ability of the tutor, steeped in the traditionalist epistemology, in fully understanding the change in role from lecturers to coaches could create an authority–dependency situation (Olmesdahl & Manning, 1999). This issue was confirmed by some student participants who demonstrated an over-reliance on direct guidance in our study. The extent to which the tutor could make the role transition becomes a major factor in successful PBL coaching. PBL coaching requires adequate student and tutor preparedness with a balance of learner- and tutor-directed learning: not only the tutor should be trained to put on a 'coach's hat', but students should also be suitably induced into the PBL coaching process and told what they are expected to get from the coaching experience.

Facilitative skills used in PBL coaching

Due to the complex and multi-skilled nature of PBL coaching, some tutors may not be sure how to determine the appropriate time to intervene and how to achieve the balance between too much and too little structure with each unique PBL group. Successful PBL coaching is largely dependent on the availability and skills of tutors who know when and how to adopt facilitative skills and strategies. The desirable attributes, skills and strategies commonly used in personal and professional coaching are also applicable to PBL. On the other hand, PBL coaching requires a number of the basic facilitative skills required in PBL tutoring, including scaffolding knowledge construction, supporting meta-cognitive development, using well-designed open-ended and reflective questions to help students make their thinking visible, modulating the challenge of the learning to meet students' requirements, and monitor ing students' progress and group dynamics (Schmidt & Moust, 1995). The tutors could mainly take a wandering facilitation mode (Hmelo-Silver, 2000). They move from group to group, adjusting the time spent with each group in the classroom according to students' needs, dynamically assessing the progress of each group and readjusting their facilitation efforts accordingly. Like PBL tutoring, PBL coaching also requires the facilitators to ensure that all students are involved in the discussion and exercise distributed expertise (Pea, 1993; Salomon, 1993). As the students divide up the learning issues, they are able to learn to become 'experts' in particular topics and bring the results together, so that the whole group can tackle problems that are normally considered too difficult for each student alone. The difference is that in PBL tutoring, expert information and guidance are offered directly to the learners through conversations or explanations of the reasoning processes (Hmelo-Silver, 2004), whereas PBL coaching greatly emphasises indirect facilitation and passing the responsibility to students themselves, and encourages the student Chair to take the leading role in each group. The Chair develops facilitative skills during the course, just like the tutors, because they function as 'junior coaches'. Once they have consulted with the tutors, the Chair assigns distinct roles to group members, such as formulating problems, summarising information, discussing results and relating predictions to theories, in order to ensure that all group members are cognitively and emotionally engaged rather than merely talking together.

Addressing emotional, psychological and empathetic aspects in medical education

Coaching psychology contributes to the PBL process by accentuating that learners' cognitive, affective, psychological, relational and social needs should be appropriately addressed and supported with appreciation, facilitation and positive regard in their own learning contexts. According to many PBL instructional documents across a variety of contexts, PBL emphasises the importance of understanding content, disciplinary epistemologies and investigative strategies, the nature of scientific research, and the practices involved (see Barrows, 2000; Hmelo-Silver, 2004; Hmelo-Silver *et al.*, 2007). PBL tutoring therefore is primarily designed to fulfil these learning goals and it is centred on facilitating the cognitive process in student learning. However, the existing literature on PBL has largely neglected the emotional, motivational and psychological aspects of PBL (Bowman & Hughes, 2005). Strong psychological and interpersonal support is especially needed within the particular context of the Chinese medical working environment. Medical workers, including clinicians, nurses, social workers and other staff in the hospital, are generally under enormous pressure and work to very intense schedules. They need to deal with various emergencies and face urgent problem-solving situations during the day. The presence of burnout, depression and stress has been shown to be related to the fundamental attributes of medical professionalism (Tavakol *et al.*, 2012; West, 2012). Therefore the promotion of psychological health and well-being is crucial for their personal health, professional performance and optimal functioning. PBL coaching explicitly involves promoting medical humanity, cultivating empathetic dispositions, enhancing psychological health and well-being and fostering a strong career identity with higher self-respect. This study provided empirical evidence that PBL tutors could be 'personal coaches' to individual students when necessary, embracing students' distinctive emotional, motivational, psychological and social needs in addition to the cognitive needs that are usually involved in PBL tutoring. The coaching can be conducted by setting up a well-structured learning environment, employing empathetic listening skills and a positive attitude towards individual students, mentoring stress management skills and role modelling experiential learning.

Empathy is increasingly understood to be fundamental to effective medical education and the foundation of the patient–doctor relationship (Burks & Kobus, 2012; Rosenow, 2000). Empathy is considered an innate ability that can be cultivated, practised and perfected in coaching, counselling and psychotherapy literature (Allan & Whybrow, 2007; Joseph, 2006; Stober, 2006; Palmer & Whybrow, 2006; Wang, 2013). Although PBL tutoring involves communication skills training to a basic extent, it has been mainly regarded as a way of providing better cognitive scaffolding, rather than an essential ingredient for developing and sustaining therapeutic doctor–patient relationships (Hojat, 2007) and the interdependent quality of a competent clinical practitioner (Grosseman *et al.*, 2014). In PBL coaching, the tutor needs to take an empathetic position in tutor–student interactions and becomes the role model in approaching clinical situations with compassionate reasoning. PBL coaching is potentially a powerful pedagogical approach for students to experience, observe, imagine and reflect on medical empathy. They can assimilate the empathetic skills into their repertoire and then transfer these skills into other contexts of learning and future clinical practice.

In addition, it seems that there may be more tolerance of errors in PBL coaching. Chi *et al.* (1994) suggested that errors are a necessary step in learning to apply new knowledge. An ancient Chinese saying indicates that 'failure bears success just like the mother bears a child'. However, in traditional Chinese education, making mistakes in the classroom is regarded as embarrassing and humiliating for both students and teachers. Chinese PBL tutors may still try to guide students to find the right solutions straightforwardly and discreetly avoid making mistakes themselves. In contrast, PBL coaching creates a more flexible, secure and friendly learning environment where students and tutors are allowed to acknowledge that they do not know all the answers, embrace mistakes that they make and clarify any interpersonal misunderstanding. By articulating incorrect knowledge and sharing the lessons learned from these mistakes, students have the opportunity to revise their false beliefs, foster correct knowledge and play with new ideas. Moreover, by openly recognising their vulnerability, students and the tutor can deepen the trust and rapport between them, which in turn helps to create an empathetic and nurturing atmosphere of learning.

The challenges of PBL coaching

PBL coaching has implications on three levels. For PBL tutor recruitment, training and continuous professional development, it seems to be desirable to include and strengthen coaching psychology, such as person-centred, cognitive behavioural or narrative approaches. From a PBL facilitation perspective, tutors need to intentionally and flexibly incorporate a range of coaching skills, strategies and models into their practices with the purpose of supporting students in a holistic way. At the level of educational administration, it is important to provide sufficient learning resources and financial support, train more qualified tutors, and allow adequate time for completion.

PBL coaching has met practical obstacles and challenges in its implementation in real medical education settings. Although participants felt confident in the successful implementation of the model, incorporating it into the existing medical educational system is a big challenge that correlates, to some extent, with reported difficulties (e.g., too time-consuming, lack of staff, students might feel compulsion) in implementing PBL in Asian countries (Jiang *et al.*, 2005; Hao *et al.*, 2005). Additional challenges in the implementation include 1) building a solid knowledge base of coaching psychology, PBL and clinical practice; 2) creating a nurturing and supporting culture using coaching principles; and 3) enhancing students' self-directed learning and teachers' continuous professional development using coaching strategies. Implementing the CPBL model could be a daunting task requiring strong support from academic administrators, well-trained and committed tutors, skilful and dedicated problem case writers, appropriate technical support and well-prepared students with a belief in the PBL and coaching philosophy.

The alignment between learning activities and assessments is crucial for participation in PBL (Hickey & Zuicker, 2005). Whether the fusion of coaching psychology and PBL is effective is a big question, and we need to find evidence from various aspects to view the whole picture. The learning dispositions, reasoning and problem-solving skills and empathy that we expect students to develop are long-term learning goals and very difficult to measure precisely after only one semester's intervention. Therefore, obtaining academic or attainment results in the traditional sense is not applicable, and simple quantitative measurements could be flawed. We propose a mixed-method approach to evaluation that comprises both quantitative (e.g., various learning outcomes) and qualitative data (e.g., classroom observations, interviews, peer assessment, narratives and learning portfolios) to give a comprehensive picture of the effectiveness of PBL coaching.

Summary

This chapter provides a rich description of the development and implication of a new pedagogical framework, i.e., the CPBL model, using the methodologies that have been described in the previous chapter. The model explicitly addresses empathy and medical humanity as key learning goals in medical education, the tutor's role as a knowledge expert and a learning coach for the students, cognitive and emotional scaffolding strongly grounded in psychological theories and effective mutual feedback between the tutor and students. Medical students' and tutors' experiences and perspectives have revealed that PBL coaching, as a systematic facilitative method, offers opportunities for students and tutors to become reflective co-learners and flexible thinkers. PBL coaching empowers medical students to consider how they would use constructed knowledge and specific learning dispositions in real clinical cases through using self-directed and collaborative learning skills. Although PBL coaching has a significant overlap with PBL tutoring, it has the advantage of suggesting a method to address medical humanity and

164   Empirical case studies

empathy, attend to effective communication in clinical environment, enhance psychological well-being and foster professional identities of medical students in a more sensitive, comprehensive and professional way.

The investigations into coaching psychology and medical PBL are useful in two ways. First, the study could serve to stimulate consideration and debate as institutions develop their own PBL concepts and procedures. Second, the study provides insights into incorporating coaching skills into professional development programmes for PBL tutors and PBL curricula for students. A future research agenda of PBL coaching may be examining tutors' facilitation more carefully and how the elements of coaching can be tailored to different goals, local contexts and developmental levels of learners. There is a great need for evidence-based instructional strategies with which medical educators could make informed choices in adapting coaching to their particular PBL approaches.

In the next chapter, I shall bring the two empirical studies together and propose a unified psychological model of coaching psychology for learning, with a focus on coach–learner responsibilities, relationships and interactions.

Recommended reading

Barrows, H. S., & Wee, K. N. L. (2007). *Principles and practice of PBL*. Singapore: Pearson Prentice Hall.

Evenson, D. H., & Hmelo-Silver, C. E. (2000). *Problem-based learning: A research perspective on learning interactions*. Mahwah, NJ: Lawrence Erlbaum Associates.

Rogoff, B. (1990). *Apprenticeship in thinking: Cognitive development in social context*. New York: Oxford University Press.

Key points for reflection

- What are the key elements of the CPBL model?
- How is CPBL different from other problem-based learning approaches?
- What are the key learning/facilitating processes of CPBL?
- Who are involved in CPBL and what is the nature of their relationships?

References

Allan, J., & Whybrow, A. (2007). Gestalt coaching. In S. Palmer & A. Whybrow (Eds), *Handbook of coaching psychology: a guide for practitioners* (pp. 133–159). London: Routledge.

Bandura, A. (1977). *Social learning theory.* New York: General Learning Press.

Bandura, A. (1997). *Self-efficacy: The exercise of control.* New York: Freeman.

Barron, B. J. S., Schwartz, D. L., Vye, N. J., Moore, A., Petrosino, A., Zech, L., & Bransford, J. D. (1998). Doing with understanding: lessons from research on problem- and project-based learning. *Journal of the Learning Sciences, 7*(3/4), 271–311.

Barrows, H. S. (1988). *The tutorial process.* Springfield, IL: Southern Illinois University School of Medicine.

Barrows, H. S. (2000). *Problem-based learning applied to medical education.* Springfield: Southern Illinois University Press.

Barrows, H. S., & Wee, K. N. L. (2007). *Principles and practice of PBL.* Singapore: Pearson Prentice Hall.

Bereiter, C., & Scardamalia, M. (1989). Intentional learning as a goal of instruction. In L. B. Resnick (Ed.), *Knowing, learning, and instruction: essays in honor of Robert Glaser* (pp. 361–392). Hillsdale, NJ: Erlbaum.

Bowman, D., & Hughes, P. (2005). Emotional responses of tutors and students in problem-based learning: lessons for staff development. *Medical Education, 39*(2), 145–53.

Brodley, B. T. (1986). *Client-centered therapy – What is it? What is it not?* Paper presented at the First Annual Meeting of the Association for the Development of the Person-Centered Approach.

Burks, D. J., & Kobus, A. M. (2012). The legacy of altruism in health care: the promotion of empathy, prosociality and humanism. *Medical Education, 46*(3), 317–25.

Chi, M. T. H., DeLeeuw, N., Chiu, M., & LaVancher, C. (1994). Eliciting self-explanations improves understanding. *Cognitive Science, 18*, 439–477.

Chng, E., Yew, E. H. J., & Schmidt, H. G. (2015). To what extent do tutor-related behaviours influence student learning in PBL? *Advances in Health Sciences Education, 20*(1), 5–21.

Collins, A., Brown, J. S., & Newman, S. E. (Eds.). (1989). *Cognitive apprenticeship: Teaching the crafts of reading, writing and mathematics.* Hillsdale, NJ: Lawrence Erlbaum Associates.

Dewey, J. (1938). *Experience and education.* New York: Simon & Schuster.

English, M. C., & Kitsantas, A. (2013). Supporting student self-regulated learning in problem-and project-based learning. *Interdisciplinary Journal of Problem-based Learning, 7*(2), 128–150.

Ertmer, P. A, & Simon, K. D. (2006). Jumping the PBL implementation hurdle: supporting the efforts of K–12 teachers. *Interdisciplinary Journal of Problem-based Learning, 1*(1), 40–54.

Evenson, D. H., & Hmelo-Silver, C. E. (2000). *Problem-based learning: A research perspective on learning interactions.* Mahwah, NJ: Lawrence Erlbaum Associates.

General Medical Council. (2009). *Medical students: professional values and fitness to practise.* London: GMC.

Gonzalez, G., & Dejarnette, A. F. (2015). Teachers' and students' negotiation moves when teachers scaffold group work. *Cognition & Instruction, 33*(1), 1–45.

Greene, J. A., & Azevedo, R. (2007). A theoretical review of Winne and Hadwin's model of self-regulated learning: new perspectives and directions. *Review of Educational Research, 77*(3), 334–372.

Grosseman, S., Hojat, M., Duke, P. M., Mennin, S., & Rosenzweig, S. (2014). Empathy, self-reflection, and curriculum choice. *Interdisciplinary Journal of Problem-based Learning, 8*(2).

Gyori, B. (2013). Mentorship modes: strategies for influencing interactive learners. *Interdisciplinary Journal of Problem-based Learning, 7*(1), 173–185.

Halpern, J. (2003). What is clinical empathy? *Journal of General Internal Medicine, 18*, 670–674.

Hao, X., Jin, G., Ma, Y., & Cui, M. (2005). Attempts at PBL in clinical teaching. *Advances in Science Education, 3*, 113–114.

Hickey, D. T., & Zuiker, S. J. (2005). Engaged participation: a sociocultural model of motivation with implications for assessment. *Educational Assessment, 10*(3), 277–305.

Hmelo-Silver, C. E. (2000). Knowledge recycling: crisscrossing the landscape of educational psychology in a problem-based learning course for preservice teachers. *Journal on Excellence in College Teaching, 11*, 41–56.

Hmelo-Silver, C. E. (2004). Problem-based learning: what and how do students learn?. *Educational Psychology Review, 16*(3), 235–266.

Hmelo-Silver, C. E., & Barrows, H. S. (2006). Goals and strategies of a problem-based learning facilitator. *Interdisciplinary Journal of Problem-based Learning, 1*(1), 21–39.

Hmelo-Silver, C. E., Duncan, R. G., & Chinn, C. A. (2007). Scaffolding and achievement in problem-based and inquiry learning: a response to Kirschner, Sweller, and Clark (2006). *Educational Psychologist, 42*(2), 99–107.

Hojat, M. (2007). *Empathy in patient care: antecedents, development, measurement, and outcomes.* New York: Springer Verlag.

Hojat, M., Louis, D., Markham, F., Wender, R., Rabinowitz, C., & Gonnella, J. (2011). Physicians' empathy and clinical outcomes for diabetic patients. *Academic Medicine, 86*(3), 359–364.

Jiang, P., Yang, Z., Shang, Q., & Guo, D. (2005). Applied analysis of PBL learning patterns in higher medical education reform. *China Journal of Traditional Chinese Medicine, 15*(3), 104–105.

Joseph, S. (2006). Person-centred coaching psychology: A meta-theoretical perspective. *International Coaching Psychology Review, 1*(1), 47–54.

Kataoka, H. U., Koide, N., Ochi, K., Hojat, M., & Gonnella, J. S. (2009). Measurement of empathy among Japanese medical students: psychometrics and score differences by gender and level of medical education. *Academic Medicine Journal of the Association of American Medical Colleges, 84*(9), 1192–1197.

King, A. (1997). Ask to think-tell why: a model of transactive peer tutoring for scaffolding higher level complex learning. *Educational Psychologist, 32*(4), 221–235.

Knowles, M. S. (1970). *The modern practice of adult education: Andragogy versus pedagogy.* New York: Association Press.

Knowles, M. S., Holton, E. F., & Swanson, R. A. (1998). *The adult learner* (5th Ed.). Houston, TX: Gulf Publishing Company.

Leinhardt, G., & Steele, M. D. (2005). Seeing the complexity of standing to the side: Instructional dialogues. *Cognition and Instruction, 23*, 87–163.

Levett-Jones, T. L. (2005). Self-directed learning: implications and limitations for undergraduate nursing education. *Nurse Education Today, 25*(5), 363–368.

McCaughan, K. (2013). Barrows' integration of cognitive and clinical psychology in PBL tutor guidelines. *Interdisciplinary Journal of Problem-based Learning, 7*(1), 11–23.

McLean, M. (2003). What can we learn from facilitator and student perceptions of facilitation skills and roles in the first year of a problem-based learning curriculum?. *BMC Medical Education, 3*(9), 1–10.

Olmesdahl, P. J., & Manning, D. M. (1999). Impact of training on PBL tutors. *Medical Education, 33*, 753–755.

Palmer, S., & Whybrow, A. (2006). The coaching psychology movement and its development within the British Psychological Society. *International Coaching Psychology Review, 1*(1), 5–11.

Pea, R. D. (1993). Practices of distributed intelligence and designs for education. In G. Salomon & D. Perkins (Eds), *Distributed cognitions: Psychological and educational considerations* (pp. 47–87). New York: Cambridge University Press.

Pierrakos, O., Zilberberg, A., & Anderson, R. (2010). Understanding undergraduate research experiences through the lens of problem-based learning: implications for curriculum translation. *Interdisciplinary Journal of Problem-based Learning, 4*(2), 35–62.

Pithers, R.T., & Soden, R. (2000). Critical thinking in education: a review. *Educational Research, 42*(3), 237–249.

Polman, J. L. (2004). Dialogic activity structures for project-based learning environments. *Cognition & Instruction, 22*(4), 431–466.

Pope, M. L., & Keen, T. (1981). *Personal construct psychology and education.* London: Academic Press.

Quintana, C., Reiser, B. J., Davis, E. A., Krajcik, J., Fretz, E., & Duncan, R. G., . . . Soloway, E. (2004). A scaffolding design framework for software to support science inquiry. *Journal of the Learning Sciences, 13*(3), 337–386.

Reiser, B. J. (2004). Scaffolding complex learning: the mechanisms of structuring and problematizing student work. *Journal of the Learning Sciences, 13*(3), 273–304.

Robinson, L., Harris, A., & Burton, R. (2014). Saving face: managing rapport in a problem-based learning group. *Active Learning in Higher Education, 16*(1), 11–24.

Rogers, C. G. (1942). *Counseling and psychotherapy.* Boston: Houghton Mifflin.

Rogers, C. G. (1951). *Client-centered therapy.* Boston: Houghton Mifflin.

Rogoff, B. (1990). *Apprenticeship in thinking: Cognitive development in social context.* New York: Oxford University Press.

Rosenow, E. C. (2000). Recertifying in the art of medicine: what I would tell young physicians. *Mayo Clinic Proceedings, 75*, 865–868.

Ryan, R. M., & Deci, E. L. (2000). Self-determination theory and the facilitation of intrinsic motivation, social development, and well-being. *American Psychologist, 55*(1), 68–72.

Salomon, G. (1993). No distribution without individual cognition: a dynamic interactional view. In G. Salomon & D. Perkins (Eds), *Distributed cognitions: psychological and educational considerations* (pp. 111–138). New York: Cambridge University Press.

Saye, J. W., & Brush, T. (2002). Scaffolding critical reasoning about history and social issues in multimedia-supported learning environments. *Educational Technology Research & Development, 50*(3), 77–96.

Schmidt, H. G., & Moust, J. H. (1995). What makes a tutor effective? a structural-equations modeling approach to learning in problem-based curricula. *Academic Medicine Journal of the Association of American Medical Colleges, 70*(8), 708–714.

Silver, M., & Wilkerson, L. A. (1991). Effects of tutors with subject expertise on the problem-based tutorial process. *Academic Medicine Journal of the Association of American Medical Colleges, 66*(5), 298–300.

Stober, D. R. (2006). Coaching from the humanistic perspective. In D. R. Stober & A. M. Grant (Eds.), *Evidence-based coaching handbook: putting best practices to work for your clients* (pp. 17–50). Hoboken, NJ: John Wiley & Sons.

Tavakol, S., Dennick, R., & Tavakol, M. (2012). Medical students' understanding of empathy: a phenomenological study. *Medical Education, 46*(3), 306–316.

Van Berkel, H. J., & Dolmans, D. H. (2006). The influence of tutoring competencies on problems, group functioning and student achievement in problem-based learning. *Medical Education, 40*(8), 730–6.

Van de Pol. J., Volman, M., & Beishuizen, J. (2010). Scaffolding in teacher–student interaction: a decade of research. *Educational Psychology Review, 22*(3), 271–296.

Veronese, C., Richards, J. B., Pernar, L., Sullivan, A. M., & Schwartzstein, R. M. (2013). A randomized pilot study of the use of concept maps to enhance problem-based learning among first-year medical students. *Medical Teacher, 35*(9), 1478–1484.

168 Empirical case studies

Vygotsky, L. S. (1978). *Mind in society*. London: Harvard University Press.

Wang, Q. (2013). Towards a systems model of coaching for learning: Empirical lessons from the secondary classroom context. *International Coaching Psychology Review, 8*(1), 35–53.

Wang, Q., Li, H., Pang, W., Liang, S., & Su, Y. (2016). Developing an integrated framework of problem-based learning and coaching psychology for medical education: a participatory research. *BMC Medical Education, 16*(1), 2.

West, C. P. (2012). Empathy, distress and a new understanding of doctor professionalism. *Medical Education, 46*(3), 238–244.

Whitmore, J. (2009). *Coaching for performance: growing people, performance and purpose* (4th Ed). London: Nicholas Brealey.

Wood, D., Bruner, J. S., & Ross, G. (1976). The role of tutoring in problem solving. *Journal of Child Psychology & Psychiatry & Allied Disciplines, 17*(2), 89–100.

Yew, E. H. J., & Yong, J. J. Y. (2014). Student perceptions of facilitators' social congruence, use of expertise and cognitive congruence in problem-based learning. *Instructional Science, 42*(5), 795–815.

Zimmerman, B. J. (2000). Attaining self-regulation: A social cognitive perspective. In M. Boekaerts, P. Pintrich, & M. Zeidner (Eds), *Handbook of self-regulation.* San Diego Academic Press.

Zimmerman, B. J. (2002). Becoming a self-regulated learner: an overview. *Theory Into Practice, 41*(2), 64–70.

Part 3

Towards a systems approach of educational coaching

This part pulls my reflections and thoughts together. It opens with an exploration into the nature of coaching psychology for learning in the domain of education, including the context, purpose, processes, people and their interactive relations. You will read about:

- The definition and psychological requisition of educational coaching.
- The relational aspect of educational coaching that explicitly demonstrates the connections between the coach and the learner when they travel through a series of learning cycles.
- The discursive aspects of educational coaching – what kind of language do we need to adopt when we talk about learning and learning facilitation?
- Reflections on how we can understand educational coaching philosophically, theoretically and pedagogically.
- Reflections on how we could conduct empirical research into educational coaching, including the research paradigm, methodologies and several practical issues.
- Reflections on the implementation and evaluative issues of educational coaching with different populations and purposes in different contexts.
- Future research and application directions of educational coaching, and a sincere invitation to continuous co-exploration.

Chapter 9

The relational and discursive aspects of educational coaching

Introduction

This chapter focuses on the integrated psychological model and language framework of coaching psychology for learning in order to scrutinise its relational and discursive aspects. Drawn from the empirical evidence and psychological theories of interpersonal relationships, the psychological model demonstrates a co-learning process between coach and learner. Moreover, the language framework underlines the importance of developing dialogues in this process and ensuring the learner's deep engagement.

The definition of educational coaching

The concept of 'educational coaching' emerges from the exploration that focuses on facilitating the growth and development of individuals in formal education. Educational coaching is the application of coaching psychology for learning. It can be defined as a designed conversation that focuses on the enhancement of self-directed learning, development and growth through increasing self-awareness and personal responsibility, using questioning, active listening, and appropriate challenge in a supportive and encouraging manner. Educational coaching is a relatively young field and it needs a growing evidence base to support this area of work. Educational coaching may entail different philosophies, psychological theories, methods and approaches, and expected effectiveness from that of executive coaching, life coaching or any other applied domains of coaching.

The psychological prerequisites to educational coaching

It is widely accepted that coach and learner have important physiological and psychological needs that are prerequisites to effective coaching. Maslow's (1954) hierarchy of human needs indicates that any intensive learning activity requires the fulfilment of a whole range of basic physiological and psychological needs. Educational coaching addresses the highest level of self-actualisation because

172 Towards a systems approach

coaching serves the need of self-fulfilment through achieving one's full potential, creative activities, learning and development. This level becomes the priority only after the physiological needs, safety needs, social needs and esteem needs have been sufficiently met and maintained. Another perspective of psychological prerequisites refers to the values that coach and learner hold. Egan (2002) provided four key values: respect as a foundation value; empathy as a primary orientation value; genuineness as a professional value; and empowerment as an outcome value. These values are helpful to guide coaches' ethical practice and clarify professional boundaries.

In Table 9.1, I offer a number of basic psychological prerequisites that people need to meet before embarking on educational coaching.

These psychological conditions can be established in social relationships like teacher–student relationships, manager–employee relationships or peer relationships. Generally, whatever is established, reinforced, supported or accepted by

Table 9.1 Psychological prerequisites of educational coaching

Psychological prerequisites for learner	*Psychological prerequisites for coach*
Feel physically and emotionally safe. Understand common humanity as well as diversity and individuality.	
Have a sense of acceptance and belongingness in a positive relationship. Address equality and democracy as integral to the coaching for learning process.	
Have a positive sense of 'self' as a learner. Willing to learn, grow and change with the facilitation of the coach.	Have a positive sense of 'self' as a facilitator as well as a learner. Willing to grow and change with the person being coached.
Have a sense of responsibility that 'it is MY learning'. Feel empowered as a learner.	Have a sense of responsibility for empowering learners ('it is YOUR learning') rather than taking responsibility for them.
Accept responsibility for making choices and have an ownership of learning.	Accept responsibility for making choices and have an ownership of coaching.
Take on and share challenging and approachable co-learning tasks.	
Acknowledge that learning needs lots of practice, involving making mistakes, taking risks and accepting ambiguity and uncertainty. View problematic situations as opportunities to uncover potential.	
Discover that learning can be enjoyable as well as difficult. Willing to work in 'the stretch zone' rather than stay in 'the comfort zone'.	
Value constructive feedback and dialogue.	
Acknowledge that learning is a socially mediated, interactive process.	
Identify the goal of educational coaching as empowerment, increased awareness and the continued capacity for growth.	

both coach and learner determines the kind of relationship the learner affiliates themselves with.

Nonetheless, the fulfilment of these needs cannot always be guaranteed. We should acknowledge that it is almost impossible to ask coach or learner to be 'fully equipped' with these psychological preparations in advance. Coach and learner may extend their existing needs to higher levels throughout the coaching process. For instance, at the beginning a learner may engage in activities to get the coach's attention with some approval-seeking behaviours. In a sense, the learner needs to feel a certain recognition and acknowledgement from the coach, and develops an emotional and social connection with the coach. When the coaching process develops further, and the learner's need for belonging and acceptance by the coach is sufficiently met, the learner may evolve into a more mature and active role in the coaching relationship. It is also possible that a learner at any time may regress back to any point in the hierarchy structure that Maslow addressed. Any shift in the learner's priorities would likely impact the whole coaching process. Moreover, these prerequisites are not meant to imply that all coaches and learners have exactly the same needs. The prerequisites are experienced at different depths depending on individual living and learning experiences. Therefore, the coach should exercise his or her professional sensitivity in order to respond to different levels of learner needs in different circumstances.

The relational aspect of educational coaching

In this section, I elaborate on the relational aspect between coach and learner by modelling the psychological process. The experiences, feedback and analysis of a series of coaching activities in my studies, in combination with participatory prototyping and psychological principles of learning, have led to the construction of an integrated psychological model of educational coaching. The model gives coaches and learners a common language of description, identification and analysis, which makes for greater intellectual clarity and collaboration. This is represented visually in the form of three U-shaped helixes (see Figure 9.1).

Learner's process and position

A learner's learning process and position can be represented by a spiral line that is continuous and always moving forward. It can be assumed that there is no reverse process, because all experiences, including negative ones, have the potential for learning and development. The personal goals and directions of the individual's learning journey can change at any time depending on internal and external events and environments. The trend is based on the opening, deepening and evolvement of the learner's willingness, readiness and capabilities as an inseparable whole during a transformative developmental process.

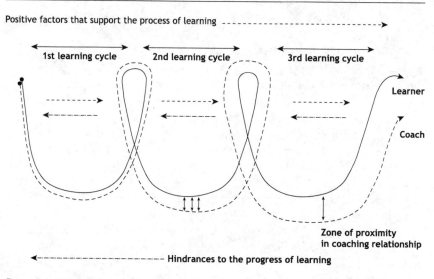

Figure 9.1 The psychological model of educational coaching

Coach's process and position

A coach's learning process and position can be represented by a spiral line that is sometimes continuous and sometimes broken. This represents the fact that a coach is only present with a learner at key points in the learning process, i.e. when the learner and the coach initially meet and begin to establish rapport and build a coaching relationship, when they meet subsequently to discuss the focus of coaching and make decisions, when they meet to co-create knowledge and make progress in learning, and when they meet to reflect on the experience and review goals. These meetings are represented by a line that shows a continuous pattern. The learner is encouraged to experiment with his or her own learning process without the coach being directly present. These periods are represented by a broken line. However, the 'internalised presence' of the coach can still be influential. The primary point in the psychological model regarding the coach's position is the awareness of coaching as a facilitative rather than a directive process, which is seen as supporting the development of a range of positive learning dispositions, especially the learner's agency, self-directedness and sense of empowerment. The coach cannot provide all the answers or solutions for the learner but rather facilitate the learner finding his or her own answers. Therefore the coach is always 'behind' the learner who is supposed to lead and take responsibility for the learning journey.

Zone of proximity in the coaching relationship

The distance between the coach and learner spirals is identified as the 'zone of proximity in the coaching relationship', representing a metaphorical space of the degree of closeness and dependency in their relationship. This distance changes during the course of the coaching/learning process. As the learner becomes more mature, independent and perhaps acquires self-coaching skills, it is assumed that the coach will play a less direct role as the learning cycles move forward, so the zone of proximity in the coaching relationship is enlarged as the learning cycles progress. However, the increased distance does not mean that the coach and the learner are gradually separated from each other. Instead, it means that the coach, as a facilitating agent, should hand over more responsibility to the primary learner. For instance, in the first learning cycle, the coach may provide information in the form of instruction, demonstration or informative feedback about what is right or wrong and what to do instead. In the second learning cycle, the coach may not give such informative guidance. The learner may be provided with challenging but still approachable tasks, and the coach will scaffold the learning process as it unfolds with tips and hints. In the third learning cycle, the learner may be the leader of learning progress. The coaching relationship is still based on the mutual affirmativeness, respect and trust in this joint learning system where the coach helps the learner to achieve critical conditions of learning, but the learner's dependence on the coach is gradually decreased. Meanwhile, there is more space for the learner's self-regulated and self-directed learning. The real skilfulness of coaching is based as much on the art of not doing things as it is on doing things. It demands the courage to 'coach less' in order to create a gateway to bring out the learner's own resources and open up a space for the learner to see things differently. The ideal development of the zone of proximity in the coaching relationship is that the learner is progressively able to conduct self-coaching with the influence of being coached, and with the learner's ability to provide for him or herself what the coach initially provides, but without the coach's actual presence and direct input to the process. This is the time for the coach to consider a withdrawal from the learning/coaching process.

Trust and authenticity are highlighted in the zone of proximity in coaching relationships. Coaching is different from counselling in that the latter attempts to stay in a client's comfort zone and aims primarily to heal. On the other hand, coaching attempts to move beyond a person's comfort zone and stretch this person's capacities, and primarily serves an educational purpose in order to enhance performance, and support change and growth. In a similar sense, educational coaching involves creating bonds of deep trust between the coach and the learner, who should be willing, able and ready to face and negotiate problems, questions, doubts and uncertainties in learning without feeling worried that this relationship might be fragile, abused, or easily jeopardised by open discussions, conflicts and confrontations. An existential approach to coaching actually sees conflict as 'an essential aspect of an authentic relationship, and confrontation is necessary from time to time in order to keep a relationship real and valid' (Peltier, 2001, p. 166). This zone of proximity in the coaching relationship is central for both the coach and the learner to gain self-knowledge and increase self-awareness through trusting the processes, opening experiences and broadening perspectives, realising

176 Towards a systems approach

and actualising intrinsic nature and energy, exercising inter-depending and inter-being (Gibb, 1978).

Supporting factors to learning

The horizontal arrows in broken lines represent the internal and external forces and influences that support the progress of learning and development. The internal factors include personal experiences and stories that have a potentially positive impact on learners' self-awareness, personal strengths, characteristics, beliefs and motivation in learning, for example, recognition and development of learning power, a growth mindset of intelligence and competence, acknowledgement and embracement of a variety of learning experiences including difficulties and challenges, a thrust of learning and curiosity, resilience and grit, confidence and positive self-image. External supporting factors include a positive learning environment, a personally tailored coaching curriculum, a well-scaffolded learning process, available resources and information, and supportive family, friends, schools and communities. The coach's role is to encourage the learner to unlock and foster the internal factors as well as acknowledge, build and strengthen the external factors.

Hindering factors to learning

Conversely, the arrows in line segments and dots represent the internal and external forces that create barriers to the progress of learning and development, or deplete energy, motivation and attention. The internal hindrances and resistance in learners can be a fixed mindset of capabilities and intelligence; fear of failure or anxiety about learning; low levels of self-esteem and low expectations; lack of resilience and flexibility; a negative image of self as a learner; underdeveloped strengths, resources and talents; or physical reasons. For students who have been trained in formal educational institutions, grasping the essence of 'being coached' is exceptionally challenging in the first place, so the feeling of unfamiliarity and frustration may make them shy away. However, a normal level of anxiety is expected when the learner attempts to change, ventures beyond the comfort zone, and thinks about the deep meaning of his or her own learning.

The external hindrances to learning include a negative learning environment, lack of time and resources, or unsupportive family and community. The coach's role is to help the learner to identify these barriers, then overcome, weaken or remove them as well as anticipate, avoid or manage the interference. These 'negative' intra-psychic or interpersonal hindrances, however, can be considered as natural, potentially adaptive balancing feedback loops (O'Conner & McDermott, 1997). They are understandable and sometimes potentially useful responses to investigate the psychological dynamics in the coaching process.

The coach needs to optimise the conditions for learning, minimise barriers and resistance to learning and allow the learner to progress or 'go with the flow'

Relational and discursive aspects 177

(Csikszentmihalyi, 1990). Also, the coach needs to be aware of and prepared for resistance and defensiveness by sharing the expectation and having genuine conversation with the learner. In such conditions, the helix cycles stretch out; transformation in learning and becoming can occur. What I mean by 'becoming' here is a process of evolvement, growth and flourishing for an individual as a learner.

It is possible to integrate psychological theories and practice in order to better understand the complex dynamics of the learning/coaching process at various stages. The psychological model of educational coaching involves a particular discourse orientation that aims not only to enhance learners' cognitive abilities through enquiry, but also to empower them with the dispositions, motivation and confidence to do so. Thus the language is of critical importance. The next section focuses on the discursive aspect of educational coaching.

Discursive aspects of educational coaching

Drawing from the current research and literature, developing a shared language within the educational context is of critical importance. The synthesis of data from previous studies indicated that teachers might not be aware of how important the element of 'knowledge co-construction' is to the concept of 'learning', or what differentiates 'coaching' from 'teaching'. Consequently, the teachers adopted ideas and practices that possibly compromised the pedagogical value of educational coaching. Language can encourage or hinder how individuals regard their ownership of learning and how educational institutions create the conditions for further engagement (Deakin-Crick, 2012). I ponder three questions related to the discursive aspect: 1) What is there in the current language that supports student learning? 2) What is missing from the language that we need? 3) Whose language is it? I use the first participatory study with secondary students and teachers as an example because the discursive issue was more obvious in this case.

The language used in the educational context

In the study of implementing coaching psychology into secondary students' enquiry-based learning, a metaphorical description of the learning journey and animal analogies of learning power dimensions were formed and adopted by teachers and students. There was a sense of developing a language in the evolving process of coaching, based on teachers' existing knowledge, their practices and experiences. They seemed to be comfortable with using coaching skills such as 'drama triangle', 'perceptual positions', 'clean language' or other vocabulary in learning power dimensions. Meanwhile the students demonstrated significant progress in describing their learning and themselves as learners. Their language of self-awareness and learning relationships was confidently owned and translated into their dispositions of learning.

However, after careful scrutiny of the case, a number of problems still existed. First of all, I was surprised to notice that very little language was used to describe how new knowledge was constructed. Though the teachers and students were provided with a personalised enquiry handbook, they seldom used it. Yet the fact that students could not articulate knowledge construction does not mean it was absent from their learning. It might have been because the language of knowledge construction was not effectively employed.

Secondly, whilst the teachers attempted to adopt a coaching language and tried to incorporate it in the process of enquiry, they did not explicitly tie the language of learning power with coaching. There still seemed to be a gap between coaching and learning. This might be due to the external coach's influence on teachers during the staff development training. The external coach introduced professional coaching vocabulary, but he did not combine it with typical learning activities in the classroom. Coaching became a tool for establishing trust and harmony in the learning relationship, which was undoubtedly important in student learning. However, the coaching conversations around facilitating students' authentic choices or scaffolding the enquiry process were less evidenced.

Thirdly, the majority of the students seemed to lack a rich language to describe their own learning power. This was shown by a sense of passivity during the interviews. Some of the students could only superficially respond to interview questions and hardly gave any active account of their own learning. Though I presented myself as a listener, not as a teacher or someone who held knowledge for them, they sometimes expected me to tell them more about their learning power, rather than telling me what it meant for themselves. This phenomenon did change during the course of the three prototypes, and the students were more open in terms of their attitudes and willingness to share ideas, but their language did not change much in richness, depth or diversity. Moreover, the students clearly stated that they did not understand words such as 'meaning-making' or 'strategic awareness', though they were using them all the time. This problem reflects my third question: whose language is it? Is this language authentically owned by the learners?

An anatomy of the language of educational coaching

Developing a language of educational coaching requires the coach and the learner to achieve an understanding of learning and facilitation of this learning, and to talk about the core processes in a shared language. It involves promoting three sub-languages: 1) a language of learning power, 2) a language of knowledge construction and 3) a language of learning facilitation. I will take a closer look at each language in the following sections.

Language of learning power

Learning power has been defined as 'a set of personal qualities or orientations towards learning which are understood and manifested in thought, feeling and action and derived from values and attitudes – sets of beliefs with affective loading' (Deakin-Crick, 2012, p. 32). The terminology of learning power incorporates values, beliefs, attitudes and dispositions. The language of learning power was originally developed by academics and introduced to schools, teachers and students. Years of studies have demonstrated that learners have developed an awareness of the value of using learning power language in secondary schools, higher education and in the workplace (ibid.). However, the efficacy with which learners, especially young people, adopt this language in their own learning remains questionable. In my study, participants found it very difficult to understand certain terms and struggled to interpret learning profiles. This superficial grasp of learning power language not only reduced ELLI to a psychometric instrument to the point where it merely served a diagnostic purpose, but it also further affected the quality of coaching conversations.

Developing a language of learning power means that individual learners could reflect in depth on their own learning profiles and even create their own terms to describe the seven dimensions. Because the online questionnaire assessing learning power produces a spider diagram with no numbers, it relies heavily on the learners' critical thinking, reasonable interpretation and use of language rather than simply pointing out which dimension is strong and which is weak. Hence, a language of learning power should enable individual learners to makes sense of what their profiles really mean to them and give them concrete examples in discussing each dimension.

Both learner and coach should understand that the imbalance of learning power dimensions exists *in place and in time*; and those strengths and weaknesses are *not traits but states* – they may develop or change over time. Therefore, the tone of talking about learning power should reflect a growth mindset (Dweck, 2000, 2006) that these dimensions are expandable and changeable through effective coaching and learning.

Moreover, the language of learning power should be critical. It is essential to realise that a learning profile is a self-reported assessment of current learning power; it may not provide an absolutely accurate measurement of one's learning capacities. Last but not least, the language of learning power should not merely dwell in the domain of school subject-based learning or formal learning but rather situate itself in a wider learning context.

Language of knowledge construction

The second sub-language relates to knowledge construction. I take a Vygotskian view that an individual's learning, which emphasises the acquisition of transferable knowledge, cognitive and meta-cognitive skills, is embedded in cultural contexts and social interactions. Learning is a collective participatory process of active knowledge construction situated in context and interaction (Cole & Engestrom, 1993). Knowledge is co-constructed, situative and participatory (Greeno, 1997; Greeno & MMAP, 1998).

The process of knowledge construction almost always entails social mediation, even if this is not immediately apparent (Salomon & Perkins, 1998). The social

180 Towards a systems approach

mediation of learning, and the individuals involved in that learning, form an integrated, complex and highly situated system in which the interaction serves as the socially shared vehicle of thoughts (ibid., 1998). Hence a language for scaffolding the process of knowledge construction is significant in establishing this learning system.

Developing a coherent, shared language of knowledge construction means learning is designed as an enquiry process (Deakin-Crick, 2009, 2012). The language of knowledge construction is captured in an authentic enquiry framework (Deakin-Crick & Jelfs, 2009). It accommodates nine sequential but iterative stages that may be revisited in a spiral formation through the actual practice of the enquiry project (Deakin-Crick, 2012): choosing and deciding, observing and describing, questioning, storying, mapping, connecting, reconciling, validating and, finally, applying. The enquiry is scaffolded through generating meaningful questions, building on a prior knowledge base, finding resources and information, engaging in in-depth thinking and understanding, making meaningful connections between the new information and knowledge structures, stretching learning capabilities, establishing positive learning relationships, and expressing findings through elaborated communication. In addition, the enquiry process includes reflexivity: determining how the implicit assumptions, frames of references, perspectives and biases of personal experiences would influence the ways in which knowledge is constructed within others. The language goes beyond knowledge acquisition or recognition; it brings a flexible structure in which learners are psychologically secure enough to move from personal choices to achievement or learning outcomes that meet formal assessment criteria.

Language of learning facilitation

The third sub-language of educational coaching regards learning facilitation. One of the most fundamental social forms of learning in the human world is that a person or a team helps another individual to learn (Saloman & Perkins, 1998). The concept of learning facilitation in this context needs a different discourse from how we speak in a traditional mechanical form of pedagogy. The teacher as an agent of facilitation and the student as an agent of learning should form a joint learning partnership where the former supports the latter to achieve critical conditions and negotiate outcomes of learning. The facilitators, or educational coaches, go beyond providing direct instruction, modelling, demonstration, informative feedback and guidance about what is right, what is wrong and what to do next. They should assign challenging yet approachable tasks, offer encouragement and inspiration to keep learners going and help them to move forward. The focus of learning facilitation should always be on learners taking responsibility for themselves.

The language of learning facilitation in my study concerned asking questions and using coaching materials. It evolved into different modes of roles, and each role indicated a different discourse. It required a teacher to be able to move between different roles and make effective professional judgements about which role to take, when to take it, and what kind of language to use in order to convey appropriate pedagogical messages to the students.

Nonetheless, teachers-as-coaches should not completely forget how to speak like a teacher. The concept of 'authentic chameleon' (Lazarus, 1993) could be useful here: the coach needs to tailor the relationship and adapt to the learner's needs in specific situations. The traditional functions of a teacher, such as monitoring, disciplining, instructing, demonstrating and telling, are still essential parts of the everyday classroom. The difference is that teachers as learning facilitators need to have a clear sense of a higher pedagogical goal (cultivating 21st century learners rather than producing knowledge *photocopy machines*', in the words of a teacher interviewee) and an art of gradually relinquishing control of what and how to learn by using an alternative language.

Thus, the language of learning facilitation is flexible in terms of when and where it is employed, what purpose it serves and who is being coached. It is mainly descriptive rather than evaluative. It denotes that an educational coach should develop an *ownership of coaching*, which means spontaneous, natural or even implicit responses in different coaching situations. It is about having distinctive and flexible coaching conversations with individual learners or groups without following a prepared script or ticking boxes. It involves recognising personal characters and strengths, transferring these strengths to coaching contexts and forming personalised coaching styles instead of accumulating coaching training knowledge or following coaching manuscripts. Most importantly, it is about taking responsibility for one's own coaching.

The interplay of educational coaching and deep engagement

The sub-languages of learning power, knowledge construction and learning facilitation strongly interrelate with each other to form a comprehensive language of educational coaching. Hence, developing one of them stimulates the improvement of the other two. For instance, a learning power profile provides a framework for coaching conversations moving between the identity of the learner and a particularly negotiated learning outcome (Deakin-Crick, 2012). Thus the discursive factors in the measurement derived from a self-reported questionnaire could reflect how learners view themselves and their own learning capabilities. These views constitute their basic language of describing identities, experiences, values and dispositions as well as articulating desired learning outcomes, learning strategies, obstacles, options and breakthroughs in the learning processes. These descriptions and articulations could be operationalised in coaching dialogues, where learners make meaningful connections of personal and experiential choice, complex thinking and learning capabilities, and existing knowledge and goals of achieving public competence. These connections happen on a platform of 'structured freedom' (ibid., p. 32), scaffolded by the teacher who is an educational coach

182 Towards a systems approach

rather than an authority holding expert knowledge. Thus the most powerful engagement for learning occurs when the personal and communal narratives share a common language through which learning is actively designed, enquiry-led and authentically owned by the learner (Newmann, 1996; Newmann *et al.*, 2001). Best understood as a complex system integrating identity, learning power and authentic enquiry (Deakin-Crick, 2012), this deep engagement goes beyond the repetition of knowledge (primary learning) and learning to learn (secondary learning); it leads to third level of learning (Bateson, 1973) involving personal transformation (Mezirow, 1991, 1996; Taylor, 1998, 2007).

The interplay of educational coaching and deep engagement supports learners in achieving the third domain of learning in Habermas' (1970) framework. The first domain concerns skills and competences, and the second domain relates to learning for personal meaning and understanding through social interactions, while the purpose of the third domain of learning regards changing the way we perceive ourselves and our contexts. In educational coaching, raising awareness of specific perceptions, meaning or behaviour *and* associated feelings is a vital part of the process. A critical level would be achieved when learners begin to reflect on their consciousness and assumptions, and this kind of reflective learning leads to perspective transformation (Mezirow, 1981). Learners at the transformative level take an emancipatory process from old, unhelpful ways of seeing the world, which constrain the way they see themselves and their relationships, to more open and meaningful schemes. For instance, students who are coached to ask themselves 'what kind of learner am I?' and 'how do I feel about being this kind of learner?' begin to address their own identities. They are coached to challenge their current way of viewing themselves and start to author new stories from a different perspective. This perspective transformation may be followed by a new sense of personal responsibility and agency leading to transformative action (Askew & Carnell, 2011). As a result, learners achieve deep engagement where they integrate experiences, act upon new understandings, explore options for new ways of learning, acquire knowledge and skills, implement learning plans and build confidence and competence in new roles that have been personally internalised as well as aligned with social expectations. In this way, learning connects its personal and public domains.

Summary

This chapter illustrates the psychological and discursive aspects of educational coaching as a living system in a greater depth. I address key pedagogical themes such as learning relationships, agency, identity and knowledge construction. In addition, I offer a bold invitation for coaches and learners to be positive, efficient, authentic and transformative in the co-learning process (including personal learning, professional learning and learning how to facilitate learning). In the next and final chapter, I will bring together the various elements of the book and enumerate the contributions of coaching psychology to learning in terms of theory development, methodological innovation, and potential impact on educational practice and policy making.

Recommended reading

Askew, S., & Carnell, E. (2011). *Transformative coaching: A learning theory for practice.* London: Institute of Education.

Dweck, C. S. (2000). *Self-theories: Their role in motivation, personality, and development.* Philadelphia, PA: Psychology Press.

Mezirow, J. (1991). *Transformative dimensions of adult learning.* San Francisco: Jossey-Bass.

Key points for reflection

- How do you understand the concept of educational coaching?
- What is the relationship between the coach and the learner when they are both engaged in learning cycles? How does this relationship evolve?
- What are the focuses of a language of educational coaching?
- How exactly is educational coaching different from teaching?

References

Askew, S., & Carnell, E. (2011). *Transformative coaching: A learning theory for practice.* London: Institute of Education.

Bateson, G. (1973). *Steps to an ecology of mind: Collected essays in anthropology, psychiatry, evolution and epistemology.* London: Paladin, Granada.

Cole, M., & Engestrom, Y. (1993). A cultural-historical approach to distributed cognition. In G. Salolom (Ed.), *Distributed cognitions: Psychological and educational considerations* (pp. 1–46). New York: Cambridge University Press.

Csikszentmihalyi, M. (1990). *Flow: The psychology of optimal experience.* New York: Harper and Row.

Deakin-Crick, R. (2009). Inquiry-based learning: Reconciling the personal with the public in a democratic and archaeological pedagogy. *The Curriculum Journal, 20*(1), 73–92.

Deakin-Crick, R. (2012). Personalisation: Integrating the personal with the public: A pedagogy for social sustainability. In M. Mincu (Ed.), *Personalisation of education in contexts: Policy critique and theories of personal improvement.* Rotterdam: Sense Publishers.

Deakin-Crick, R., & Jelfs, H. (2009). *The personalised enquiry project handbook: Strategies for implementing the personalised enquiry project.* University of Bristol.

Dweck, C. S. (2000). *Self-theories: Their role in motivation, personality, and development.* Philadelphia, PA: Psychology Press.

Dweck, C. S. (2006). *Mindset.* New York: Random House.

Egan, G. (2002). *The skilled helper* (7th Ed.). Pacific Grove, CA: Wadsworth.

Gibb, J. (1978). *Trust: A new vision of human relationship for business, education, family, and personal living.* California: Newcastle Publishing.

Greeno, J. (1997). On claims that answer the wrong questions. *Educational Researcher, 25*(1), 5–17.

184 Towards a systems approach

Greeno, J., & MMAP. (1998). The situativity of knowing, learning and research. *American Psychologist, 53*(1), 5–26.

Habermas, J. (1970). *Toward a rational society: Student protest, science and politics.* Boston, MA: Beacon Press.

Lazarus, A. A. (1993). Tailoring the therapeutic relationship or being an authentic chameleon. *Psychotherapy, 30*, 404–407.

Maslow, A. H. (1954). *Motivation and personality.* New York: Harper.

Mezirow, J. (1981). A critical theory of adult learning and education. *Adult Education, 32*(1), 3–24.

Mezirow, J. (1991). *Transformative dimensions of adult learning.* San Francisco: Jossey-Bass.

Mezirow, J. (1996). Contemporary paradigms of learning. *Adult Education Quarterly, 46*(3), 158–172.

Newmann, F. (1996). *Authentic achievement: Restructing schools for intellectual quality.* San Francisco: Jossey-Bass.

Newmann, F., Bryk, S. A., & Nagoaka, J. (2001). *Improving Chicago's schools: Authentic intellectual work and standardised tests: Conflicts or coexistence?* Consortium of Chicago School Research.

O' Conner, J., & McDermott, I. (1997). *The art of systems thinking: Essential skills for creativity and problem solving.* San Francisco: Thorsons.

Peltier, B. (2001). *The psychology of executive coaching: Theory and application.* New York: Brunner-Routledge.

Salomon, G., & Perkins, D. N. (1998). Individual and social aspects of learning. *Review of Research in Education, 23*, 1–24.

Taylor, E. W. (1998). Transformative learning: A critical review. *ERIC Clearinghouse on Adult, Career & Vocational Education: Information Series*, 374.

Taylor, E. W. (2007). An update of transformative learning theory: A critical review of the empirical research (1999–2005). *International Journal of Lifelong Education, 26*, 173–191.

Chapter 10

Reflections and concluding remarks

Introduction

This chapter concludes the book by consolidating various elements that have been progressively constructed in previous chapters, demonstrating the significance in theory development as well as practical implications, and clarifying new perspectives of coaching psychology for learning in educational contexts. The chapter begins with a brief recapitulation of my initial intention and key questions regarding coaching and learning. I link the purposes of empirical studies and questions to the main findings and arguments in order to revisit the existing debate and concisely indicate its highlights. Following that, I enumerate the implications in broader contexts and directions of future studies related to coaching psychology for learning.

A reprise of the book

To recap, the key purpose of this book is to explore how coaching psychology could be used to facilitate students' learning, development and growth in education, particularly in formal educational systems. I have been trying to understand: 1) students' and teachers' experiences and perceptions of coaching psychology; 2) the incorporative process of coaching in their actual learning and teaching practices (e.g., enquiry-based learning and problem-based learning); and 3) the potential influence of coaching psychology on the development of students' learning dispositions and learning agency, as well as teachers' professional development.

In order to answer these questions, I designed exploratory participatory studies in different contexts. This book includes studies with a mainstream UK secondary school, and a medical school in Mainland China. I adopted a modified participatory research methodology and invited students and teachers as co-researchers. After years of extensive fieldwork collecting survey questionnaires, interviews, observations and a series of documents, the substantive purpose of this book has been fulfilled by making modest contributions to the existing literature of coaching and coaching psychology and explicitly connecting them to educational psychology and learning theories in the context of formal education. The relationship between coaching psychology and learning in an educational context could be theorised as a participatory living system that involves coaches and learners in different roles and positions for different purposes in various circumstances along the individual learner's personalised learning journey. Educational coaching can be taken in various approaches that are strongly associated with enquiry approaches in real classroom settings. It should support knowledge construction, and development of positive learning dispositions and learning agency, including a sense of responsibility and ownership of learning. Interpersonal relationships play a critical part in the system that engages the complex psychological mechanisms of both the coach and the learner. In addition, understanding the discursive aspect and developing a shared language of educational coaching are essential to capture the nature of it. It can be concluded that educational coaching entails a sustainable learning system where teachers and students share personal and collective power in learning. It enhances students' learner agency, autonomy, confidence, self-esteem and self-expression, and it extends the scope and content of teachers' CPD programmes.

How do we understand educational coaching?

The evolving concept of educational coaching

In this book, I establish a new concept of educational coaching and originate a systems model with psychological depth. The studies are generative in terms of bringing the concept of educational coaching into existence and allowing this concept to evolve through a series of dynamically repeated processes. When I decided to coin the term 'educational coaching', I found a similar idea has been used on different occasions by other researchers (see Turnbull, 2009; Adams, 2016), who use the terms 'coaching for learning', 'coaching psychology in schools', and that the authors mainly use coaching as a method in teacher training, professional development for school principals and general learning issues. This is very helpful literature that readers may want to refer to. I want to introduce my innovative model of educational coaching by providing a critical description of its process, with the clearly defined purpose of developing students' learning agency and dispositions. The concept of educational coaching also engenders a systematic investigation of coaching psychology in formal education regarding its application in scaffolding enquiry-based learning, problem-based learning and other kinds of learning methods that are socially constructive.

Philosophical integration and pedagogical paradigm

In Chapter 2 and 3, the philosophical connections have been made between the participatory paradigm, systems thinking, humanistic psychology, positive psychology and a socio-cultural perspective of learning. This paradigmatic foundation offers multiple perspectives for my investigation into coaching psychology for learning without losing its own complexity. In doing so, I have established a philosophical integration that denotes 'learning-centred education', which is a pedagogical paradigm different from a conventional content-centred view or a more personalised, liberal learner-centred approach. This pedagogical paradigm makes a strong link between teachers, students and knowledge, and thus has the potential to inform a gentle educational transformation that is characterised by participation, contextualisation, interaction and wholeness.

The theoretical framework of educational coaching

The innovative theoretical framework underpinning coaching psychology for learning can be seen in Chapter 3. This seems to be an appropriate thinking device for combining the two most important aspects of the book: the psychology of learning and the psychology of coaching. The particular strength of the theoretical framework is identifying a relationship between learning and coaching rather than simply putting them together, thus it articulates the sense of purpose and direction in coaching psychology for learning.

The integrative models of coaching psychology for EBL and PBL

From Chapter 5 to Chapter 8, I have presented two participatory studies and proposed two integrative, pedagogical models of coaching psychology for enquiry-based learning and problem-based learning. The model used in the UK secondary school includes 1) context: it is a system embedded within a wider educational system; 2) the main purpose: it aims to develop learning agency and positive learning dispositions, i.e. learning power, confidence, ownership and responsibility for learning; 3) people: it takes at least one coach and one learner to form a dialogic and participatory relationship; 4) four main simultaneous processes with their own sub-processes; and 5) mixed methods to evaluate its effectiveness in the evolving educational discourse. The model used in the Chinese medical school includes 1) core learning goals: it aims to develop lifelong learning capacities, clinical reasoning and problem-solving skills, and empathy and humanistic concerns; 2) student and tutor circles that indicate their distinctive and connected learning/coaching activities; and 3) three main processes in the co-learning experience: preparation, process and conclusion.

Although these two models are constructed with different participants in their own educational contexts with different purposes, they demonstrate their characteristics as a living system of emergence, interrelatedness, adaptation, development and sustainability. This dynamic perspective on coaching psychology for learning is valuable in offering sufficient substance to understand its definition, processes, purposes and people engaged in the system.

The original psychological model of educational coaching

Acknowledging the essential role of relationships and communication in the process of coaching psychology for learning, I have proposed a comprehensive psychological model in Chapter 9, explicitly pinpointing the relational aspect of educational coaching as learning with psychological prerequisites, positions, processes, and supporting and hindering factors. In addition, the psychological model proposes a new concept of 'zone of proximity in the coaching relationship', describing the space where coaching functions. The overall model indicates the *developmental trend* of the relationship between coach and learner when the co-learning process becomes mutual and interdependent.

How do we study educational coaching?

The benefit of using participatory methodology in educational research

To study coaching psychology for learning, I mainly employ a modified participatory approach with teachers and students in real learning settings for co-constructing knowledge, triangulating evidence and informing the directions of change. The details of this modified participatory methodology have been presented in Chapter 5 and Chapter 7. The findings from the two studies show that the relationship between coaching and learning is best understood as a participatory living system.

This participatory methodology is firmly based on the paradigmatic and philosophical position elaborated in Chapter 2. It has a number of potential benefits for studying coaching psychology for learning. First, this approach could foster trust between participants and researchers as two equal parties in a research dialogue, and as a result it could enhance the authenticity and trustworthiness of the research. Second, the level of involvement and engagement will be decided by the participants themselves in order to ensure the democratic dialogues between them and the researchers. Third, the coaching interventions to facilitate learning would take natural, dynamic prototypes; they will not be intrusive to students' subject learning in their formal curriculum. Fourth, in educational studies taking classic experimental approaches, students and teachers may think they are doing researchers a favour, and sometimes they do not know what benefits that research could bring them. As an interesting contrast to passive attendance, participatory methodology ensures that students and teachers take active roles in the whole process as co-researchers rather than appointed subjects. Participants' agency and exercise of their ownership are recognised, so that people know they can learn and benefit from the research. Fifth, the participatory methodology could eliminate a demand effect on the participants: they might face less pressure to report progress or to report only positive aspects in order to please researchers due to social desirability; they would be more open about their queries, doubts, concerns, mistakes and ideas to improve their own practices. Therefore, the participatory studies could display rigour and authenticity in their efforts to bridge research and practice.

Furthermore, I need to point out that it is generally not easy to get access to a real classroom as a research site, whether it is in the UK or in China. Teachers and students usually have their own agendas and bear the pressures of school achievement and accountability. Therefore, participatory approaches may not be fully conducted on some occasions. However, we should try our best to encourage high levels of involvement and engagement in the research process, as long as it reflects the value of emancipation and empowerment.

Utilising repeated multiple methods

The methodological enquiry of coaching psychology for learning, in my studies, generally used mixed methods in data collection from various perspectives. These methods include self-reported survey questionnaires of students' learning (e.g., learning power, school engagement, academic self-efficacy, self-regulated learning and learning motivation), semi-structured interviews and focus groups with teachers and students, narrative interviews with students, observations of behaviours and dialogues in the classroom, and documents of teaching/coaching plans and students' learning outcomes (e.g., assignments, products, presentations, grades). If necessary, repeatedly collecting interview data, observational data and documents with the same cohort of participants across many prototypes will be useful for researchers to ensure a rich, high quality data base and understand the development and change in the research site. For instance, in the first study, I integrated three types of interviews in order to scrutinise every account of each participant on different occasions. The art-based narrative interview was perhaps the most innovative part, because it could function as a *coaching intervention*: when it was blended into the whole empirical process, it served as a data collection method. It provided the opportunity for students to tell their own learning stories in a holistic, art-inspired and adult-facilitated way, which could be a powerful strategy in educational coaching.

Conducting critical thematic analysis

There are numerous possibilities for dealing with a large data set, especially when a study has accumulated data from a variety of sources over an extended period of time. In order to better understand coaching psychology for learning, I argue that one of the most important approaches to data analysis is critical thematic analysis of qualitative data and effective synthesis of both quantitative and qualitative analysis. The critical thematic analysis method would be particularly useful in dynamic prototyping with multiple sources of data. Due to its sophistication and rigour, the framework used in my studies has a strong transferable applicability to other research in participatory research design.

How do we apply educational coaching?

This section explores the concrete implications of coaching psychology for learning and it stresses students' and teachers' authentic accounts of their lived experiences. Educational coaching is seen as a creative, ever-deepening journey of exploring how to build a culture that breeds confident, resilient, self-determined lifelong learners, rather than a quick fix for solving educational problems. Although the empirical studies on coaching psychology for learning are inevitably limited due to design issues and pragmatic problems, they have stimulated numerous good practices, and practices that need to be improved with joint efforts. The emerging pedagogical themes raise a number of important implications for educational practices, centred on promoting educational coaching at the secondary level as well as in higher education. The implications include a range of audiences at different levels, and I would like to enclose all of them to raise common consciousness.

Committing to participatory and learning-centred values

The philosophical and psychological themes underpinning educational coaching are central to pedagogical practices. The ideological and ethical perspectives determine what purposes are, which direction to go in, and what actions should be involved in pedagogical interventions. The implementation of coaching psychology for learning needs a commitment of participatory and learning-centred values, which requires the development of a broad range of underlying ideologies and rationales that bring about radical shifts in how we view the relationship of knowledge, teachers and students as a whole. It also requires the expansion of moral imaginations and mindfulness of everyday professional responsibilities. Current educational policy initiatives and reports seem to overly emphasise raising attainment and achievement in examinations; these initiatives do not give enough vision as to how to realise students' academic potential, appreciate students' and practitioners' voices and accentuate the processes of constructing knowledge. The studies on educational coaching suggest policy makers pay more attention to the ultimate values of education, form strong connections and build schools as communities of co-learners. This commitment endorses innovations in political infrastructure that create places for deepening democracy through participatory decision-making and bringing together diverse stakeholders.

Establishing a systems view of school and a climate of experimentation

Applying educational coaching in real learning settings should consider the culture of the classroom and the educational institution in which it is situated. As Leadbeater (2010) stated, instead of seeing schooling as a system of years and grades with key stages and examinations, targets and regulations, it should be seen as a set of relationships between teachers, pupils, parents and the wider community.

This reflects a systems view of schooling, where children need to have the relationships and joint efforts for better learning. The vision of where learning takes place and the initiatives taken by teachers cannot be understood in isolation from the support of parents and the wider community. The interventions and experiences of teachers and students in particular classrooms are informed and shaped by their environment.

Leading and managing educational coaching is harder than it might at first appear. It tends to have its roots in counselling and psychotherapy, where trust is paramount and confidentiality is assured, but a typical school may come from a managerial culture characterised by hierarchical relationships and monitoring processes. Therefore, it is critical to recognise educational coaching as a creative means to construct new knowledge and practices, rather than an accountability tool in organisational procedures. This involves a significant mind shift on the part of educational administration, management and leadership.

Educational coaching may not be the choice for everyone: this practice is based on voluntary participation rather than obligatory involvement. It may not be initiated and mandated by policy makers, governors, administrators, researchers or legislators. The approach comes into existence when school teachers and senior management teams are propelled by a vision of learning as a route to emancipation and liberation: they have a common understanding and concern with the current issues in their schools and they want to effect a transformation. They work with local authorities and professional scholars to further investigate these issues and to act upon them in order to make a change. The outstanding feature of such an institution is its determination to innovate and courage to experiment, especially in extremely challenging circumstances. The only way out of difficulty is *through* it. This climate of collective curiosity and spirit of experimentation cannot be forced by any authority or external factor if deep change is to happen. The educational institution must have ownership of where the change is taking it; hence the crucial inputs into the innovation would be sustainable without the need for constant intervention.

Aligning pedagogical purposes with learning approaches

Coaching should function as an effective method of scaffolding students' learning processes. For instance, coaching needs to become reconciled to different pedagogical purposes in different enquiry approaches. In general enquiry-based learning, coaching mainly facilitates students' research skills and knowledge building regarding their enquiry topics. In authentic enquiry, coaching serves four functions at different stages of enquiry: coaching for aspiration and personal motivation; coaching for developing learning power and enquiry capabilities; coaching for knowledge construction; and coaching for authentic performance. In problem-based learning, coaching focuses on clarifying the key problems, developing clinical reasoning and diagnostic skills, and enhancing empathy and medical humanity. In project-based learning, coaching emphasises initial goal setting and project management.

192 Towards a systems approach

Therefore, different learning approaches would have an impact on where the starting point of educational coaching is, what kind of situation needs to be created to challenge students, how information and knowledge is organised, sequenced and framed, what kind of relationship is appropriate, and how to publish and present the learning outcomes. The emphasis on coaching is different in various learning approaches, and coaching should be flexible enough to serve different purposes. Designing a learning-centred curriculum determines that educational coaching functions mostly close to its nature.

Including educational coaching in teachers' professional development agenda

The link between teachers' learning and students' learning acts as the main layer for the development of educational coaching – it could provide a means of collaborative continuous professional development (CPD) and thus be a strong dimension for teachers' professional learning. Educational coaching could support self-development activities, exploring and clarifying the relationships between values, knowledge and the practices of teachers. Teachers' traditional understandings and long-held assumptions of professionalism may be challenged: they need to take multiple roles and various conversational approaches to support students' learning. Each coaching conversation with each individual student can be unique, so teachers are invited to respond differently and equip themselves with the ability to make professional judgements appropriately along the continuum of roles in educational coaching.

Changing the habits of a defined professional teacher is not easy. To become educational coaches for their students, teachers need to unlearn their traditional skills in teaching, telling and transmitting knowledge, relearn new mixed roles and skills in educational coaching, explore their professional identities and stories, exercise their own learning capacities and coaching efficacy, and consequently, inspire and guide other colleagues. If teachers encourage their students to be more mindful of their learning, they will probably at the same time take more ownership of their teaching and coaching. When teachers' learning is based on their genuine understanding of students' learning, they can start to make adaptations to their practices which lead to real differences in outcomes.

Furthermore, I recommend that teachers' perezhivanie should be included in a CPD agenda, because teachers' lived experiences in the classroom – their feelings and responses to social situations of development – are strongly connected to their professional development. The desired change is in how teachers spontaneously act and talk in the classroom, and how their behaviours are authentically congruent with their feelings and beliefs in learning.

Practical ideas for CPD include (but are not limited to) teachers' EBL or PBL, collaborative learning, action learning groups and educational coaching as repeated cycles. These could offer structured opportunities for teachers, coaches and researchers to work collaboratively on the development of educational coaching with the aim of satisfying the researchers' need to create a strong evidence base whilst drawing on the expertise of teachers as regards implementation in educational context. Such activities could be seen as more powerful than one-off activities such as conferences or workshops, because they promote ongoing, sustainable communities of learning. Good coaching encourages teachers to become more reflective, articulate and exploratory in relation to their work. Thus they would be more confident in deploying a wider pedagogical repertoire suited for the roles, in developing heightened meta-cognitive skills for planning, and in observing and refining coaching to ensure the importance of its quality.

Enhancing the quality of coaching relationship

The quality of a relationship is central to the process and outcomes of educational coaching. Learning is a process as much about feeling and reflecting as it is about seeing, listening, thinking and taking action. The quality of a relationship is validated by teachers' and students' lived experiences and how they express their experiences. It is a product of what they do, what they say, how they interact and, essentially, who they are. In particular, students' experiences of interpersonal relationships are a primary determinant of effective educational coaching.

Knowing an optimal relationship by intuitively sensing is one thing, taking action to enhance communication and relationships is another matter. We could coach teachers to acquire skills of co-creating ideal connections with their students, look at the flow of classroom interactions and communications and study the nature of emergent processes. However, a positive relationship is not built by teachers *only*; the nature of mutuality in a relationship requires students' active contributions. Introducing, modelling and discussing a deliberately created set of social habits, practices, behaviours and expectations is necessary for coaching students in building a positive relationship with their teachers. In addition, teachers-as-coaches should create agreed ground rules; invite students to note, reflect on and distill good actions; and, finally, positively reinforce improvement.

How can we tell if the quality of a coaching relationship is high or not? The process of building, maintaining and enhancing a relationship could be captured in descriptive and observational data. Alternatively, since personal stories and voices are trustworthy resources for evaluating the quality of a relationship, interview and narrative data can offer detailed commentaries and measurable warmth, excitement and the presence of positive emotions via verbal language, vocal tones or non-verbal expressions. The evaluation results can be used to inform improvement of the relationship.

Developing a shared language in educational coaching

It has been clear from the empirical studies that there is relatively limited language available when discussing educational coaching practices, and it is difficult to define the precise nature of effective coaching conversations. The knowledge-creating process is enhanced when the coach, learners and stakeholders share a language. Though a more nuanced or formal language is helpful in persuading policy makers of the seriousness and validity of the educational coaching approach, translating it into a more accessible and straightforward set of terms when talking to teachers and students is crucial if the approach is going to take root. So we should explore the discursive aspect of educational coaching in order to make our vocabulary more vernacular without losing its precision and rigour.

In Chapter 9, I have provided a language framework of educational coaching that integrates a language of learning power, knowledge construction and learning facilitation. A productive language includes adopting a tone of voice that varies from neutral to positive, which can suggest a hidden agenda, an emotional state or a learned behaviour. Having this language enables teachers and students to plan, concretely and creatively, how to develop positive learning dispositions through the process of co-constructing valid knowledge with the facilitation of coaching. In practice, teachers and students could customise the language, play with the vocabulary and create their own versions of the words and metaphors. They could also expand the vocabulary and add more words to it. And they could try different ways to blend the words into their everyday classroom life. Moreover, an educational coaching dialogue includes a shared understanding of the language and a positive relationship between speakers and listeners so that each voice is respected and heard. It is linked to the importance of a coaching relationship.

Providing responsible freedom for making choices in learning

Educational coaching supports students in becoming more proactive and independent in making responsible decisions about their own learning. Making one's own choice stretches learning power by placing students in situations of cognitive, emotional and experiential complexity. It focuses on students' self-awareness, self-regulation, self-assessment and self-monitoring once they have made their own decision of what, when, how and with whom to learn.

However, this freedom does not mean an absolute hands-off without any structure or direction. Teachers should remain in close contact with students, scaffold learning through a series of tasks with clear goals, encourage freedom to experiment and take risks, secure learning opportunities and monitor the learning progress. Students need to be coached to take responsibility for their freedom in learning and not abuse this freedom. This is what I would call 'responsible freedom', which plays an essential role in educational coaching.

Cultivating a sense of ownership and partnership in learning

As Watkins (2010) observed, the more students are supported as autonomous learners, the higher their overall academic performance will be. Developing students' sense of autonomy, ownership and a sense of agency in learning is one of the central purposes of educational coaching. It relates to the previous section about responsible freedom in making choices of content, context, processes and people in learning. Ownership means that learners feel they are the architects or designers of their own learning; they shape what and how they learn, and they are able to articulate the values and meaning to others.

Equally important is the sense of partnership in learning that goes beyond responsibility for one's self and suggests taking responsibility for others. However, it does not mean that learners need to take care of others' feelings all the time; it means attending to a *shared ownership* of togetherness and collectiveness in learning because no one is the sole decision maker in a collaborative learning environment. It means students need to develop mutual respect and recognition in relationships with teachers and among the students themselves. Thus I suggest a balanced power relationship in the classroom, giving respect to each learner's autonomy and ownership as well as the partnership between them.

Providing time and space for reflection

A key feature of educational coaching in classroom is that students and teachers have time and space for reflection about each step of learning and about themselves as co-learners in the process. It is encouraged at the individual level, in pairs, in small groups and at a whole class level, depending on the theme of reflection. Spending time and allowing space to attend to reflection in the classroom is not an easy task: teachers are required to be conscientiously aware of when reflection is necessary and to actively prioritise this over other academic demands. This implication is particularly crucial in meta-learning because the time and space for reflection could host the strategic and managing sides of learning. Students can take the chance to review what has been achieved so far, anticipate needs and obstacles, rethink and revise their approaches as they go along, envision applications for future tasks and reappraise themselves as learners. Learning materials supporting reflection need to be prepared and allocated to the students in advance, but they should not be in an overwhelming amount that takes away students' attention and consumes too much energy. What could follow reflections is to share the reflections and engage in more sophisticated learning conversations.

Using coaching tools in educational coaching

Coaches, teachers and students need appropriate tools to develop coaching practices. Generally, coaching tools to facilitate goal setting and scaffold the learning process, perspective taking and comprehensive evaluation can be used in educational coaching. In my studies, teachers and students planned to draft a handbook or toolkit of coaching based on their experiences (although this plan was not realised due to financial and practical limitations). Good practice of educational coaching means allowing it to develop and extend organically through networks for the dissemination of success stories within and beyond the school.

The perspectives of teachers and students have added valuable information for a handbook. Producing a handbook would be very useful for sharing the concept and strategies of educational coaching in schools, universities and other educational institutions. After defining its purpose and nature, the handbook could suggest procedures and steps and recommend effective coaching strategies, skills and tools to facilitate students in any socially constructive approach to learning. It could also include the use of qualitative and quantitative methods to collect evidence, the development of coaching guidance for specific pedagogies, a language to describe educational coaching, and a framework by which coaching quality can be developed over time. Practitioners need to understand that educational coaching needs support and adequate resources from the field of coaching psychology if it is to achieve maximum impact.

Developing peer coaching and parent coaching

In my studies, the educational coaches for students were mainly school teachers and university lecturers. However, coaches are not limited to these people. It has been found that peer coaching has a positive impact on CPD for teachers (Prince *et al.*, 2010) as well as mid-career and senior faculty members (Huston & Weaver, 2008). These studies and many more all show the utility of peer coaching in adults. The peer critique in my studies gives rise to the possibility of peer coaching among young students themselves. Employing peer coaching radically in students could be an opportunity to enhance their learning dispositions and self-coaching capacity.

Equally important is the involvement of parents in students' learning. Coaching parents with essential philosophy, principles, models and skills of coaching psychology in relation to their children's learning could be a promising area where educational coaching can be implemented. The systems models of coaching psychology in different approaches to learning and the psychological model of educational coaching can offer generic and practical ideas about how parents can become educational coaches for their children at home.

Future research directions of educational coaching

As an educational psychologist and a coaching psychologist, I have been thinking about a range of new questions and highlighting a number of interesting areas for future studies on educational coaching. In this section, I identify pathways that draw attention to new horizons, new investigations, new territories and new possibilities.

Evaluations on the effectiveness

A common question asked about coaching intervention is: does it work? It is the same with educational coaching. What we have discovered about educational coaching requires a rigorous, systematic assessment of its effectiveness. So far, the empirical studies only involve a small cohort of students and teachers as the sample and it is difficult to claim the changes in student learning have statistical significance. Future research with an interest in the evaluation of educational coaching could employ a random control trail (RCT) experimental design or a quasi-experimental design, with larger samples to examine the effectiveness of educational coaching on motivational, cognitive, emotional and social aspects of student learning. Factors such as gender or socio-economic status can be further explored. However, we need to be aware that the variables can never be tightly controlled in an organic, complex learning system. We should be careful in interpreting any result and try to employ multiple methods of evaluation in order to draw a complete picture. I recommend a mixed methodology in conducting evaluations. Indicators of outcomes and success need to be identified with the subjective and complex nature of educational coaching itself.

Longitudinal studies

After the coaching interventions, how do students learn and develop? What do they think about their learning after six months or a year? What are the impacts of coaching that can last for a prolonged period of time? We expect that the students who have been coached would be equipped with learning power, confidence and capacities that are transferable and sustainable. Longitudinal studies of the same cohort of students over two or three years would generate insights of educational coaching in terms of its long-term impact.

Interpretative phenomenological analysis of coaching experiences

Whilst numerous studies of coaching practices have focused on organisations, schools and communities, there is a growing yet still small amount of research examining whether coaching is better suited as an approach for some type of individuals. To explore educational coaching from an individual's perspective requires in-depth studies on personal psychological experience. The qualitative method of interpretative phenomenological analysis (IPA) could be used to explore the lived experiences of learners and how they make sense of their major events when they are coached in different learning scenarios. The aim of IPA studies of educational coaching is to enable an understanding of individual experiences and to explore the potential value of coaching as a pedagogical method for different learners. The IPA method can be employed as independent research or be tied into a participatory design.

Studies in other contexts

More attention should be given to what educational coaching means in different contexts. Future research could be extended to different educational contexts, such

198 Towards a systems approach

as with vocational, undergraduate and postgraduate students. I am particularly interested in first-year university students because they are in a transitional stage from secondary education to higher education. The complexity and uncertainty involved in this transition would pose particular challenges and opportunities for young people to become more effective learners if they are well supported.

Cross-cultural studies

Further research could take a cross-cultural and comparative perspective. In this book, I present one study conducted in the UK where an individualistic cultural construct is dominant, and another study conducted in Mainland China that is coloured by collectivism. Culturally comparative studies stimulate these questions: how would educational coaching look in different socio-cultural educational environments? How would we implement educational coaching in a Chinese/Japanese/British/Canadian/American classroom? How would teachers and students from different cultural backgrounds understand educational coaching? Would they do so differently? I assume that answering these questions requires a higher level of sensitivity to cultural contexts where people have different ways of understanding what learning is, of knowing what to learn and learning how to learn.

Educational coaching for cultural adaption

Cross-cultural adaption is one of the most challenging kinds of real-life learning. Since the phenomenon of international students studying abroad is becoming very common, there is a large body of literature which suggests that to live and study in another cultural setting involves learning. My master's dissertation explored the interrelationship between learning power and cross-cultural adaptability and I found a very strong positive correlation. There are countless questions we can ask relating to educational coaching for cross-cultural adaptation and learning. For instance, how can we coach international students to become more adaptive and powerful learners? How do international students establish their support systems through effective coaching? These questions would be interesting and meaningful for both universities and students and extend educational coaching studies to a cross-cultural perspective.

Exploring interdisciplinary research topics

Educational coaching can be applied to explore a wider range of research topics based on a scientist–practitioner model. The scope for application is wide and varied, and it can include the following areas:

- improving general educational services;
- enhancing the learning dispositions and motivation of young talented and gifted students;

- supporting people who have experienced slight underperformance and aiming to unlock their potential and opportunity development;
- conducting inter-disciplinary studies, such as social psychology, counselling, neuroscience, science education, business management and human resource development.

Concluding statement: an invitation

When I was writing this book, I occasionally received emails and text messages from some participants in my studies. In these messages, they indicated that the studies they participated in have brought many observable and inspiring changes to their learning: they have been taking more initiatives and becoming more engaged in learning, they have achieved higher grades in exams, they have produced high quality products that amazed their parents, they have been really enjoying what they were doing, and they still talk about the excitement of educational coaching.

It seems that the story of educational coaching continues to have an impact on students' learning. I am encouraged that this is what I expect my research to do: to *bring positive changes in people*. These changes may be regarding teachers' new understanding of their professionalism, students' engagement and ownership of their learning, parents' deepened involvement in their children's learning and living, or the school's development towards an authentic learning community. Although we cannot guarantee these changes will definitely create enormous impacts, nor expect that the effects will be long lasting without being challenged, I am very pleased to participate in and witness this innovative endeavour.

The exploration of coaching psychology for learning was indeed a rewarding adventure for me and, I hope, my participants. As a researcher of educational psychology, I have the impression that many educational psychologists may not be well equipped for working amid chaos and complexity. This may be because our theories tend to be grounded in a linear empirical model and over-focus on prediction, evaluation and control, rather than engagement with ongoing, unpredictable emergent processes in authentic learning contexts. One of the 'remedies' is to learn how to make sense of ambiguity and embrace multiple perspectives. The participatory, systematic studies on educational coaching are congruent with the values: individuals take responsibility for identifying meaningful questions/problems, work out their own solutions to new processes and new procedures, acquire new knowledge, skills and competences, develop positive dispositions and attitudes, and empower themselves as learners.

Educational coaching does not intend to solve educational problems directly or demand a wholesale replacement of familiar ways of teaching with completely new ways. Instead, it provides a vehicle for change through evolution, not revolution. It is about a subtle shift in the way we think about learning and what we have always done. Young people's identities as lifelong learners and their learning power dimensions will certainly be of use, whatever their paths of life will be.

The task for 21st century education is not only to build learning power in the context of school, but to make sure that it can be transferred outside the school gate and used in the wider world, in people's professional and personal lives. It is an attempt to connect what happens in school and what will happen in the wider world in which students will have to take responsibility for their own learning and make their own choices.

In the midst of the research and implementation of coaching psychology for learning, there is still much more to be done. However, I invite readers who care about their learning to experiment with the idea of educational coaching in new ways and different places and join the innovation towards a positive change in learning and being. In doing so, we could add to the growing body of knowledge about how to better facilitate students' learning, how to make learning authentically owned and shared, and how to cultivate each student to be the author of their own learning journey.

The journey of coaching psychology for learning continues.

Recommended reading

Adams, M. (2016). *Coaching psychology in schools: Enhancing performance, development and wellbeing.* London: Routledge.

Turnbull, J. (2009). *Coaching for learning: A practical guide for encouraging learning.* London: Bloomsbury Academic.

Key points for reflection

- What are the philosophical and theoretical foundations of educational coaching?
- How will you design and conduct research on educational coaching if you work in the field of coaching psychology and education?
- How will you apply educational coaching in your everyday teaching if you are a teacher/lecturer?
- What does your own model of coaching psychology for learning look like?

References

Adams, M. (2016). *Coaching psychology in schools: Enhancing performance, development and wellbeing.* London: Routledge.

Huston, T., & Weaver, C. (2008). Peer coaching: Professional development for experienced faculty. *Innovative Higher Education, 33,* 5–20.

Leadbeater, C. (2010). *What's next? 21 ideas for 21st century education.* Innovation Unit. Retrieved from: http://charlesleadbeater.net/wp-content/uploads/2010/01/Next2.pdf

Prince, T., Snowden, E., & Mathews, B. (2010). Utilising peer coaching as a tool to improve student–teacher confidence and support the development of classroom practice. *Literacy Information and Computer Education Journal, 1*(1), 72–82.

Turnbull, J. (2009). *Coaching for learning: A practical guide for encouraging learning.* London: Bloomsbury Academic.

Watkins, C. (2010). Learning, performance and improvement. *Institute of Education International Network for School Improvement. Research Matters Series, 34.* Retrieved from: www.mantleoftheexpert.com/wp-content/uploads/2010/06/Watkins-10–Lng-Perf-Imp.pdf

Index

Entries in *italics* denote figures; entries in **bold** denote tables.

academic performance: assessment of 21; and coaching 64, 72, 76; as primary goal 12, 51
achievement motives 34
acquisition metaphor 39
action research 136
active learning 49, 134, 153
adaptability 23, 48, 97
adaptation effect 101
adult-development approach 67
adult learning approach 67
adventure-based model 67
affections 34, 37, 46, 141
affirmativeness, mutual 175
agency: and CfL 116, 128; and coaching relationship 174; and complexity theory 24; in CPBL 151, 153; in discursive perspective 40; and intentionality 44; and L2L 43–4; in participatory research 188; sense of 2; and transformative learning 182; *see also* learner agency
ambiguity, tolerance for 48
analytical thinking 11, 20
andragogy 158
'Another Way' classroom **13**
anxiety, in coaching relationship 176
APA (American Psychological Association) 1, 41
aspiration 45, 53, 63, 72, 75, 191
assessment criteria 121, 127, 157–8, 180
authentic chameleon 181
authentic enquiry 47, 49–50, 53, 182, 191
authenticity: in axiological orientation 19–20; in coaching relationship 175; conceptual roots of 47–8; and learning 48–9; in participatory worldview 15

authentic learning experience 149
authentic performance 116, 191
authentic relationships 42, 47, 175
autonomy: in axiology 19–20; and CfL 113, 116; in cognitive coaching 68; developing sense of 194–5; need for 34, 62, 158; sharing 149
axiological orientation 19–20

balance, internal 127
behavioural psychology 34
behaviour-based approach 67
behaviourism 11–12, 41, 79
belongingness 154, 159
bottom-up development 14
boundaries 43, 64–7, 116, 133, 172
BPS (British Psychological Society) 1, 61

Cartesian dualism 11–12
case study methodology 25
CfL (Coaching for Learning) 3; context of *115*, 116; definition of 113–14; effective relationships in 121–2; evaluating 125–6; knowledge construction in 120–1; people in system 122–5; stations of 116–17, **118–19**, 128; systems model of *114*, 115, 126–8
Chair, of student learning groups 155, 161
change, principles of 22
China: author's experience in 2–4; medical education in 132, 135, 135–48, 158, 161–3, 187; traditional education in 162
CLASS approach 73
classroom discourse 36, 40
classroom environment 107

clinical logicality 132, 134
clinical supervision 67, 123
coaching: and coaching psychology 62; in educational contexts 71–8; as facilitative tool 51; and learning-centeredness 53, 149; origin and definition of 60–1; and other supporting approaches 64–6; and PBL 133–5; personal narrative of 2–3; and person-centred learning 42; problems and potential solutions of 100–2; psychological approaches of 67–71; as role-modelling 149; and teaching 96, 177; and traditional pedagogy 46–7; *see also* educational coaching; life coaching
coaching and learning: literature gap 79; research on 78–80
coaching communications 108
coaching conversations: content of 178; in CPD 192; creating 111; engagement in 109; increasing awareness 50; and reflection 70–1; as scaffolding 46
coaching dispositions 97
coaching for parents *see* parent coaching
coaching knowledge, basic 97
coaching lessons 93, 98, 107–11
coaching psychology: definition of 1, 61–2; in education 1–2, 14, 71–2, 185–6 (*see also* educational coaching); and learners' needs 161; meta-theory of 62–4, 69; and PBL 134, 136, 148, 163; (*see also* CPBL); recent changes in 1; research on 19, 91–5
coaching relationships: building 121, *122*, 173–4; enhancing quality 193; expectations of 42; feedback in 128; flexibility in 65–6; as learning platform 76; in PBL 155–6, 159–60; research on 95–8; zone of proximity in 174–5, 188
coaching skills: and counselling 64; in PBL 135, 138, 164
coaching tools and materials 81, 107, 180, 195–6
coach-learner relationship 42
co-construction of knowledge 2, 16, 38–9, 79, 194
cognitive behavioural therapy 65
cognitive coaching 60, 67–8, 71, 73
cognitive load 2, 150
cognitive psychology 34, 67
cognitive skills, higher-order 148

coherence, emergent 127
co-learning: in CfL 115; and coaching relationship 188; in CPBL 149
collaborative enquiry 75–6
collaborative learning 52, 93, 117, 140, 147, 155, 192
collaborative reflection 79, 94
comfort zone 149, 175–6
communication, effective 121–2, 134–5, 148, 164
communication skills 147, 150, 154, 157, 160, 162
communities of practice 39
competence: need for 34, 62, 158; range of 38
complexity theory 11, 20, 23–6, 91, 127
computers 107, 117
confidence: and coaching 99, 110–11; and trust 42
content/curriculum-centred model 51
context 19
control beliefs 34
conventional classroom **12**
counselling, and coaching 2–3, 60, 64–5, 191
courage to fail 97
CPBL (Coaching and Problem-Based Learning) 3; challenges in implementation 157–8, 163; features of model 148–9; feedback in 151; model 145, *146*; origins of model 139; scaffolding 148–50; structure of model 147–8
CPD (continuing professional development) 72–6, 99–100, 102, 162–3, 192–3, 196
creativity: and coaching 64, 105, 110; in complexity theory 24; in CPBL 147, 153; and internal balance 127; as quality of coach 97
critical thinking 42, 111, 134–5, 153, 158, 179
cross-cultural studies 198
cultural adaption 198
CUREE (Centre for the Use of Research and Evidence in Education) 72
curiosity: collective 191; critical 100, 102, 110
curriculum, prescription 12, 14

data collection 91, 94, 121, 139–40, 189
decision-making, local and institutional 14

Index

deep engagement 17, 48, 68, 110, 171, 181–2
deep learning 149
deep thinking 138
dialogue: and learning 40; therapeutic 65
discursive psychology 36, 39–40

EBL (enquiry-based learning) 19; as authentic design 49–50; and coaching psychology 91–3, **95**, 96–8, 100–4, 110, 177, 187, 191; in learning-based model 53; parents and 125
educational coaching: application of 190–6; and deep engagement 181–2; discursive aspects 177, 194; evolving concept of 186; psychological model of *174*, 188; psychological prerequisites 171–3, **172**; relational aspect 173–7, 188; research on 177, 188–9, 196–200; theoretical framework 187; use of term 171
educational innovations 14
educational paradigms: 20th century 11–12; 21st century 12–14
educational psychology, and learning 31, 34
educational research, methodology in 18, 188–9
effectiveness evaluation 125–6, 163, 187, 196–7
ELLI (Effective Lifelong Learning Inventory) 94, 179
emancipation 15, 19–20, 39, 182, 189, 191
emergence 23, 126–7, 187
emotional support 97, 122
empathetic skills 148, 161–2
empathy: in CPBL 146–9, 157, 163–4; and educational coaching 172; medical 148, 162; modelling 124, 135; in person-centred education 41–2
empirical research 18, 91
empowerment 172, 174, 189
Enlightenment 11
enquiring, spirals of 47
epistemology: extended 15–18, *17*; traditionalist 160
errors, tolerance of 35, 162
executive coaching programmes 72–3
Existentialism 19, 47
experience, integrating 50
experiential knowing 16–17

experiential learning 14, 49, 61, 133–4, 161
exploratory learning 14
extroverts 154
eye contact 108–9

facilitation: indirect 161; nondirective 150; wandering mode 160
facilitation of learning: effective 38; and intentionality 44
facilitative skills 160–1
failure, fear of 162, 176
feedback: and coaching 128, 175, 180; fast cycle 91; immediate 108; mutual 146, 151, 156, 163
feedback loops 21, 115, 176
field theory 23
fixed mindset 35, 100, 176
flourishing, human 19, 63, 177
focus groups 92, 94–5, 139, 189
freedom: existential interpretation of 47–8; responsible 194–5; structured 181
freedom of choice 48, 96, 98
freedom to learn 14

general feedback 151
genuineness 41–2, 160, 172
goal attainment 69, 133
goal-oriented approach 67
goals: setting 74, 173; *see also* learning goals
group dynamics 148, 150, 154–5, 160
group facilitation 133–4, 148, 151, 154
growth mindset 35, 176, 179

Habermas, Jürgen 182
hard systems 21
humanism 34, 41
humanistic concerns 147–8, 157
humanistic perspective, in coaching 67
humanistic psychology 48, 62–3, 150, 186
humanistic teaching 52
human resources, limited 100–1

identities: and narrative 70–1; *see also* learning identities; professional identities
information management 154–5
innovation, and complexity theory 24
institutional change 24, 75–6
instruction, design principles of 36

intellectual growth 68, 147
intellectual responsibility 151
intentionality 21, 44
intentional orientation 70
interactive-relational approach 94
interactive whiteboards 107, 117
interdisciplinary research 198–9
interest development 76
interrelatedness 14, 115, 117, 126–7, 132, 181, 187
inter-subjectivity 66, 134; critical 15–18
intuition 17
IPA (interpretative phenomenological analysis) 136–7, 140, 145, 152, 197

knowledge: in extended epistemology 16–17; implicit 70; objectivity of 12; overlapping systems of 13; predefined 46, 51; professional 74; shared 36, 134
knowledge acquisition: and coaching 75; quality enhancement of 46–7
knowledge construction 178–80; and coaching 79–80, 120, *121*, 128, 191; interdependent 100; and language 40, 177–80; learning as 31, 44, 177; in learning-centred model 52–3; and participatory inquiry 136; personal 98–9; and scaffolding 66; through problem solving 159; *see also* co-construction of knowledge
knowledge management 24
Kuhn, Thomas 18

L2L (learning to learn) 43–4, 182
language: in coaching lessons 102, 109–10; of educational coaching 178–81, 193–4; and learning 6, 38–40, *120*, 128, 177–8; shared 124, 177–8, 180, 186
laptops 107, 117
leadership development 1, 72–3, 147
leadership programmes 72
learner agency 126, 186
learner-centeredness 14, 40–2, 122
learning: and coaching *see* coaching and learning; holistic metaphor of *45*; how to learn *see* L2L; humanistic perspective 41–2; making choices in 194; motivational theories of 34–6; new 37, 75; outcome-oriented 100; personalised 14, 72; social interactions of 37, 66; social perspectives on 36–40;

supporting and hindering factors 176; views of 31, **32–3**; *see also* co-learning; lifelong learning; professional learning; student learning
learning agency *see* agency
learning alliances 154
learning approaches 4, 74, 191–2
learning capacities, higher-order 53, 154
learning-centred model of education 51–4, 187, 190
learning coaches, teachers as 91, 97, 104, 107–10; *see also* teachers-as-coaches
learning cycles 49–50, 147, 175
learning dispositions: and CfL 113, 116, 125; and coaching relationship 174; and cognitive coaching 68; and CPBL 153, 163; and EBL 99, 102, 106, 111; and learning power 46; lifelong 2, 153; in soft processes 21
learning engagement 48, 76
learning environments: collaborative 13, 195; creating *120*, 128; and L2L 43; and learning-centeredness 52; and meta-theory 64; motivating 36; supporting and hindering factors in 176; supportive 147
learning facilitation: language of 180–1; PBL and coaching psychology 134
learning facilitators, teachers as 2, 54, 96–7
Learning Futures Engagement surveys 94
Learning Futures project 92–4, 110
learning goals: clarifying 120; in CPBL 147; functional 35; in PBL 50, 135
learning identities 46, 50, 107
learning journey 44–51; and CfL 116–17; and coaching relationship 173–4; student narratives of 102, *104*, 105, *106*
learning outcomes: and EBL 100, 110; evaluation of 31, 126
learning power: coaching for developing 191; and cultural adaptability 198; improved 110–11, 125; language of 177–9; parents and 125; and positive psychology 78; supporting and hindering factors 176; surveying 126, 189; use of term 45–6
learning process and position 173–4
learning progress 175–6, 194
learning relationships 21–2; in CfL 116; and coaching 96, 99; dialogue in 40; and L2L 43; students valuing 103–5

206 Index

lecturing, mixing with coaching 152–3
LH2L (learning how to learn) 43
life coaching 77–8, 171
lifelong learning 43–4; capacities 13, 147, 187; and CfL 124, 126; and coaching 100; and cognitive coaching 68; and PBL 132
listening: active 108, 135, 138, 171; attentive 109, 156; empathetic 97, 150
living systems 21–2, 24, 115, 182, 186–8
logical thinking 153–4
longitudinal studies 197

Marx, Karl 15, 36
Maslow, Abraham 63, 171, 173
Me and My School surveys 94
meaning-making 110
medical education: learner needs in 152, 161–2; PBL in 131–2, 136–42, 152–8, 163–4
medical humanity 135, 146, 156–7, 161, 163, 191
mentoring: and coaching 65–6; and CPD 74–5; school discourse on 78–9; three-mode process of 149
mentors, teachers as 97
meta-cognitive coaching 134, 160
meta-cognitive skills 44, 50, 149–50, 179, 193
meta-learning 50, 195
metaphors of learning 38–9, 45
mindfulness 63, 190
mind mapping 107, 121
mindsets, of coaching and learning 152–3
mindset theory 35
mixed methodologies 4, 197
motivation: affective and cognitive models of 34–5; and coaching 72, 80; intrinsic 132, 135, 158–9; and self-efficacy 35; situated and social perspective 35–6; supporting and hindering factors 176
multimodal therapy 65

narrative analysis 82, 94
narrative coaching 2, 60, 70–1
narrative evidence 4, 92, 94, 102–6, 126, 189
narratives, personal 45, 48–9
narrative therapy 2, 67, 70
Navig8 humanities curriculum 92
NVC (non-verbal communication) 107–8

observational evidence 4, 92, 107–10, 126, 189
ontology 5, 14–16, 18
open systems 21, 23, 115, 126–7
outline of work 4–6
ownership: in CfL 113, 116, 125; of coaching 100; of knowledge 52, 99; of learning 42, 44, 71, 151, 177; in participatory research 188; in PBL 136, 147; of problems 135; sense of 110, 194–5; terminology of 39

paradigms, use of term 11
paradigm shift 5, 81, 126
paralanguage 107–8
parental involvement 92, 123–4
parent coaching 5, 124–5, 196
participation metaphor 39
participatory methodology 18–20, 26, 91, 136, 188–9
participatory research 19, 135–8, 142, 189
participatory values 190
participatory worldview 11, 14–15, 20–1, 26, 117; extended epistemology *17*; ontology 15–16
partnership 25, 74, 116, 194–5
PBL (problem-based learning) 11, 19; and coaching psychology 133–5, 138, 145, 187, 191; and EBL 49–50; tutoring and coaching 132–3, 135–42, 145–6, 151–4, **152**, 157–64; *see also* CPBL
pedagogical relationship 46, 52
peer coaching 73, 75, 77, 196
peer critique 99, 196
peer mentoring 92
peer-networking 74
perezhivanie 37, 192
personal cognitive constructivism 36
personal growth 41, 61, 120, 123
personality dispositions, positive 64
personal stories 48, 193; *see also* narrative
person-centred psychology 41–2, 52, 62–3, 69
personhood 47, 52
philosophy of education 25
Piaget, Jean 36
pluralism 24, 39
positive education 78
positive psychology 48, 186; and coaching 63–4, 67, 78; and SFBT 69
positivism 11, 15, 24
power relationships 154, 195

practical knowledge 16
pragmatism 16
presentational construing 16
presentational knowing 16
problem-based enquiry 50
problem-focused therapy 68
problem-solving: in coaching psychology 14; in CPBL 149–50
problem-solving skills 50, 147, 163, 187
professional development: continuous *see* CPD; in CPBL 156
professional identities 156–7, 159, 164, 192
professional learning 73–5, 100, 182, 192; *see also* CPD
professional skills 148, 154
progression rates 14
project-based learning 191
propositional knowing 16–17, 117
prototyping: dynamic 91, 189; and feedback loop 115; interventions in *93*; participatory 173
psycho-educational model 52
psychological health 156, 161
psychotherapy: and coaching 64, 191; person-centred 42
public domain 46–7, 113, 182

qualitative research 25, 94, 136
quantitative evidence 94, 110–11
quantum leaps 18
questions, open 4, 108, 110, 135, 138

rational emotional behavioural therapy 65
rationality 11
reductionism 11, 20
reflection, time and space for 195
reflective coaching 70
reflective learning 131, 182
reflective practice 22
reflexive research 24, 136, 141, 180
regulation, identified and integrated 159
regulatory styles 34
relatedness 14, 34, 49, 62, 154, 158
relationships: hierarchical 141, 159, 191; interpersonal 42, 128, 171, 186, 193; multiple 65; positive 78, 98, 193–4; with self 127
re-professionalisation 47
research methodology: for complexity theory 24–5; and educational philosophy 18

resilience: building through coaching 64, 69, 77, 97, 99; in CPBL 147; student narratives of 102, 105–6; supporting and hindering factors 176
respect, as value 172
responsibility for learning: and CfL 116; developing 51; and intentionality 44; transferring to students 66, 99, 109
Rogers, Carl 41–2, 48, 62
role-and-task model 123
role modelling 73
role playing 157

scaffolding 2, 38; and coaching 66, 98, 101, 110, 175, 191; cognitive 135, 146, 150, 162; emotional 135, 146, 149–50, 156, 163; of enquiry process 180
school leadership development 72–3
schools, as living systems 21–2
SDT (self-determination theory) 34, 62
self-actualisation 48, 171–2
self-assessment 148, 194
self-awareness: and CfL 116; and coaching 51, 64, 71, 102, 105–6, 194; and critical inter-subjectivity 17; and knowledge acquisition 46; and L2L 43–4; supporting and hindering factors 176
self-coaching 175
self-concept 35, 43, 68, 70
self-determination 128, 134; and emotional scaffolding 150
self-directed learning 43; and coaching 61, 99, 171, 175; and CPBL 155, 158–9; and SFBT 69
self-directedness 35, 64, 74, 134, 153–4, 159, 174
self-efficacy 2, 35–6; and coaching 99, 111; and feedback 151; and SFBT 69; surveying 189
self-empowerment 128
self-esteem 34, 43, 68, 176, 186
self-evaluation 42
self-identity 48, 77
self-image, positive 176
self-knowledge 48, 117, 175
self-organisation 22–3
self-reflexivity 19, 48
self-regulation: and coaching 194; of learning 67, 158–9, 189; parents modelling 124

Index

self-theories 2
semi-structured interviews 4, 94–5, 139, 189
SFBT (solution-focused brief therapy) 65, 68–9
SGCP (Special Group in Coaching Psychology) 1, 61–2
social cognitive theory 34–5
social congruence 151, 160
social constructionism 37, 69, 134
social mediation 39, 66, 179
social relationships 37, 96, 127, 172
socio-cultural theories 36–8, 43, 51, 141, 186
soft systems 21
solution-focused coaching 60, 68–9, 71, 77
specific feedback 151
speech, and learning 39–40
storying and re-storying 2
storytelling 70–1
strategic awareness 99, 111, 178
strategic thinking 44, 80
strengths coaching 64
structuralism 24
student engagement 94, 109
student group collaboration 154
student learning: and coaching 76–7, 98; narratives of 102–7; and teachers' CPD 74–6
students, psychological well-being 77–8
subjective-objective interaction 14–16
sustainability, coaching for 115, 126–7
systemic approach 67
systems theory, complex adaptive 24
systems thinking 11, 14; in education 21, **22–3**; key ideas of 20–1; and philosophy of education 25–6
systems view of schooling 190–1

teacher efficacy 75
teachers: in educational models 51–4; as life coaches 78; professional development of 73–5 (*see also* CPD); roles in CfL **123**
teachers-as-coaches 100–1, 104, 108, 123–4, 181, 193
teacher–student communication 107–8
teacher–student relationship 12, 42, 92, 128, 172
teacher training 72, 74–5, 186
temporal connectivity 46
thematic analysis 95, 101, 139, 189
therapeutic relationship 65
thinking, spirals of 47
Tongji University 137, 139
transactionalism 39
transference 122
transformative learning 22, 68, 127, 173, 182
trust: between parents and students 125; in coaching 68, 121, 175, 191; establishing 72; and feedback 128; in inner experiences 48; and participatory research 188; and person-centred education 42
tutor circle 147, 187
tutors, in CPBL 151; *see also* PBL

values, in coaching 70
voice: confidence about 110; quality of 108–9
Vygotsky, Lev, socio-cultural perspective 36–7

wholeness 15, 19–20, 22, 187
wisdom, systemic 17

Zen Buddhism 16
zone of proximity 174–5, 188
ZPD (zone of proximal development) 37–8, 45–6, 51, 66, 73, 150